CUCKOOLAND

CUCKOOLAND

Where the rich own the truth

Tom Burgis

**WILLIAM
COLLINS**

William Collins
An imprint of HarperCollins*Publishers*
1 London Bridge Street
London SE1 9GF

WilliamCollinsBooks.com

HarperCollins*Publishers*
Macken House, 39/40 Mayor Street Upper
Dublin 1, D01 C9W8, Ireland

First published in Great Britain in 2024 by William Collins

1

A catalogue record for this book is
available from the British Library

HB ISBN 978-0-00-856474-2
TPB ISBN 978-0-00-856475-9

Set in Garamond Premier Pro
Printed and bound in the UK using 100%
renewable electricity at CPI Group (UK) Ltd

For Delilah and Fred

CONTENTS

The most potent weapon in the hands of the oppressor is the mind of the oppressed

Steve Biko

Part I

Living the dream

One

Hard-won truths

'I'm glad this recording shows how heated I am because you are a dishonest journalist. There is no honesty in you at all. And I hope you will play this recording to your publishers as well, before they fucking publish a pack of lies.'

Mohamed Amersi is extremely cross. I am not doing what he wants. Mohamed just wants everybody to do what he wants. To accept that what he says happened is what happened. That who he says he is is who he is. Then he can get back to his philanthropy.

We are sitting across a boardroom table at the offices of Amersi's lawyers in London. The mere name of the firm – Carter-Ruck – is enough to induce a jolt of anxious nausea in journalists. Nigel Tait, most formidable of the partners, once remarked that he gets a buzz from suppressing free speech. Letter after letter after letter (to the reporter but also to their editors, and sometimes only their editors, to make the point that the reporter is not to be trusted) threatening legal proceedings of scarcely imaginable expense. That usually does the trick. The book, the article, the documentary will vanish from view, if it ever made it into view in the first place. Should these muckrakers, these tittle-tattle merchants, these grubby hacks defy his clients, Tait will ensure they spend months, years, in court. The lawsuit he engineers will go to war on their reputation, their career, their sleep. Funding this is no problem: his clients tend to possess inexhaustible quantities of money.

Nigel Tait is Mohamed Amersi's lawyer. He's somewhere in the building, I suppose. In this room, as agreed, it's just me and Mohamed. Plus a piece of corporate art that looks like a hatching egg, a plate of deluxe chocolate biscuits and a dozen blue ring binders. In these, I have been told to expect, reside the proof that Mohamed Amersi is right about everything.

For two and a half years I have been trying to figure out who this man really is. Since I first heard that a major donor to the ruling party – the Conservatives – had hired Nigel Tait to go after a former MP. Charlotte Leslie's offence was to have raised questions about Amersi, about his past, about how he made the money with which he was now purchasing access to the most powerful people in the UK (yes, even to Boris). Amersi, on his charitable foundation's website, is 'an entrepreneur, philanthropist and thought leader'. Leslie googled around a bit and wrote a memo suggesting there might be some more chapters to this man. No bombshells, no skeletons or smoking guns, no allegations of the kind of great crimes that are said to lie behind many a great fortune, just some apparent gaps between his words and his deeds, plus some traces of business dealings – hardly uncommon – in the former Soviet Union. So why, I wondered, had she produced such an aggressive response in Amersi.

From Mayfair to Kathmandu, I looked for the real Mohamed Amersi. And as I went, I felt his story connect with a bigger one. Once you spot it, it's everywhere. The Chinese Communist Party bullying respected scientific journals into withdrawing research on the origins of Covid-19. A serving UK prime minister and recently departed US president respectively resigning for lying and facing jail for lying. Putin's troops captured in Ukraine saying they came to free their fellow Russian-speakers from annihilation by the Nazis in Kyiv. Hannah Arendt would have recognised what is happening. Everywhere, the powerful are making a renewed claim to the greatest prize of all: to own the truth. The power to choose what you want reality to be and impose that reality on the world.

A few days ago I sent Amersi a long list of what I've learned about him in these two and a half years. The letter that came back from Nigel Tait and his sidekicks invited me to their office. This morning, a sticky Friday in July 2023, I walked down Chancery Lane, past the glass towers of the law firms sparkling like pristine teeth in a perfect smile. On the way I listened to an interview with Andrew Malkinson. He's just been freed after seventeen years in prison for a rape someone else committed. 'I was in total shock for the first few years, not even weeks but years, trying to get my head around the fact that the world now thinks I'm this person, but I'm not that person. I contemplated suicide many times.' Although his conviction was transparently wrong, the interviewer asked if he ever did what lots of prisoners who begin long sentences protesting their innocence do, and after a while just give up. 'No. No, no, no. The truth is the most fundamental thing. I've always had an interest in science and mathematics and stuff. These are fundamental, hard-won truths.'

I am, I'm told, about to see another injustice unravelled. What I have heard about Mohamed Amersi is wrong. If, as he explains, I'm not too fucking thick to understand, he will set the record straight. He wants to help me. So that when I sit down to write this book it won't be full of lies and bias and hogshit and misinformation imparted by wankers.* So that I will write the truth.

---

* The word 'hogshit' appears to be a portmanteau, forged in fury, combining two of Mohamed's other preferred terms for information that displeases him, bullshit and hogwash. At the back of this book are comprehensive notes explaining the basis of every significant fact herein, including what people say and think. Sources are either named or, to protect them, described as fully as possible short of making them identifiable. Corroborating documents are cited. When it comes to Amersi's interjections, I've used footnotes, in case the reader is as fucking stupid as me and needs easily accessible assistance with his technical jargon and other challenging language.

Two

Take-off

Who is it that Mohamed Amersi wants to be? He wants to be the man who is due aboard the private plane scheduled to depart RAF Northolt on Sunday January 20, 2013. A private plane carrying Mohamed Amersi to his well-earned place among the highest in the land.

Everything has been arranged. Ben Elliot's people have taken care of it.

Amersi adores Ben. As a person: his decency, his warmth. His friendship. Ben understands what I'm trying to do, Amersi thinks. None of this would be happening without Ben. Mohamed says so himself. 'Unless you have somebody like him who opens these doors for you, it's not possible.'

For Quintessentially clients, there is nothing Ben can't provide. When Madonna's mucous membrane cried out for the soothing properties of slippery elm, Elliot's people airlifted teabags of the stuff to her in Los Angeles. Others have wanted penguins, false eyelashes (and a plastic surgeon to repair the mischief the St Tropez hostess had done herself by tearing out the originals), llamas, backstage passes to Beyoncé, a football signed by Lionel Messi, albino peacocks.

Tall, handsome, his Eton accent customised to Mockney, Ben can get you into places others cannot go. If you want the Sydney Harbour Bridge to yourself, Ben's people will get you the Sydney Harbour Bridge, and you can propose on it. They will have the doors to Shanghai's couture boutiques closed to the public so that your wife is undisturbed while she shops on her birthday. Quintessentially's clients party beside pyramids and dine on icebergs. If they want to stay at home but wish their home was the Batcave, a Batcave Ben's people will build.

Yet even Ben cannot control the weather. You'd have to be Vladimir Putin, sending jets to spike the clouds, and Ben's not Putin. As Amersi makes ready the evening before take-off, the temperature falls below zero. After midnight, snowflakes fill the air. They carpet the runway at RAF Northolt.

Needs must when the devil drives. When the devil drives, sometimes you just have to fly commercial. British Airways to Glasgow. Ben was going to come along but now he won't. Amersi's host, Ben's aunt's husband, will be there to welcome him.

The plane flies north. How far he has come, Mohamed from Mombasa. The Amersis' roots run through the old empire. His forebears, in Iran then in India, were in the business of moving commodities. A lot came from Africa. So it made commercial sense for Amersi's grandfather to send his son to Kenya. To Mombasa, the port city where the Indian

Ocean winds have carried centuries of traders, slavers, missionaries and invaders. When little Mohamed was born in 1960, Kenya was still a British colony. Three years later came independence. It had taken decades of rebellion to throw off colonial rule, but the British did not simply leave. Across the former colonies, there was oil to be drilled, mines to be dug, arms to be sold, markets to be opened. And the old mother-land was willing, for a suitable fee, to take delivery of the promising offspring of thriving families from the former colonies such as the Amersis for moulding.

Merchant Taylors' School was founded by guildsmen five hundred years before the adolescent Amersi arrived in 1976. A generation earlier, it had been uprooted from central London and shifted to roomier grounds in the heartlands of English propriety, the Home Counties. The new pupil from Mombasa, with his accent and his pigment and his Islamic name, was not in the image of the bishops and generals and translators of bibles who had preceded him. This was the England of Paki-bashing and the National Front. On April 20, 1968 – young Mohamed's eighth birthday – Enoch Powell had prophesied a river of blood. Sometimes Amersi has wondered what his life would be like if he were John Smith, white man.

Because you can climb all the way to the top. But as you haul yourself onto the summit, you will find a wall, a wall that you couldn't see before. And in the wall, a single door, oaken and locked. Entry is secured by birthright alone. You can't buy your way in.

Except that you can. This is what Ben Elliot has in his pocket: a key to the final door.

And why not? Did the triumph of capitalism over communism not teach us that wealth is the badge of worth? That money gravitates towards merit? And Mohamed Amersi has made money. It might even be said – by no less an authority than Mohamed himself – that he has been *the* premier mergers and acquisitions adviser in the emerging markets telecommunications space. The master dealmaker.

When they disembark in Glasgow, a chauffeur awaits Amersi and his partner. Not Annar, the Mombasa girl he married in 1981 when he was not yet twenty-one. At his side today is Nadia Rodicheva, a beauty seventeen years his junior. Mohamed, short and always smart, a neat greying plume above his hawkish features, takes his seat beside her in the car. No longer just some Kenyan and some Russian. They are about to become someone.

Past picturesque Scottish farms they are carried, past the town Johnnie Walker comes from, past a hamlet called Moscow. Closer, closer ...

Ben's people emailed the itinerary a few days ago. Arrive. Meet host. Host personally conducts tour of exquisite Georgian mansion, with its Chippendale furniture and the Gobelin tapestries that were a gift, according to a fictional passage in the old place's history, from the Sun King, Louis XIV. Tea. Rest. Gather for dinner at half past six.

The car enters the grounds. Through the trees, Dumfries House peeps like a pearl. The garden is an hors d'oeuvre of neat conifers and sculpted lawn. The gravel of the drive crunches under the wheels. A dozen solid steps wide enough for the fullest of retinues lead up to an ochre stone front topped with silvery chimneys. And within, all set to receive his guests, is Charles.

Three

A furnace for the past

The other Mohamed Amersi – the Mohamed Amersi that Mohamed Amersi does not want to be – did not board the flight to Dumfries. He was left behind. Left behind in the past.

The thing about the past, though, is that it's forever ambushing the present, forever buzzing into the picture like a fly in the projector. It is an unceasing effort, keeping the past under control. Sometimes you can burn it. Sometimes you can buy it. Which is what one of Mohamed's business partners is seeking to do right now, on September 6, 2004, behind the heavy velvet curtains of a private room at the Ritz.

'I will be around for forty-seven minutes,' says Jeffrey Galmond. 'One hour or so. And then running off to another meeting. I have got meetings tomorrow all day. And then I have got meetings on Wednesday. Thursday, I think, I am out of here. I keep moving. I stay in the same place for about two or three days and then move to another place. I don't make any bookings in advance. I use a lot of private aeroplanes.

They come from another country, come to pick me up and fly me out.'

The previous day's *Observer* has declared Jeffrey Galmond to be what he wants to be: 'the newest conqueror of the Wild East'. A billionaire. 'The 54-year-old built a modestly successful legal practice in Denmark before starting to advise numerous European clients on Russian investments in the early nineties. Details of his subsequent career are not widely known but he seems quickly to have become a serial investor himself, making canny plunges into Russia's property and telecoms markets.' The writer notes: 'Galmond's story is all the more remarkable for being so little recognised until now.'

Jeffrey Galmond has revealed his remarkable story in the long witness statement he has been forced to make after a rich Russian accused him of not being who he says he is. Under oath, he's described in this affidavit how he became a titan of the Russian telecommunications industry without anyone noticing. 'I have been assisted in this process by the maintenance of a low profile,' he states. 'It is my firm belief, and I would suggest it is plain common sense, that if one trumpets one's activities from the rooftops and signals one's intentions when building up businesses in this way, one is asking for trouble. It will invite envy, animosity and competition.'

Thankfully for Jeffrey, doing business with the man he says he is can be lucrative. Mohamed Amersi's share will be four million dollars.

It used to be easier, managing the past. Before information went digital. Paper was so much more flammable. Just look at the Russian before us now, on December 5, 1989, in a detached, custard-coloured house near the north bank of the Elbe, shovelling documents into a furnace.

He has the thick neck of a judo champion, though four years of German beer have pudged him out. A stern parting bisects his soft hair. The way his lips twitch up at the sides, it's like he's suppressing a smirk. But there is no tarrying over the incineration, no time to relish a few of the secret words printed on these secret pages. Outside, crowds are pressing against the gates. Weeks ago, up in Berlin, the wall was breached. The Russian knows his time here in Dresden is over.

Since he was a boy, he'd wanted this life, to belong to the Soviet Union's most exclusive club: the KGB. It would deliver him from the Leningrad grind, the communal flat with the rats and the appalling toilet. It would make him an author of events. One spy, he said to himself, one spy can decide the fate of thousands. All through his law degree, he hoped for the call. For the tap on his shoulder. Eventually it came. And with it, the chance to be someone else.

They all had pseudonyms, the recruits. Keeping just the first letter of their real name, like a memento of who you really were. Platov, that was his. These other people that they became, they could leave the commons behind, depart the realm of the many, enter the zone of the few. 'Nobody can go here,' he told a friend one day, when his KGB credentials gained them access to an antique church to see its magnificent altar. 'But we can.' Tickets to any theatre, no problem. You could even leave the country.

Lyudmila was pregnant with their second when they left Leningrad. She has liked it here in Dresden. The driver, the picnics with the Stasi guys. The family's apartment is next door to the KGB office. He goes home every day for lunch and sees her oval face, those big eyes accentuated by stark, dark lashes.

The Russian's professional performance is monitored like the output of a factory under a Five-Year Plan. It is measured in 'the quantity of realised units of information'. Today, information is being unrealised. The most valuable documents have been sent to Moscow. They have buried some of the others. The rest, handful by handful, he and his colleagues are throwing into the flames. He must make an expert judgement of each file's worth, set against its danger. A secret is like a hidden passage beneath your citadel. It could be your salvation. If your enemy discovers it, it could be your ruin.

The crowd is growing. He can hear them. Here in Dresden, as across the Soviet empire, the prevailing reality is breaking down. The Russian has grown up in a system run on *vranyo*, a term defined thus: 'You know I'm lying, and I know that you know, and you know that I know that you know, but I go ahead with a straight face, and you nod seriously and take notes.' He has requested guidance from KGB headquarters. No answer comes. Moscow is silent.

Vladimir Putin hurls more papers into the fire. More and more until the furnace bursts.

Lyudmila hates the queues back in Leningrad. Chapters of history are said to be ending and beginning but everything is the same. The empty shelves, the coupons, the ration cards. They've no savings – in Dresden they spent his KGB salary on the car. At least they have the washing machine their German neighbours gave them before they left.

Her husband has found a new way to make money: politics. He has established himself as a fixer for Anatoly Sobchak, leader of the city's democrats. Putin is the liaison between this law professor and the security forces. When the Communist hardliners' tanks approach the city, Putin negotiates with them through the night. Their coup fails; the transition to something called capitalism proceeds.

Leningrad becomes St Petersburg once more. Sobchak is its mayor, Putin his deputy. They take offices in the old Soviet headquarters. Putin installs a KGB comrade called Igor Sechin, veteran of Cold War conflict in Angola, as his gatekeeper. On the hook where Lenin's portrait hung, Putin chooses not the customary image of the newly elected president Boris Yeltsin but an engraving of an emperor, Peter the Great.

When Putin is summoned to the capital, Lyudmila is still getting over the crash. The light was green. She didn't see the car that smashed into them. Into the front, mercifully: Katya was asleep in the back. The child was only bruised. Lyudmila was knocked out. When she came to, she grabbed a bystander and gave them the number to call Sechin. The public hospital the ambulance took her to was full of the dead and dying.

Corpses lay on stretchers, left there by a state that had fallen apart. Only when they brought her to the military clinic did an X-ray show the crack in her spine and a fractured skull. She was there for two months. It would be three years before she felt normal again.

She falls in love with Moscow. It feels like a place where life is in full swing. Putin is getting a promotion a year. Into Yeltsin's presidential administration, then back to the KGB – they call it the FSB now – as boss. Then secretary to the security council, then prime minister in 1999.

How strange, Lyudmila thinks, I'm married to a man who yesterday was just an unknown deputy mayor of St Petersburg, and now he's prime minister. A few months later, he is president. Putin takes Lyudmila to places others cannot go. They pop their New Year's champagne in a helicopter over Chechnya. But she and the children see less of him. Like when the kids want him to watch that new movie they love with them. The one where you have to take a blue pill or else reality falls apart. *The Matrix*. He says he doesn't have time.

These days Putin keeps the highest company. 'I found him to be very straightforward and trustworthy,' George W. Bush declares after they meet. 'We had a very good dialogue. I was able to get a sense of his soul; a man deeply committed to his country and the best interests of his country.'

All the attention can be unpleasant for Lyudmila. It's unpleasant when the media dig into their background. It's unpleasant, she says, when they lie. The family's life has gone on show. Her husband still has his secrets, of course.

Everybody does. One of them features Lyudmila herself. For a while after they move to Moscow, she takes a job at a telecoms venture. She gives it up before Putin becomes president in 1999, but the company continues to enjoy the aura of association with the big man. Once Putin is in the Kremlin, it grows into one of the country's most valuable. Its owner goes unnamed, hidden inside a shell company. Until, in 2004, the shell jiggles and cracks, and there emerges a hitherto unremarked Dane, the new conqueror of the Wild East, Jeffrey Galmond.

Being the new conqueror of the Wild East has its perks. The private planes, the meetings at the Ritz.

'That's very lovely,' says James Hatt, listening to Jeffrey Galmond describe his jet-set existence.

'Pardon?'

'Lovely,' repeats Hatt, who has arranged this private suite to allay Galmond's concerns about eavesdroppers. He speaks with the sonorous precision of the English barrister he used to be. 'I am very happy for you. You must be having a lovely life.'

'You would not like to be in my shoes,' says Galmond, whose moustache, like the rest of his hair, is greyer than it was back in St Petersburg.

'That is true,' Hatt says. 'I wouldn't. I don't want to be in your shoes. And I was having a very happy, comfortable, quiet life. A very different life. And then, one day, my life got complicated.'

Like a great many other western bankers and lawyers and management consultants, at the fall of the Soviet Union, James Hatt went to Russia to do business. He ended up in telecoms. After a decade, he moved to Massachusetts to do what he really wanted: train to be a psychoanalyst. He has been studying Jung's concept of splitting, how we are able to be two people at once. And then, the other day, the past turned up at his door, in the form of a man called Tim asking Hatt to meet Kroll. Agents from the private intelligence industry do not track you down because they want to hear your thoughts on Jung. Kroll is on a mission from the rich Russian who's trying to prove that Galmond is not who he says he is.

I've read your affidavit, Hatt tells Galmond. Your big thick fucking affidavit. Jesus Christ, it's full of holes. The Kroll spies are very interested in it. And they've found Tony Georgiou, another character from the past that Hatt and Galmond share. Tony Georgiou doesn't believe Galmond's story either. Georgiou's review of Galmond's account is even blunter than Hatt's: he calls it 'fabricated'. And he's gone and written an affidavit of his own.

The cigars-and-caviar heir to an Italian furniture business, Tony Georgiou had been in St Petersburg fitting out exclusive hotels in the late eighties when, waiting in the ten-hour queue to use a phone at the Astoria for four minutes at a cost of forty-five dollars, he saw an opportunity. Gorbachev was opening the economy. Georgiou decided to start a telecoms business. His associates made introductions to St Petersburg's new rulers. Georgiou met Sobchak, the charismatic mayor, and his inscrutable deputy, Vladimir Putin. And he heard of a young official who everyone said was destined for great things.

Leonid Reiman's friendly face and congenial manner distinguished him from the stolid apparatchiks who disdained and distrusted the foreign capitalists. Reiman, by contrast, they could deal with. His mother taught English and Reiman's was flawless; he caught nuances that would escape all but native speakers. Georgiou arranged to meet him at the Astoria. The young Russian's intelligence, his ability to understand intricate corporate apparatus – these qualities, instantly apparent, demonstrated to Georgiou that he had found his man.

Although he was not formally the boss of the officials who ran St Petersburg's public telephone system, Reiman was clearly in charge. Georgiou cultivated him. An invitation to a Christmas gathering in London. The promise of proximity to western splendour that glimmered when Georgiou dropped a name, such as that of his personal friend Lord Beaverbrook, Conservative Party treasurer.

In return, Georgiou was after a telecoms licence. The Soviet apparat had not so much been swept away as clunkily repurposed for capitalism. A telecoms licence required sixteen signatures. 'Mr Reiman,' Georgiou has written in his affidavit, 'was able to take the document around the relevant ministry officials and to ensure that at each level those involved were persuaded to sign. Although I was not involved in this, I understand that this would have involved Mr Reiman paying an appropriate "fee" to each of the officials in return for their help. I should add, at this stage, that it is a fact of life of doing business in Russia that it is necessary to take care of everyone whom you need help from. Mr Reiman seemed an expert in "oiling the wheels" and had no compunction about doing it. He told me what it would cost and I provided the money.'

Reiman himself, a civil servant in his thirties, got a million. On October 12, 1992, Georgiou wired the payment to Reiman's Swiss bank account. 'I queried whether Mr Reiman, as a State employee, could legally receive such a payment,' Georgiou says in his affidavit, 'and I was assured that this was a private arrangement and not prohibited by Russian law.' The final payments were for 'people without whose support the licence would not be forthcoming'. Georgiou didn't know who all these shadowy powers were. His affidavit does not record whether there was any inducement for the senior official who approved a change to the shareholdings in PeterStar, his telecoms venture. The owners were originally to be Georgiou himself and the Russian people. But the Russian people's interest was shifted into a private company incorporated on the Isle of Man, owned by just one of them, Leonid Reiman. Achieving this needed the consent of the chair of St Petersburg's committee for foreign relations. The chair obligingly signed his name: Vladimir Putin.

Putin has kept Reiman close. The telecoms venture where Lyudmila worked when the Putins moved to Moscow is the one Reiman founded. This venture has been acquiring more and more assets, becoming one of the biggest companies in Russian telecoms. To begin with, it belonged to the Russian people. But like their stake in PeterStar, this one too has quietly changed hands. It now belongs to a private company in Luxembourg called First National Holding. There is no public record of who owns it. But in his affidavit, Jeffrey Galmond has unmasked the human being behind First National Holding: it's him, Jeffrey, conqueror of the Wild East. And this is rather bewildering for James Hatt, as he sits with Galmond behind the Ritz's heavy velvet curtains.

'Leonid Reiman was always in control of First National Holding,' Hatt says. 'You and I know that to be true. The reality.' And this reality is rather important now. Because these days Leonid Reiman is President Putin's telecoms minister. He oversees an industry worth countless billions, the bedrock of Putin's surveillance state, and in which, if Hatt is right, Reiman himself secretly holds an enormous illicit stake.

'When Leonid became a minister and went to Moscow,' Hatt reminds Galmond, 'you and I were sitting together in St Petersburg. Leonid would phone you at one in the fucking morning. And if he'd been in St Petersburg he used to come and see us at one in the fucking morning. Remember the nights we spent together? It's no wonder I never got laid in St Petersburg. I was always in your fucking office.'

'On the small red couch,' says Galmond.

'On the small red couch.'

'Yeah, yeah,' says Galmond. 'That's true.'

But if Jeffrey Galmond is not who he says he is, who is he? Tony Georgiou says in his affidavit that Galmond in the nineties was a mere lawyer – 'arrogant and not that bright' – whose wife happened to be close to Reiman's. That's what Hatt remembers too: that Jeff Galmond was one of the lawyers who helped Leonid Reiman covertly assemble and run his telecoms empire. You were there, Hatt tells Galmond. You were there when we drew up the paperwork to describe the owners of PeterStar in a way that would nicely disguise Reiman's stake. The owners, Hatt points out, were described as 'persons interested in telecommunications in north west Russia'. The paperwork did not, Hatt observes, say 'I, Jeffrey Galmond, own it'.

'Right,' says Galmond.

This is just the sort of thing the Kroll spies are looking for. 'They are unpicking your affidavit,' Hatt tells Galmond. 'This is a big issue.'

'For whom?' Galmond asks.

'For you,' says Hatt.

It's true, this scrutiny of the galaxy of companies Galmond purports to own is most incommoding. Even the authorities in Bermuda, usually one of the easiest places to maintain corporate camouflage, are examining the ones he's set up there. They are constantly asking him questions. Why are you making this payment? Where does the money come from? I can't move a dime, he complains, not a fucking dime, without producing a great big binder.

The spies are closing in. They want to show that Jeffrey Galmond is a frontman concealing an immense corrupt scheme within Putin's regime. Yet there are still those who take Galmond at his word, who will believe that he is who he says he is, and who are thus able to join him in his money-making. He's recently met one such person, by the name of Mohamed Amersi.

After Merchant Taylors, university at Sheffield and Cambridge, one prestigious law firm, Clifford Chance, another, Jones Day (a 'star' of its Swiss office, the trade press says), Mohamed Amersi is a most impressive character when he meets Jeff Galmond. And some experience in Russia: when Yeltsin sold off the Soviet economy in the nineties, Amersi worked on a bid for telecoms assets. He knows God and the devil and everybody, Galmond thinks; he's shrewd, intelligent. They see each other again in London and Dubai and St Tropez.

By now, Amersi has departed the law. There is a way to monetise this ability he possesses, the ability to make everyone feel he's on their side. To be what they call a 'dealmaker'. It's how Mohamed has long seen himself. That has been the recent verdict of a High Court judge.

Mr Justice Smith observed Amersi in his witness box. The case was brought by two former clients of Mohamed's old firm Jones Day, the Saab brothers of Lebanon, who claimed that Amersi two-timed them. They thought he was their lawyer on a property deal but he was also working for the Saudi bank on the other side. No, Mohamed told the court, the Saabs are mistaken, there was no wrongdoing. His testimony, Mr Justice Smith concluded, was 'unreliable', 'incredible', 'extraordinary', 'generally unsatisfactory', detailed when it suited him but vague when it did not, and contradicted by contemporaneous correspondence. In Amersi's sworn witness statement, the judge remarked, Mohamed denied that on September 14, 1994 he had discussed a retainer with one of the Saabs. The Saabs' barrister pointed out that Amersi's own case relied on this conversation having happened. Mohamed 'therefore produced a fresh witness statement,' the judgment recorded, 'not only saying he now recalled a conversation on the 14 September but giving detailed evidence as to what was discussed about the retainer.'

As he peered into the psyche of the man before him, the judge concluded that Amersi saw nothing amiss in his own conduct. The holes in his records, those were his secretary's fault, he said – the incompetent woman struggled with the office computers. As for a conflict of interest, Mohamed made himself blind to it. 'In reality,' Mr Justice Smith found, 'Mr Amersi saw himself as a dealmaker.' He 'was so attracted personally because of the success fee, because of the size of the transaction, that he lost a proper sense of objectivity' and 'forgot that he was a lawyer who owed duties to different clients that might cause conflict. It is clear that he purported to act for both sides at stages during this saga. Of that there is no doubt.'

_____

'He was a bloody farmer and he is a fucking farmer and he lost his job because he behaved like a farmer.'

Mohamed and I are getting started. Fortified with a swift yoghurt en route to Carter-Ruck, I listen as his rage swells, subsides, then swells again.

'Sorry, can I just ask, I know this might seem like a strange question, but why farmer? I don't understand the insult,' I say. 'Why's being a farmer a bad thing?'

'They are generally seen as peasants.'

'I see what you mean.'

And this peasant of a judge had not believed Amersi, siding instead with the Saabs.

'Well,' Mohamed says of his former clients, 'fuck them.'

The Saabs sued Jones Day and Amersi together. The claim against Amersi himself was stayed before the trial. But Mohamed wishes to set the record straight anyway. There was that 'one fucking mail' that showed he was doing work for both sides, the one Mr Justice Smith 'made a song and dance about'. Yet Amersi was always in the right. He explained this to Mr Justice Smith but the judge 'didn't understand it because he's too thick'. As am I, Mohamed tells me. 'I'm talking to a two-year-old that doesn't understand anything.'

He shows me some of the paperwork from the case. 'I know in your little head you have said my modus operandi, it's conflict, acting on both sides blah blah blah.'

'That's what the judge said.'

'Fuck him. If he doesn't understand it, fuck him. Please quote this. Fuck him. I don't give a shit. I've had enough of this nonsense, of being made a poster boy for their nonsense. He doesn't understand how a transaction is done, that's why they fired him. Did you see what a court of appeal said about him?'

I did. Mr Justice Smith's seniors on the bench found that he'd refused to recuse himself from a case despite being angry with the law firm that brought it because said law firm had recently declined to hire him. Another time they detected 'a deeply worrying and fundamental lack of understanding of the proper role of a judge'. Among his misadventures was the awkward incident when he demanded that the British Airways lawyer before him in court find his lost luggage.

This happened years after he ruled in Amersi's case, I say.

'The spots on the leopard never fucking change. Once an imbecile, always an imbecile.' So much so, in fact, that Smith was simply unable to grasp the kind of complex international deal-making for which Mohamed was billing three hundred dollars an hour.

But if this peasant in robes got it so wrong, I ask, why didn't Jones Day appeal? 'If you're saying it was such an outrageous mischaracterisation of your character, did you not wish to have it corrected?'

'Jones Day decided that they would rather pay the money and go home, end of story.' Thanks to 'this wanker judge', the

Saabs were able to extract a seven-figure settlement, Amersi says.

'It didn't bother you that there was this public record that gives this quite damning account of your behaviour?'

'It didn't change anything.'

———————

By the time Mr Justice Smith hands down this judgment in 2002, Amersi has unleashed the dealmaker the judge divined in him. A dealmaker with a philosophy: everyone wins. 'When making deals,' he says, 'you need to know the constituency that you are engaged with. That means that when you walk into a room, you've literally got two or three minutes to size people up. You need to speak to them in a language they understand and make them feel that they have just met their very best friend for the first time.'

Jeffrey Galmond soon has reason to believe that he has met his new best friend. The spies are on his tail, the Bermudan authorities are asking questions, but Mohamed Amersi is committed to Galmond's cause. In August 2004, Amersi sends him a message regarding a new idea.

'At the outset, I would like to stress that on a personal note I very much enjoy working with you as we look at "life" in a very identical manner. We share a number of common interests and that usually bodes well for a strong partnership.' He turns to the matter at hand. 'As I had promised you personally, Enigma has now been set up.'

Enigma, aptly enough, is a collection of opaque offshore companies. It's similar to the one in Bermuda that Kroll is crawling all over, searching for evidence that Galmond is a front for the Russian telecoms minister, Leonid Reiman. Only it's registered in another paradise of secrecy in the Caribbean: the Cayman Islands. The idea is for Enigma to become the new corporate vessel for the telecoms assets Galmond purports to own. Money starts to move. By the end of 2004, millions have landed in Luxembourg, at another company Amersi's helping Galmond run. It's called Industrial Development Corporation and in a few short months its records show a shift from handling a few thousand dollars to many millions.

Mohamed introduces Jeffrey to his Swiss bankers, helps him apply for a Coutts account. They are furnished with the tale of the spectacularly successful series of breaks and brain-waves through which Galmond acquired his telecoms empire. It's the same story that he's given in his recent affidavit. The one that explains how in the nineties he arrived in Russia to practise law but got into business, how he grew fond of a Russian telecoms expert called Leonid Reiman, how their families would go on holiday together, how they still meet for dinners in Moscow every couple of months now Leonid is Putin's telecoms minister, but that any suggestion that 'I have been, and remain, accountable to him' – that Reiman, not Galmond, is the owner of the telecoms empire – is 'completely false'.

As the Ritz's diners and drinkers come and go in the plush halls below their private room, Galmond tells James Hatt that Leonid Reiman is adamant. He will not give in. He doesn't fucking want Mikhail Fridman's company getting a chunk of MegaFon. MegaFon: the pan-Russian communications giant that has long been Reiman's dream. It is to be listed on the London Stock Exchange, worth billions. And there is a dispute over who owns one large stake in it. Jeffrey Galmond says it's his. No, says the oligarch Fridman, it's mine. It is he who has set the Kroll spies on Galmond.

'If Fridman doesn't understand the music,' Galmond tells James Hatt, the pair of them still cloistered in the velvet curtains, 'he should have a word with Mr Khodorkovsky.'

Mikhail Khodorkovsky was Russia's richest man, for a while. Under Boris Yeltsin's drunken rule, the oligarchs could do as they pleased, take what they want, boss the Kremlin around. Times have changed. Khodorkovsky continued to believe that all that money he made actually belonged to him. Thought it bought him power. That he could ignore Putin's warning to stay out of politics. Now he's on trial, bound for the gulag.

But Fridman came up from the streets; he will not easily be scared off. A student in Moscow when perestroika began, he made his start in capitalism with a window-washing concern. Then selling perfume, cigarettes, rugs, computers – things Russians wanted and were now permitted to buy. Soon he was a banker and an oilman and a telecoms mogul. Yes, Reiman knows Putin from St

Petersburg. But Putin runs a feudal court. He permits his barons to fight over the spoils of power. This keeps them divided, and so more easily ruled. So Fridman is free to prosecute his campaign against Reiman. Fridman's lawyers are using information from Kroll's spies to bring legal proceedings wherever the companies Galmond says he owns are registered. If they can prove that Galmond is just a front for Reiman, Fridman can be sure the courts will find that the fabulous MegaFon stake is rightfully his. And Kroll might have turned up an ace. The sleuths have found James Hatt. They are asking him to spill what he knows about Leonid Reiman and Jeffrey Galmond.

Galmond needs this fixed. Reiman is growing angry with him. 'You don't have to make any statements to anyone,' he tells Hatt. 'Yes, I think it would be better to say, you know, "I am suffering from a very strong attack of Alzheimer's."'

I spoke to Leonid about this, Galmond goes on. And the message Reiman wishes to convey to James Hatt is: 'We are not interested in collecting enemies. We are interested in finding friends, you know? We would be also happy to make sure that this, it will not be an additional expense to you. Or any inconvenience. And we will make up for that.'

It's just a case, Galmond tells Hatt, of finding the right hidden passage through the global financial system to get the money to you safely. Kroll is sniffing around everywhere. 'We have to be extremely cautious,' Galmond says.

Fridman's side are offering me an extraordinary amount, Hatt says.

Galmond counters: 'I have Leonid saying to me that we will do whatever it is, whatever we need to support you.' And don't forget, he adds, how tight are the bonds that tie Putin to Reiman. Who was it who was in charge of the Moscow office? Who was making tea and coffee? And meeting people at the airport? Lyudmila. Putin's wife. 'I mean,' he assures Hatt, 'they go back a long time.'

Hatt is giving every indication he will agree to sell Leonid Reiman his silence. He and Galmond discuss the logistics of sending his pay-off incognito.

Hatt looks at the time. 'It's 10.30 p.m.,' he says. 'We'll talk tomorrow.'

Don't trust phones, Galmond says. 'You're sure no one has been watching us?

'I have spent a small fortune to make sure that didn't happen,' says Hatt, who's picking up the bill at the Ritz.

Jeffrey rises and departs into the London night. When he's gone, James Hatt stands up. He crosses to the velvet curtains to make sure the camera hidden inside them has worked.

On August 1, 2005 Mohamed Amersi is about to make millions by orchestrating a vast international business deal on behalf of Jeffrey Galmond, respectable Danish tycoon. And on August 1, 2005 Mohamed Amersi is about to make millions by orchestrating a vast international business deal on behalf of Leonid Reiman, corrupt crony of Vladimir Putin. It depends which truth prevails.

While Galmond is at the Ritz negotiating the price of James Hatt's forgetfulness, Mohamed has been negotiating the acquisition of a majority stake in the St Petersburg telecoms network PeterStar. The sellers are some Americans who bought into PeterStar back in the nineties, after Tony Georgiou and Leonid Reiman set it up. The buyer is First National Holding. 'Leonid Reiman was always in control of First National Holding. You and I know that to be true. The reality.' That was what the hidden camera recorded James Hatt saying to Jeffrey Galmond a few months ago at the Ritz. And this reality is seeping out.

In November 2004, while Amersi is in talks with the Americans over PeterStar, the *Wall Street Journal* reports on a dispute before a Swiss arbitration tribunal. It concerns Russian telecoms assets purportedly owned by Jeffrey Galmond and to which Mikhail Fridman's company lays claim. The arbitration panel is looking into Galmond's dealings. Its initial finding is that 'there might be a group of corrupt government officials in the telecommunication industry acting in a concerted way'. A British newspaper, the *Sunday Business*, prints a story days later based on a sworn affidavit in the dispute. It is the testimony of Tony Georgiou. 'Mr Galmond's story about how he claims to have built up his alleged telecoms empire in Russia is fabricated,' goes the quote from Georgiou's affidavit. 'His dealings in that field to my knowledge have always been on behalf of a number of powerful individuals in the Russian state, but most particularly Leonid Reiman.'

This does not halt Mohamed Amersi's work on the PeterStar deal. The Russian people themselves have generously agreed to supply the funding. Two hundred and fifteen million dollars, equivalent to a year's income for forty thousand of them. They will loan the money to First National Holding through state-owned Sberbank, an institution directed by Putin's Kremlin.

In July 2005, more than a year into the PeterStar negotiations, the *Wall Street Journal* runs another story. It's about 'an intensifying money-laundering investigation into whether Russian telecommunications assets now worth hundreds of millions of dollars were diverted through a company set up by a longtime ally of Russian President Vladimir Putin'. The investigators want to know more about a friend of the Russian telecoms minister called Jeffrey Galmond.

Less than a week later, the PeterStar deal is completed. There's a press release. It includes a line from Amersi, declaring himself 'proud to have played a part in this landmark transaction'. Proud, and quite a bit richer. First National Holding – the Luxembourg company at the heart of what is said to be a Putin crony's illicit telecoms empire – pays him four million dollars.

The thing I must get into my thick head is this: Jeffrey Galmond speaks truth.

'I did believe at all times,' Amersi says, 'that Galmond was a telecoms entrepreneur.' He's told me before – the first time we spoke, two years ago – that when he was doing the PeterStar deal he had never even heard an allegation that Galmond was a front for Reiman.

'Have you read this or you haven't?' he says now, as we turn the next tab in our blue binders.

'The Galmond affidavit I've read, yes.' I've also read what James Hatt said of this affidavit at the Ritz: 'Jesus Christ, it's full of holes.'

'That is his idea, which is how he explained through due diligence that he shared with banks, with lawyers and with everyone, as to how he made his money in telecoms. Full stop. And people asked him questions on it and generally believed him. Full stop.'

'Which people?'

'We just talked about it half an hour ago.' The American sellers of the PeterStar stake, plus some lawyers. 'Why are you so dumb? Or are you just making me angry for nothing? You're really dumb and that's why I worry about your senility writing a book because you are dumb.'

'My senility?'

'Yes. You are dumb. I'm telling you this. This is not facetious; you are genuinely dumb. You may think you are very bright but you are really dumb.'

'No, I don't think I'm very bright, don't worry.'

'You are really dumb.' So much so that the point must be rammed home. 'You don't know what you're talking about. You are such an imbecile on this book that you do yourself a disservice and get sued in the process, I'm telling you.'

I hold my senility at bay sufficiently to re-read how Jeffrey Galmond's affidavit starts. And my dilapidated neurons manage a spark. Amersi insists that while he was working for Galmond he heard not so much as a rumour that his client was a front for Leonid Reiman. Any suggestion to the contrary elicits his spleen. Despite being doolally, I can read the date on the affidavit: July 2004, more than a year before Amersi finished the PeterStar deal. In the first paragraph, Galmond says he's given this sworn evidence 'to answer the allegations' that 'myself and numerous other associated companies and individuals are not engaged in legitimate business activities but are vehicles to launder the proceeds of corrupt and other criminal activities of Russia's telecommunications minister, Leonid Reiman.'

But Mohamed is sticking with Jeff. Moron that I am, I am failing to grasp that refuting Galmond's word demands a standard of evidence beyond that required for criminal convictions. Why should these accounts of Jeff being a front for Putin's crony be believed, Mohamed wants to know, in the absence of 'unquestionable proof'? Besides, just as Amersi's secretary was to blame for the debacle with the Saabs, checking such things was 'the responsibility of the lawyers – not me – especially where large sums of money were received or paid'.

We have a lot of documents to get through, and Amersi is going fast. Now and then I ask why one of them is, say, a draft rather than a final signed version. This angers Mohamed. 'I can share what I can share. I'm not going to do your dirty work for you. You fucking go out and do it. Find the shit and come back and ask me proper questions, not bullshit, okay. Go do it. How useless you are. Look at you. You have no idea what you're talking about. No fucking idea, do you know that? You are dangerous.'

―――――――――

The state of Room 5330 suggests its occupant is unravelling. There are dents in the wall. A flower pot is broken. The leg of a chair is damaged, the dresser scratched. The plasma television has been ripped from the wall. When the housekeeping staff at the Mandarin Oriental by Central Park see the damage, they call the police. An NYPD officer arrives and arrests Jeffrey Galmond.

Christmas is nearly here, and the end of 2006. In the two years since Galmond strode assuredly into the Ritz, his reality has imploded. In May, an arbitration tribunal gave its judgment in the MegaFon case. James Hatt testified for Fridman's side, accepting a payment that he said would free him to reveal the truth by covering the costs and risks of giving evidence against powerful Russians. Tony Georgiou took payment as well. The arbitration judges said they would treat such witnesses 'with caution'. But there were documents and other evidence to back up what they said, including the footage captured by the camera Hatt had slipped into the Ritz's curtains.

The judges considered Galmond's evidence too. They concluded that he had 'intentionally misled' them. He is just a front for Leonid Reiman, Putin's minister of communications, the arbitration judges ruled. Leonid Reiman, meanwhile, arranged deals to 'misappropriate for his personal enrichment' assets that belonged to the Russian state.

If they are right, then Mohamed Amersi's four million dollars may have come from the proceeds of crimes against the Russian people.

Fridman has won. But that is not the worst of Galmond's problems. If he is feeling concerned that he may be an object of the Kremlin's wrath, it's a distressing time to be so. Two months ago, Anna Politkovskaya, a journalist who revealed the barbarity of Putin's war in Chechnya, was shot dead in Moscow. Her killer left the pistol at the scene – the signature of a hit. Four weeks ago, Alexander Litvinenko, an exiled former KGB officer investigating Putin's corruption, met two Russians at a London hotel. They slipped a lethal dose of polonium into his tea. Galmond does not need to be paranoid to feel scared. Judges and journalists are discussing what look like the innermost secrets of Putin's kleptocracy – because Jeffrey has let them slip. Others who do that fall from high windows.

Galmond can't sleep. The stress is awful. From the Caribbean to Germany, the authorities have been investigating suspected money-laundering by Leonid Reiman. And Galmond believes he's been betrayed – by Mohamed Amersi.

Amersi set up Enigma for him. Introduced him to Coutts. Arranged the PeterStar deal. Then, this past summer, Amersi switched to Mikhail Fridman's side. That's how Galmond sees it. After Fridman's lawyers prevailed in the Swiss arbitration, Mohamed came to see him with an offer from the victor. Fridman will sell you the MegaFon stake for two billion dollars. And if you don't pay, Fridman and his associates will have you locked up. That was the version Galmond put in a court filing. He told people Amersi was actually rather more colourful, sketching the prospect of Galmond living out his days in a bamboo jail.

The thing I must understand is this: Jeffrey Galmond is a liar.

'That wanker Galmond is not to be trusted to tell the truth,' Amersi tells me. What actually happened is that Mohamed sought to make peace. He spoke to Fridman.* He spoke to Galmond. He met Leonid Reiman himself (never suspecting, he insists, that the minister was up to anything illicit). I ask some questions, trying to establish details.

'This sounds like I'm sitting in a fucking tribunal or a judge. I don't give a shit. I'm telling you what I'm telling you. You want to believe it, you believe it. You don't want to believe it, you'll be sued if you misrepresent it, full stop. There's nothing more to it.'

And the bamboo jail?

* Fridman told me he had no recollection of this. To which Amersi responded: 'Fuck him then, screw him.'

'Those words were not words I ever used. That's my absolutely million per cent confirmation, once and for all. I will not discuss that shit one more time. I never used those words, full stop.'

'So, Galmond was lying about that?'

'Whatever, I don't give a fuck if he's lying, misleading, making it up, it's his problem.'

During exchanges like this with Amersi, a cuckoo comes to mind. A cuckoo needs two opposing realities to be true at once. One is that the egg in that nest over there is the cuckoo's offspring. This truth is the cuckoo's very reason for existing – to reproduce. But at the same time, the cuckoo's egg will only be nurtured if the bird into whose nest the egg has been snuck believes it is its own. But of course, only one of these things can actually be true. The other is an illusion.

If the Swiss judges are right, the cuckoo has been rumbled. The truth, it would seem, is coming for Jeff Galmond. And then, just when its jaws stretch open, ready to swallow him, the truth flops to the ground, motionless. The hunt has been called off.

This fight inside Putin's feudal court is in danger of getting out of hand. It has dragged in half the Russian regime, not just Mikhail Fridman and his allies, but the boss himself, plus the boss's wife, Lyudmila. At the Ritz, Jeff Galmond revealed that Putin had been asking Leonid Reiman: Are you sure you've got this under control?

The highest Swiss court upholds the arbitration ruling that Putin's minister of communications has been embezzling the nation's telecoms assets. But the German authorities investigating Reiman's suspected use of Frankfurt bankers as proxies receive a letter from their Russian counterparts assuring them that no crime had been committed in Russia, scuppering any money-laundering case. In the Caribbean, four of the companies holding Russian telecoms assets that Jeff Galmond maintains belong to him have forty-five million dollars confiscated for perverting the course of justice and furnishing false information. But it is the companies, not the human being, that are convicted.

Days later, it's over. Alisher Usmanov, portly ex-prisoner, billionaire, metals mogul, newspaper proprietor, superyacht owner, Arsenal shareholder, lord of a Moscow mansion guarded by attack dogs and Kalashnikovs, friend to the Putin Kremlin – he starts buying everyone out of MegaFon. Fridman's company gets five billion dollars for its stake. Even though Jeffrey Galmond was found by the arbitration judges to be a front for Leonid Reiman, he remains the named owner of another MegaFon stake of about the same size as the one Fridman has wrested away. Usmanov pays far less than it's worth; perhaps that's what comes of losing. Still, Jeffrey Galmond – or Leonid Reiman, if Galmond is his frontman – receives two hundred million dollars.

Usmanov's munificence brings an end to the hostilities.

Leonid Reiman leaves government, free at last to live openly as a rich man. Oh yes, he declares, that Jeffrey Galmond is a successful investor; he's not some front for me. 'Finally,' he says when the last criminal case fizzles out, 'this whole dirty story has been brought to an end.' Galmond abides in Swiss luxury, troubled only by occasional inquiries from the Danish tax authorities about how he came by his fortune.

Having demonstrated his mastery of the information industry, Mohamed Amersi's horizons widen. He finds a client whose ambitions span what used to be the Soviet empire.

Four

The host

Here in Scotland, he is not the Prince of Wales but the Duke of Rothesay. Titles aside, though, Charles no longer has to be his own double. Those miserable years are gone, when he was married to Diana and in love with Camilla. What joy to wed her at last, back in 2005. Handy, too, to bring Camilla's nephew into the family. Ben Elliot had just started Quintessentially then. Look at it now: two thousand staff, offices in sixty cities. Nigeria, Ukraine, China, a big one in Russia. Even that Roman Abramovich is a client. Knowing the right people, that's what it's all about, Ben says. Being able to ask the right person for the right favour.

When Ben sends Quintessentially clients Charles's way, they get what money can't buy. And Charles, he gets money. Not for anything so crude as his personal expenses, of course. That's covered by the taxpayer. Thirty-three million they're forking out for the royal household in 2013. No, Ben's Quintessentially clients are invited to support the prince's charitable works. Few of which in recent years have caused him more bother than saving the very building at which today's clients have just arrived. For the nation – saving it for the nation.

When Charles heard to his horror that the Marquess of Bute was selling Dumfries House, he acted at once. How could he not? How could he stand by while its unique furniture was carted off and the mansion doubtless left to fall into ruin? The way the light plays on the plasterwork in the Pink Dining Room alone is a wonder to behold.

It was a close thing. Lorries stuffed with gorgeous Chippendales were already barrelling south to Christie's to be auctioned off. They'd got as far as Cumbria when at 1 a.m. Charles had them turn round. The prince raised from charities more than half the forty-five million the marquess wanted. The rest, his foundation had to borrow. Then came the financial crisis. The value of the land the debt was secured against fell to less than the amount of the loan. 'Help!' the prince would think as he lay awake at night.

This is why you have to know them. The rich. A Russian banker gathered a few donors to help make the money problems go away. That's the thing about the rich: recessions don't happen to them. Take Quintessentially's clients. Everywhere there's poverty and hunger and austerity but Ben's firm has had to set up a dedicated new Russia team at its office near Regent's Park to handle all the demand. Brazilians too. And wanting top-tier membership. The fee's fifteen grand a year or more.

Tonight's guest, Mohamed, is a Global Elite member. Ben's people, they get the little things done for you: sending flowers, renting cars, restaurant reservations. Amersi likes that. He likes this too. Being here, this place where others cannot go.

Sometimes one might invite a few of them – the others – up to Dumfries, to receive their gratitude. A few months back, the television gardener Alan Titchmarsh came to make a documentary. Before the cameras, droves of locals with shovels tamed the overgrown Walled Garden. There are to be allotments yielding vegetables for nearby schoolchildren.

Amersi dines with the prince. Like the heir to the throne, Mohamed wishes to give – to give back. Ask Amersi what he thinks on the subject of philanthropy and he says: 'Muslims and Hindus and Jews and Christians – end of the day, we all have the same red blood. We eat the same food. We're all mortal. When we were born, we did not choose our name, our faith, our colour or our parents. They were given to us. Yet we spend all our lives fighting and killing each other. For what?' In short, now he has made his fortune, the calling to which Mohamed Amersi is to devote his talents in these times of division, these times of walls and fences, is this: How to bring humanity together.

When Mohamed and Nadia depart the next day, CNN runs an interview with Charles's younger son, Harry. He's at Camp Bastion in Afghanistan, flying helicopters. The interviewer asks about the photos the *Sun* published the other day: Harry, naked in a Las Vegas hotel room apart from cupped hands shielding cock and balls. 'I probably let myself

47

down,' Harry concedes. 'I let my family down, I let other people down. But at the end of the day I was in a private area and there should be a certain amount of privacy that one should expect.'

At 10.11 that morning, an email arrives for Amersi. It's from Kenneth Dunsmuir. He used to be headteacher at the private school near Dumfries House. Now he helps run the trust that owns the mansion. 'It was a real pleasure to meet both you and Nadia during your visit to Dumfries House at the weekend. I very much hope that you enjoyed your short stay with us and that your onward journey yesterday passed smoothly.' Michael Fawcett, a courtier Charles finds so indispensable he keeps reappointing him each time he resigns in disgrace, has asked Dunsmuir to send Amersi some documents, along with his warmest regards. The documents are attached. They contain funding opportunities at the estate. One is an Outdoor Activity Area.

Mohamed Amersi emails his banker at Coutts. There's plenty in his accounts: he's just finishing six years during which one of the world's biggest communications corporations has paid for his services at a rate of nineteen thousand pounds a day. Send a hundred and thirty thousand pounds to Dumfries House, Amersi commands. Just a week's fees for Mohamed, but it's much appreciated by the royals. When Charles's courtier Fawcett sends word that the bankers have safely delivered his generous donation towards the Outdoor Activity Area, Amersi forwards the message to Ben Elliot. Elliot has achieved the win-win: Amersi, a Quintessentially client, has a place among the highest in the land, and the highest in the land – Elliot's relatives – have the benefit of Amersi's money. 'Well done,' he replies within a minute. 'Lots to discuss with you.'

Five

Protection

It is Boxing Day, 2009, and there is one present left to give. The Princess has asked for just under a quarter of a billion dollars. The demand for payment goes to a multinational telecoms corporation.

The Princess is many things. The scholar certified by Harvard Business School. The pop star Googoosha ('You look fine,' she sings, 'but what do you hide in your soul?'). The diplomat. The 'exotic beauty', according to her Twitter bio. The government minister. The fashionista. The delegate to the World Economic Forum. The mezzo-soprano. The martial artist. The poet. The dictator's daughter.

The executives at TeliaSonera receive the request for money. You don't write to one of the world's biggest telecoms companies and say: Pay the Princess. Instead, the email from her representative goes like this:

I hope you had wonderful Christmas Holidays!

Enclosed you may find the Valuation Report as promised to be send for your attention. Please advise on the next steps.

Call me if we need to discuss any matters related to the upcoming Trasaction.

The upcoming Trasaction is the latest instalment in a series of payments by TeliaSonera to its local partner in the Central Asian ex-Soviet republic of Uzbekistan. From their headquarters in Stockholm, TeliaSonera's bosses have taken care to maintain their ignorance of who exactly this Uzbek partner is. The ignorance is helpful as they go about their mission of spreading democracy one business deal at a time while delivering a healthy return for their shareholders, the people of Sweden and Finland. This latest business deal needs expert counsel on how to get it done. So among the senior TeliaSonera people the email gets forwarded to is the specialist adviser the company has retained at great expense, Mohamed Amersi.

A quarter of a billion is a fair old present, sure, but the Princess does not only take. Gulnara Karimova gives too – the gift of protection. From the punishments she inflicts on the unprotected. Woe betide those who forfeit her protection. Even her own husband.

They meet at her nineteenth birthday party. It is thrown at Daddy's place: the presidential residence in Tashkent.

Mansur Maqsudi grew up in the States but his clan is influential in Uzbekistan. Six months later, he and Gulnara are married. The couple desire a fine American education for their children, so it is in New Jersey that they make their magnificently appointed home. Islam arrives, named after his grandfather, then a daughter, Iman. A security detail befitting her status watches over Gulnara. The family goes back to Tashkent now and again. Mansur has to look after his Uzbek business: after he weds the tyrant's daughter, the makers of Coca-Cola select him as a local partner. Mostly, though, it is a western life with all the trappings of American affluence: Pokémon cards and nannies and Chuck E. Cheese birthday parties for the children, graduate degrees at Harvard for the parents.

Yet there are arguments, and they get worse. A series of marital rows escalates day after day one summer until the shouting grows so loud that little Islam runs frightened into the room. Mansur turns to walk out. The Princess's bodyguards block his way.

You have gone too far, he tells her. I want a divorce.

The next day, while Mansur is at his parents', he sees a message on his phone from his wife. She, her entourage and her children are boarding a plane.

Within three months, an Uzbek judge grants Gulnara an uncontested divorce and custody of the children. The court has been informed of the situation by the Princess herself. At an initial hearing Gulnara tells the court she's phoned Mansur and let him know about the divorce proceedings. She says she has no idea where he is but nonetheless he has been formally notified of his right to appear by way of notices that have been posted to him two days before the court issues them. At the second and final hearing Gulnara tells the court that she has not, in fact, spoken to Mansur since she left him but knows that he is reluctant to come to Uzbekistan because of a forthcoming tax audit.

Reality soon catches up with the Princess's words. Gulnara's Washington propaganda consultants build a website devoted to exposing Mansur's wrongdoing. Government auditors discover his 'illegal schemes'. Tax laws have been violated, sales regulations have been violated, human rights have been violated. A larcenous, fraudulent, tax-dodging, money-laundering, bribe-taking extortionist: the real Mansur Maqsudi is unmasked. And this degeneracy extends to his family. The secret police round up Mansur's relatives by night. His hundred-and-fifty-million-dollar Coca-Cola bottling business is liquidated by court order. Six months after the Uzbek anti-monopoly agency approves some share transactions at his company, the same agency brings legal action on the grounds that the transactions were in fact illegal. Uzbek judges, paid the equivalent of forty dollars a month, endorse these alternative facts. A financial adviser to Gulnara who flees reports that she reviewed, edited and approved their rulings. Sometimes she simply wrote passages of them herself, to get the words just right. Coca-Cola is said to have found a new local partner to replace Maqsudi, a successful entrepreneur called Gulnara Karimova.

The Princess learns how to turn power into money. She just needs her father to do what is required to maintain this power.

On Uzbek television screens, the face of the protector appears. Jowly, pock-marked Islam Karimov addresses his people. They need to hear the truth.

Yesterday, he tells them, May 13, 2005, a tragedy befell this country. In the town of Andijan, extremists shed innocent blood. Heavily armed, they seized the regional administration building. For human shields they brought elders, women and children. Immediately, says Karimov, I, your president, set up a field headquarters nearby, under my personal command. First of all, we had to protect the people. To restore calm. The extremists had already attacked and killed servicemen.

Karimov asks his flock to consider the divine will, which he, their leader, can reveal to them. 'Why did God create us in this world? For happiness. To bring up children. To leave our footsteps in the future. For something good. Who thinks it is sensible to take someone's life, to leave someone orphaned or to leave someone widowed?' Not to spill innocent blood. And yet, in his long years ruling over his dear Uzbeks, Karimov has learned to be merciful. He spoke directly to these ungodly killers, holed up in the regional administration building they had seized. What is done is done, he told them. We will send buses for you to leave. Do that, and no one will harm you. Of course, there will be a full investigation. And the guilty will be punished. But for now you should get on the buses. No one will touch you. Not a hair on your head. 'This is the president's promise,' Karimov says. 'Has the president ever lied to his people? Has he ever achieved his goal by deception?'

'I speak sincerely,' Karimov tells the nation. 'God is my witness. If they had accepted this proposal, nothing would have happened.'

But the extremists had demands. They wanted other extremists freed from prison. They refused to get on the buses. They gave the president no choice. How could he allow the chaos that has afflicted other post-Soviet republics to engulf his dear Uzbeks? The rose revolution in Georgia, the tulip revolution in Kyrgyzstan, the orange revolution in Ukraine – these insults to the natural order must not be allowed to spread.

'A total of more than ten people, including the military, police and innocent people, were killed. There are far more killed on their side,' Karimov says. 'What happened is an incongruous event that is absolutely at odds with the Uzbek people, our society and nation. I will be happy if everyone comes to this conclusion.'

The broadcast ends.

In Andijan, a leaflet marinates in a puddle of blood. The incarnadined words are still legible. 'We could tolerate it no longer.' The poverty. The corruption. They have slung in jail the local businessmen who'd used their success to pay decent wages, cover their staff's medical bills, hand out free meals.

They say we are Islamists. 'When we make demands, the authorities should hear us,' the leaflet says. 'If we stick together, they will not do anything bad to us.'

Before this, when the blood that will become the puddle is still in veins, hundreds gather in the town square. A podium goes up, with a loudspeaker. The charitable businessmen have been sprung from prison. They speak of their show trials, of what was done to them inside. A handful of those who gather are armed. Most are talking, listening, picnicking. Parents bring their children. It is still early in the day when a green car with black windows approaches the square. A bullet hits a boy's head. He is about ten. His life ends.

Protesters rush the shooters, overpower them, tie them up. They seize a prosecutor and a tax inspector too. The protest grows. There are thousands here now. More vehicles drive by sporadically, spitting bullets that pass through a stomach, a neck, a skull. But a wonderful rumour spreads. The president is coming. Karimov is coming. He will hear our grievances.

Troops are gathering at every exit to the square. At 5 p.m., armoured personnel carriers appear. The soldiers inside do not aim. They just fire. The man on the podium shouts: Run. A wall of military vehicles lies ahead. There are soldiers behind a line of sandbags. More on top of the apartment blocks, on top of the cinema, up in the trees. They are all shooting. One man looks around him. This is like a bowling alley, he thinks, when the ball hits the pins. Hundreds die.

Following the massacre, Karimov rounds on the Americans. They are helping refugees from Andijan to escape. How could they betray him like this? After he pledged allegiance to their War on Terror. He gave them a base from which to attack Afghanistan. They trained his troops. The Chinese want him. Putin wants him. The Americans can go.

The US forces are ordered to leave their Uzbek base. And the Americans who have set up a phone network in Uzbekistan decide to leave too. But a deal to sell their network to the Qataris falls apart when Karimov's authorities suspend its licence. At the US embassy in Tashkent, the diplomats detect something other than 'bias against American companies' at work. A deeper force: 'simple greed'.

As they seek a buyer the Karimov regime will find acceptable, the Americans receive an email written in cryptic business-speak. The mysterious sender calls himself Gergiy.

Dear Sirs

this message was prepared with intention to prevent and avoid unnecessary complications arisen during last months around your company in Uzbekistan. It goes without saying that it contains strictly private and confidential information, so source cannot be named and unnecessary words are intentionally omitted.

As you are aware, the ongoing process of selling the company didn't receive so called final approval for reasons you might wish to understand better:

1. Local facilitators or supporters on your side
evidently aren't right party to ensure the final
approval that would mean smooth finalization.
Without final approval, realization of selling to new
owner is not realistic.

It is necessary, Gergiy explains, 'to reach fair, mutually win–
win solution'. The Americans think Karimov's daughter
Gulnara has had a hand in the attacks her father's regime has
waged on their company. The Princess, as she's known, is now
a 'notable interlocutor' in a new prospective buyer's negotiations. By May 2007, two years after Islam Karimov spelled out
his power over Uzbekistan in blood at Andijan, his daughter
is on the cusp of spectacularly monetising her influence. A
'preliminary hand-shake' between her representatives and
those of the Scandinavian telecoms multinational TeliaSonera
swiftly becomes a formal agreement.

In the holiday lull at the end of 2007, TeliaSonera's chief
executive lands in Tashkent. It is four months since Lars
Nyberg took over. Previously, he was known as the high-
est-paid Swede abroad. Bald and wiry, he is described
admiringly by fellow business winners with words such as
'unsentimental' and 'hard-nosed'. After years at Philips, he's
been a CEO in America, running a tech company, mixing
with Bill Clinton and displaying a readiness to fire droves of
workers to improve the numbers.

The courting of the Princess took place on Nyberg's predecessor's watch. The paperwork on the Uzbek deal TeliaSonera's

directors signed off on had said merely that the company was going into business with 'a strong local group'. This strength takes human form in a discreet corner of the Tashkent restaurant at which Nyberg presents himself. The lights are low. He is led past tables filled with traditional cuisine to where a petite woman sits with two heavies. What strikes Nyberg about Gulnara is her fingers. Each of them is freighted with diamonds.

The Princess asks him: TeliaSonera wants what in Uzbekistan?

Growth, Lars replies.

Because Europe is full of phones. America too, even Russia. Not the Stans. In the former Soviet provinces, hardly anyone has a phone yet. But they will. These expanses between Arabia and China are stuffed with oil and gas and coal and metals. Those industries are dominated by corporations like ExxonMobil and Glencore. The communications industry is virgin territory. Bringing the power of information to the masses so long enslaved under communist rule: it is the noblest of vocations. But you might want to take care not to have too much information yourself. It can get in the way of the noble vocation. Information, for instance, about the Uzbek man who has escorted TeliaSonera's chief executive to dinner with the Princess.

Bekhzod Akhmedov is still in his teens when he splits in two.

It is 1990. The USSR is giving way to the new order. The new old order: one day Islam Karimov is the ruler of Soviet

Uzbekistan, the next day he is the ruler of post-Soviet Uzbekistan. Yesterday the Uzbek sun shone on communists. Today it shines on capitalists. Bekhzod enrols at Tashkent State University to study international economic relations. His sister, studying in another department, meets Karimov's daughter. A decade later, Tashkent State alumni gather for a reunion at a café. Bekhzod's sister introduces him to Gulnara. Come to work for me, Gulnara says. Bekhzod agrees. Who refuses the Princess?

Formally, Bekhzod becomes the manager of her fashion company, the one selling Benetton and Levi's to the Tashkent new rich. In reality – if that's the right word, because reality is just what Gulnara says it is, what she says it is today, this morning, this minute – he's working for some western investors who have hired him to run their Uzbek telecoms venture. Uzdunrobita, it's called: Gateway to the World.

Bekhzod's western bosses learn that he knows the Princess. They want to meet her. He arranges it at the Four Seasons in London. Let's be partners, the westerners tell Gulnara. Another gathering is arranged, this time in Dubai. Cut me in, Gulnara says, or I will destroy your company. The westerners give her a stake in Uzdunrobita, Central Asia's first mobile phone service.

The Princess makes no secret of this. In 2004, after her ex brings US legal proceedings over the divorce, she grants an interview to a sympathetic journalist from the *Independent*.

When I meet Ms Karimova in the foyer café of a smart Moscow hotel, the 31-year-old seems an unlikely source of such controversy. She wishes to reply to her critics, she tells me. Yet she appears quiet, almost shy, but very beautiful. In a city full of new-rich exhibitionists, she is modestly dressed, with almost no make-up and her hat pulled far down over her forehead. But this fugitive from US justice, accused of 'kidnapping' her children, is determined to set the record straight.

'It is all a terrible mess,' she says. 'I didn't want it to turn out like this. I just wanted a normal, civilised divorce.'

The *Independent* article quotes Gulnara 'angrily' denying allegations that she is an 'extravagantly wealthy woman' who has 'made a fortune' in Uzbekistan 'through her family connections'. She does, though, confirm that she owns two ventures. One is in jewellery design. That one's just a hobby. The other is 'a major share in Uzdunrobita, the country's main mobile-phone company, which she claims she personally built up to 150,000 subscribers'. This stake in Uzdunrobita is valuable. Soon a Russian oligarch buys it. His company pays three hundred and fifty million dollars.

Gulnara retains her control over Bekhzod, Uzdunrobita's chief executive. It is Bekhzod who negotiates with TeliaSonera's people – who are investing in a competitor to the network he runs. It is Bekhzod who takes Lars Nyberg to a restaurant to meet the Princess with the sparkling hands when the TeliaSonera chief executive comes to Tashkent. And it is Bekhzod who sends the email on Boxing Day, 2009, requesting a payment.

'FYI and for Monday's call!'

A TeliaSonera executive forwards Bekhzod's email to three senior colleagues, one of the finance guys, and Mohamed Amersi, the corporation's senior adviser on dealmaking in Eurasia.

Amersi has known these Scandinavians for years. On Europe's sometimes blurry northern frontier with Russia, they were quick into the post-Soviet telecoms industry, gaining a shareholding in the Russian giant MegaFon. Amersi served as a MegaFon director during the legal battle over a disputed stake in the company between the oligarch Mikhail Fridman and the mercurial conqueror of the Wild East, Jeffrey Galmond. As regards the allegations that their partner Galmond is merely a front for Leonid Reiman, Vladimir Putin's old crony and telecoms minister, Amersi and the Scandinavians are of one mind: there's no truth to it. Galmond, they maintain, is who he says he is.

And Amersi encountered TeliaSonera a second time in Uzbekistan in 2006. For clients in the Gulf – Qataris and Emiratis – he worked on bids to buy the mobile network there that some Americans had put up for sale. Don't compete with us, Amersi would recall TeliaSonera's chairman telling him, we have deep pockets.

Evidently, the Scandinavians liked what they saw. In 2007, TeliaSonera retained Amersi to advise on the acquisitions through which it was expanding into the former Soviet Union and the rest of Eurasia. Although he wasn't involved in the original Uzbek deal, his expertise is deployed on the payment Bekhzod has requested.

Amersi gets to work on a reply. In the beginning, TeliaSonera made an initial thirty-million-dollar down payment to its local Uzbek partner, and gave a pledge to buy the local partner's stake in their shared phone operation if the partner wanted to sell it later. This pledge is what Bekhzod – or the anonymous partner Bekhzod represents – now wants honoured. Bekhzod has supplied a Russian bank's valuation of the stake. Amersi suggests ways to let the Uzbeks have the payment and also keep them as partners rather than buying them out entirely. The response Amersi drafts is relayed to Bekhzod by Tero Kivisaari, the young, thrusting Finn that Lars Nyberg has put in charge of TeliaSonera's Eurasia unit. On New Year's Eve, Tero emails the team to say Bekhzod likes what Mohamed's suggesting.

'Tero: this is great!' Amersi replies. He proposes tweaking the financial instruments involved for TeliaSonera's benefit. 'Let me know if you wish to discuss.'

'Mohamed, thanks,' writes Tero. 'Let's not discuss today but over the weekend. I've been on the phone all the time and my wife does not appreciate it :)'

A week later, Tero emails again. He has spoken to Bekhzod. 'The discussion was very friendly. However, after reflecting with his "partners", he did not like our proposal.'

'I think,' Tero tells Amersi and the rest of the team, 'the situation is as follows: after reflecting on our paper, they felt offended.' Bekhzod is saying that they 'protected our company and now when they ask for our support, we send them a paper that is only serving TeliaSonera interest and ignoring their needs. Now they say you can keep your stinking offer.' Bekhzod wants 'proper incentives', such as more money.

We've got to think carefully about our next move, Tero says. The team tinkers with the terms, seeking a way to keep the Uzbeks sweet. In exchange, the Uzbeks agree to give an undertaking in writing to help TeliaSonera keep hold of its licences and acquire more as needs be. If there is any discussion of how it is in these Uzbeks' gift to secure such advantages from Karimov's regime, it is not recorded in the TeliaSonera team's emails.

Finally the two sides agree on a number: two hundred and twenty million dollars. Equivalent to the annual income of more than a hundred thousand of Bekhzod's fellow Uzbeks. More money than they can imagine in Andijan. Enough, if it were going into the national budget, to fund all Uzbek higher education for four years. Except that isn't where it's going. In fact, it isn't going to Uzbekistan at all but to a company incorporated four thousand miles away on Gibraltar. Provided, that is, that TeliaSonera's directors in Stockholm approve the deal. One of the team working on it sends Amersi and the others the memo that has been written to persuade the board. By keeping this obscure Gibraltar corporation as a partner, the directors are informed, 'we increase the likelihood of a successful development' of TeliaSonera's Uzbek mobile phone service.

The board signs off. The money moves. On March 10, 2010, Mohamed Amersi sends TeliaSonera an invoice for his 'success fee': half a million dollars, payable to his Swiss bank account with Coutts.

In time, TeliaSonera will pay the highest fine ever levied for corruption after admitting the true identity of its local partner in Uzbekistan, shielded within the Gibraltar shell company: the Princess with the diamond rings, Karimov's daughter Gulnara. To Mohamed Amersi, he insists, this comes as a great shock – checking whether the TeliaSonera deals he advised on were corrupt was not, as he frequently remarks, what he was paid for.

'You can write what you want, say what you want.'

I'm asking Mohamed if he knew that the two-hundred-and-twenty-million-dollar payment he helped TeliaSonera send to a company in Gibraltar was bound for the Uzbek dictator's daughter.

No, he says, I did not know. It was not my job to know. TeliaSonera bought into Uzbekistan before I went to work for the company, Amersi reminds me. Figuring out who really owned their local partner should have been done then, he says. The lawyers and the banks and the TeliaSonera staff whose job that was – they should have done it.

They did – some of them did. It's right here in the present blue binder. We have turned to a copy of the report of the internal investigation that TeliaSonera commissioned from a law firm after Swedish journalists unmasked Gulnara as the secret partner in 2012. The report says people working on TeliaSonera's entry to Uzbekistan back in 2007 were told that their interlocuter, Bekhzod Akhmedov, was her representative. The source of this information was Bekhzod himself. This knowledge, the report goes on, was recorded in a memo that describes Bekhzod as 'Chief Executive for Gulnara Karimova's investment group'.

But no one told Mohamed when he arrived at TeliaSonera months later, he says.

He had by then, I remind him, also seen an investment bank's report that said a stake in Uzdunrobita, the Uzbek mobile phone company Bekhzod ran, was 'thought to be held by affiliates of Gulnara Karimova, the daughter of the country's President'. As with the allegations that Jeffrey Galmond was a front for a Putin crony, Amersi says he disregarded this for lack of proof.

Gulnara herself had told a reporter from the *Independent* that this was true, that she was co-owner of the company Bekhzod ran. Bekhzod: the Uzbek whose email on behalf of TeliaSonera's local partner had been forwarded to Mohamed. But even if all this had passed Amersi by – passed by a man so expert in this field that he was paid millions upon millions as a consultant – did none of the other details of what he was asked to do over Yuletide 2009 make him wonder if there was anything fishy going on? That this mammoth payment was going to some company in Gibraltar? That Bekhzod represented both TeliaSonera's local partner in its Uzbek venture and this venture's rival, Uzdunrobita?

'Everybody says, "Woo ooh ooh, he was at Uzdunrobita." It's all hogwash.'* Bekhzod, Mohamed says, had told TeliaSonera's head of Eurasia – the thrusting Tero Kivisaari – that he was going to resolve this conflict of interest by ceasing to be the boss of the rival network. 'When it came up in the discussions in 2009 December, the three weeks that I spent on this bloody deal, it was raised amongst us. Tero Kivisaari said: "Yes, he's already resigned, we have seen paperwork and he will officially announce his stepping down in January." That's all that was said.'

If Bekhzod had indeed been telling the TeliaSonera people this, they were showing considerable patience: he'd been saying so for two years, ever since their first meetings. And he would not resign for a further two years. I point this out to Mohamed.

'I have no fucking idea. I'm not a babysitter.'

To buttress his point, Mohamed brandishes the report a Swedish law firm produced for TeliaSonera on the Uzbek affair. 'I interviewed with them. Bjorn, whatever his name was. I interviewed with him.'

---

* It's hard to render in prose the 'woo ooh ooh' sound Mohamed made here. It's the sarcastic noise you make before saying 'big fucking deal'.

This report notes it was 'peculiar' to have the boss of a rival firm as the representative of your local partner. So I try again and ask Mohamed: You didn't think there was anything strange about it?

'Did he criticise me in the fucking report? No, fuck it. Did he criticise me? Show me, if you read it, which page does it say that Amersi, this was your fucking task, to police this guy? Fuck off, okay. Fuck off.'

'It says no such thing,' I reply. He is right. TeliaSonera's executives, assisted by their lawyers, were responsible for keeping the deals clean. Decisions to approve deals were taken collectively by the board of directors. But Amersi was charging many millions as a specialist on making deals in Eurasia. On at least four occasions, he was directly involved in payments: TeliaSonera sent money to Amersi's company and Amersi's company sent it on to the ultimate recipient, so-called 'back-to-back' agreements that were used, he says, for 'sensitive security and other reasons … particularly in relation to oversight and accountability'.* Amersi personally

---

* Lawyers from Norton Rose Fulbright who TeliaSonera hired to investigate its Eurasia operations discovered these back-to-back arrangements. Amersi confirms them in a letter to Norton Rose, a copy of which was in the binders he gave me. Amersi says there was a payment of $135,000 related to 'Kazakh frequency' and one related to 'Nepal tax' of $1 million. The other two have codenames: 'Project Stingray' (£135,000) and Project Blue Waters ($3 million). After I read through the documents following our meeting, I emailed Amersi to ask him about this. Here are my questions, with his replies:

a) What were each of these projects?

negotiated with influential figures in countries where corruption is rife. So it strikes me that he could have had reason to think that some of the money paid to win TeliaSonera business in Eurasia might have amounted to buying the authorities' favour.

'What I'm trying to ask you is that with all your expertise—'

'Fuck off. Don't put words in my mouth. My role was not that.' He is very cross again now. 'I am not the fucking policeman who diligences KYC and who looks which toilet paper they use.* It's not my job. My job is to do valuation, my job is to validate valuation and my job is to optimise transaction structures. That's what I was paid to do as a professional.'

I wonder what he thinks in hindsight. Now that police have opened the wall safe at the Princess's Swiss apartment

NONE OF YOUR BUSINESS

b) In each case who was the third party to whom you paid the money?

NONE OF YOUR BUSINESS

c) What service did these third parties provide in exchange for these camouflaged payments from TeliaSonera?

NONE OF YOUR BUSINESS

* KYC = 'Know Your Customer', as in finding out who you're really doing business with. And 'to diligence' is one of those business-speak nouns-as-a-verb (see 'to onboard' for showing someone new around, 'to rightsize' for firing loads of people, 'to language' for using words). It means performing due diligence – checking whether your counterparty is what they say they are.

and found documents proving that Takilant, the Gibraltar shell company to which Amersi helped send hundreds of millions of dollars, was indeed hers. Now that TeliaSonera has admitted corruption and paid a record fine. Perhaps now Mohamed wonders how he didn't figure it out, a man of his gargantuan capabilities?

'You don't feel, looking back, knowing what we know now about Takilant—'

'I am not here to forensically KYC people. It's not my job. Do you understand that? Is your job to do investment banking here today? No. You are dumb, you don't understand anything about transactions. Your job is to ask stupid questions. Do I ask you to diligence anyone? No, because you'd be useless. Do I ask you to read the financial statement? No, because you'd be useless. So, why would you ask me to do things which is not within my competency or my mandate?'

'I understand your point.'

'Finished, nothing more to say. Fuck off on that. All of you. Every one of you.'

———

The Princess's message comes through on a BlackBerry. Dark bags under his eyes, Bekhzod Akhmedov reads her words and realises he will have to flee Uzbekistan.

'Everyone is tired of repeating that the sooner you put things in order, the sooner this will all be over ... your situation is getting worse and worse ... we came to your home to talk to you but you stubbornly refuse to understand ... you are responsible for everything entrusted to you ... you need to pay the entire debt – the cost of the Moscow house, the cost of the Tashkent apartment ... this may well be your last warning ... events will develop in accordance with your immediate results ... if there are consequences for your kids, wife and family, you should have thought of that earlier.'

It is June 2012. Two years have passed since Bekhzod secured the two-hundred-and-twenty-million-dollar payment that Mohamed Amersi helped to arrange – and which TeliaSonera will later admit was a blockbuster bribe for the Princess. But Bekhzod no longer enjoys the Princess's protection. Now she wants what he has.

Gulnara has sent word that he is not to leave the country. At his house in Tashkent, in front of his parents and sister, one of her minions reads out demands for money: A million by the end of the week, or else Bekhzod goes to jail. Sell your father's house, if you must. He pays but more demands follow. A bill for a quarter of a million, the cost of the Princess's fashion brand sponsoring the Clinton Foundation gala at the Cannes film festival. The authorities – her father's authorities – have found unpaid tax bills. Bekhzod, it transpires, has mismanaged the advertising budget, charitable donations, sponsorship.

A couple of times Gulnara herself calls. She swears at him. 'Every dollar of your property belongs to me.' Then one of her people shows him the message on a BlackBerry. 'If consequences fall on your kids, wife and family ...' Bekhzod's wife and children are in Moscow. It's where his youngest has been undergoing treatment. Gulnara is having the borders watched but he sneaks across the Russian frontier. He carries her secrets with him.

Bekhzod applies for the Russian witness protection programme. A few blocks from Red Square, agents from the organised crime squad interrogate him. He tells them about the Princess, about TeliaSonera, about the shell companies and the bank accounts.

His escape seems to have panicked her. He's heard that at one of her Swiss banks, there's been an arrest.

Six

The right path

In Cotswolds sunshine, the philanthropists pose for photographs before the honey-coloured stone of the Royal Agricultural University. It is July 2014. Mohamed Amersi's highly remunerative career in the telecommunications industry is over. Eighteen months have passed since Ben Elliot arranged for him to become the latest of Quintessentially's Global Elite clients to be inducted into royal circles with dinner at Dumfries. Dressed in white slacks and blue blazer, a yellow pocket square matching his tie, Mohamed beams at the camera. He is becoming the person he wants to be, the righteous one – press releases say so.

It is Prince Charles, the Royal Agricultural University's alumnus and patron, who Amersi credits with inspiring his conversion to the cause of the less fortunate. The heir to the throne, Mohamed says, 'has shown himself to be a global champion for how to ensure that the world we leave behind for our children and grandchildren is better than the one we inherited when we became adults'. Amersi says the future king shaped a lot of his thinking on such important topics as environmental stewardship, modern-day slavery and inclusive capitalism.

To advance the latter, Amersi has created Inclusive Ventures. He came up with it during an MBA at Oxford. It's about upskilling, rural-onshoring, and above all reverse-innovating. 'We now live in a world of conscious capitalism,' begins Amersi's business plan for Inclusive Ventures. 'The disparity between the rich and poor widens daily.' The 'perfect storm' is about to descend on us: 'population growth, food scarcity, clean water, environment, etc'. What's more, 'the Bottom of the Pyramid will be demanding their fair share of the earth's resources. To address these developments, social impact investing is gaining acceptance.'

Looking down from the Top of the Pyramid, Amersi has chosen for Inclusive Ventures' logo a multi-coloured arc, to symbolise the project's inclusiveness, its diversity. Inclusive Ventures 'is not restricted by colour, class, creed or culture'. 'The most powerful colour in the arc is magenta,' Mohamed explains in the business plan. 'This is a "Royal Colour" and applies aptly' to Inclusive Ventures, 'given its access to and partnership with Royalty'.

Amersi lives in Dubai these days. But he also enjoys various residences that befit his status back in the UK. There's the magnificent London townhouse behind the Dorchester in Mayfair, the hotel where elite dealmakers gather. If life is Monopoly, he's living on exclusive purple. For a verdant contrast, he has what *Country Life* calls 'a picture-perfect

Georgian house', right here in the Cotswolds. Endowed with extensive servants' quarters, Bledisloe Lodge is said to have sold for some seven million pounds. Sometimes it seems they run the country from here. David Cameron's place is nearby. His friend Rebekah Brooks. And the voice of the people, Jeremy Clarkson. Mohamed and Nadia let the less prominent locals use the barns for their fêtes.

Amersi is a welcome visitor next door at the Royal Agricultural University. By buying a tract of its land to add to his own thirty-eight acres of landscaped gardens, he's putting a little money in its monarchical coffers. At the end of today's gathering of philanthropists, the university's principal will furnish the press release with an effusive quote.

Sharing with Amersi the chocolate-box backdrop to the photoshoot is another example of a charitably minded High Net Worth Individual. Like Amersi, Ajeya Sumargi is dressed for the English countryside. Peach shirt and duck-egg jacket with bold white stripes. Like Amersi, he is, as the press release will say, here to help transform the world for the good of the poor. He has come to give – to give back. To the needy, to the young, of whom there are many back home in Nepal. Sumargi's admirers like to say he lives up to his name's Nepali meaning: One who always treads the right path.

Seven

Mr XY

No one can say for sure why Prince Dippy does it. Perhaps because the king will not let him marry the woman he loves. They met while he was at Eton, being equipped to rule alongside such promising contemporaries as Ben Elliot, and having his name, Dipendra, rendered into its diminutive by the other chaps. She was in England too, under the care of the same British lord. Her family descends from an Indian maharajah. But his are living gods. They have ruled Nepal for two and a half centuries. Other candidates for future queen are considered more suitable.

Or perhaps it's that his father has been giving away the powers Dippy is supposed to inherit. He has diminished himself, from absolute to constitutional monarch, of his own volition. His own volition, plus the uprising for democracy that arrests and bullets failed to quell. Perhaps, a flunkey thinks, the prince hasn't been loved enough. As a child he liked to burn cats and mice, you know. Perhaps there is no explanation. No story. Perhaps there is only what happens.

On June 1, 2001, the royal family gathers for dinner at Dippy's residence in the palace compound. Dippy, not yet thirty, begins the evening with billiards and booze. He knocks back two tots of Famous Grouse and smokes some of his laced cigarettes. This, at least, is the tale that's told afterwards.

By the time the king arrives, Dippy's been taken to his bed chamber. He phones his girlfriend. He throws up. He takes off his clothes. At nine o'clock, he emerges from his room. His orderly notices that the prince has changed into camouflage jacket and trousers and black army boots. Nothing unusual about that. Dippy enjoys warlike things. His gun collection comprises pistols, hunting and assault rifles, submachine guns, all sorts. He is carrying three of them.

The orderly assumes he is heading out. Does sire need anything else? 'It's not necessary now,' the heir to the throne replies.

The family is in the billiard room. Isn't he a bit old to be showing off those guns, one of his cousins thinks when Dippy walks in.

He fires first at his father.

'What have you done?' the king says, and sinks.

The gun rears up and bullets hit the ceiling.

An uncle approaches. The prince shoots him. He shoots his sister, his aunts and his brother. He goes up to the king's corpse and kicks it.

His mother calls to him: You have killed your father, you have killed your brother, kill me too. Her red glass bangle shatters where she falls.

Following the line of succession, the homicidal Dippy is proclaimed king. He is, however, insensate, having been shot in the head, apparently by himself, at the conclusion of his onslaught. The Nepali people hear rumours of deaths at the palace. Their bewilderment is soothed by the senior conscious royal, Dippy's uncle Gyanendra, who missed the deadly dinner. Gyanendra issues a statement explaining that the deaths were a tragic accident. They 'took place after an automatic weapon suddenly exploded'.

When Dippy dies of his injuries after a comatose forty-hour reign, Gyanendra is crowned. Not for him the concessions his liberal brother made to the people. King Gyanendra restores absolute rule. For his household, this is quite the competitive advantage. His son-in-law is to be found in the exclusive nightspots of Kathmandu, the casinos and the hotels. Not so exclusive, though, that the ambitious commoner Ajeya Sumargi is unable to encounter him.

As a boy in Hetauda, six hours along nauseating switchbacks from Kathmandu, Ajeya Sumargi's prospects were decent enough. His father established a limestone factory. But death came for him one day while he was riding his motorbike, and the family's fortunes darkened. They were not as poor as the hand-to-mouth pastoralists and hashish farmers out in the valleys. But when she came to buy dinner at the poultry farm, Ajeya's mother would forgo the plumper birds, instead carrying home the budget option known as 'boiler chicken'. Young Ajeya's money-making schemes, a local reporter wrote, extended to a spot of allegedly illegal logging for which he was briefly detained.

Ajeya gambled what resources he could muster on a move to the capital. With startling speed, he grew rich. Not just rich enough to afford fatter chickens. Rich as any Nepali. Richer than most who have ever lived, in his country or anywhere else. How did he find these riches? By finding the rich.

Rotund and ponytailed, a dash of lipstick or some make-up around the eyes, jolly Ajeya makes himself useful to King Gyanendra's money-minded son-in-law. To one visitor, Sumargi seems a factotum, welcoming guests. Others hear he is doing sensitive work, helping to transfer property from the murdered king's family to his successor's. Sumargi demonstrates enough flair to be entrusted with a venture in the boom industry: communication. When Gyanendra's son-in-law receives a telecoms licence, he appoints Sumargi as his representative.

And then, once more, the path forks. Gyanendra's autocracy is failing to achieve its stated aim: to vanquish the Maoist rebels who have for a decade fought from bases amid the medieval destitution of rural Nepal. Sixteen thousand Nepalis have died in this war. A whiff of Maoist leanings is enough to get you disappeared by the king's forces; the Maoists do the same to suspected collaborators. By 2006, the heavy yoke of Gyanendra's rule has brought Nepalis once more to the streets. Once more, they ask for freedom. Once more, they meet bullets. A shoot-on-sight curfew is imposed. It is not enough. 'Burn the crown!' they chant. The king blinks. He accedes to the formation of a people's assembly. It votes to abolish the monarchy. Gyanendra is banished from the palace to a two-bedroom apartment.

When the Maoists win the elections that follow the revolution, their commander becomes prime minister. Despite having largely observed the war from India, he goes by his nom de guerre, Prachanda, the Fierce One.

In power, Prachanda's Maoists set about tackling poverty. Starting with their own.

During the war, the Maoist commanders robbed banks. There were weapons to be bought and other supplies, but now the war is over, the commanders find they have leftover cash. A seductive feeling, even for these avowed champions of the downtrodden. Under the deal in which, following Gyanendra's abdication, the Maoists lay down their arms, the rank and file are granted a monthly allowance from the state. It is duly paid out, including to thousands of ghost soldiers, whose allowances the leaders pocket. They also pocket a cut of stipends paid to the ex-fighters who actually exist, plus a percentage on rations for the cantonments where they are housed. The pocketing continues until the pockets are fit to burst with loot worth some ninety million dollars.

The Maoist bosses are in possession of large quantities of what's called black cash – money they would have to use in secret, perhaps by passing it to someone else, some trusted business partner whose career they can use their newfound power to advance. Corporate intelligence operatives, hired by a western telecoms company that invests in Nepal, will identify what they believe is one such partner. His name is Sumargi. 'The unanimous opinion of our sources,' they report, is that 'possibly in return for such favours, Ajeya invests unaccounted money for various Maoist leaders including Pushpa Kamal Dahal (commonly referred to as "Prachanda").'

Where once they plundered banks, upon becoming the biggest party in the new parliament, the Maoists can plunder power. It is not long before their corruption has surpassed even the monarchy's. Before, child soldiers believed that to shake Prachanda's hand would be enough to get to heaven. Now his crew have an earthlier moniker: Cash Maoists.

What pushes the demobbed foot soldiers over the edge is news that Prachanda has taken up residence in an opulent pile in the desirable Kathmandu district of Lazimpat. Well away from the shanties in which his brethren get by. Still further from the deserts of the Gulf, where desperate former Maoist fighters seek manual work, often returning in coffins.

Mithered by angry cadres at a party conference, Prachanda concedes both to vacating the Lazimpat house and to ordering an investigation into corruption within the movement. He appoints one of his senior officials to run it. The report that is eventually produced is not published. Prachanda informs the rank-and-file that he has read it, and that it thoroughly exonerates him. It even recommends that he stay put in his splendid house for lack of appropriate alternative accommodation.

It isn't, in fact, his house. The local press gets hold of the deed. It's in the name of a close relative of Ajeya Sumargi.

Sumargi caters to others of Prachanda's needs. After the long years of a bush war, the guerrilla-in-chief likes a taste of whisky. Sumargi keeps a good bottle. For the boss, it flows like a river. So close is the Maoists' legendary leader (the mind behind the Prachanda Path, a fusion of Maoist thought with Marxism-Leninism) growing to this unashamedly capitalist moneybags that there are mutterings in the movement about 'sleeping with the enemy'.

If, as the spooks come to suspect, the Maoist leaders launched Sumargi into the big time with their black cash, he's gone on to find others who also value his services. Among those he must thank for this windfall is his fellow future philanthropist, Mohamed Amersi.

Conjuring a scene, Amersi transports me from a law firm's office in London to the prime minister's in Nepal. Present are Lars Nyberg, TeliaSonera's chief executive, two of Lars' lieutenants, the head of TeliaSonera's Nepali mobile phone network, their local partner (another rich Nepali), and the company's senior adviser, Mohamed Amersi. Their conquest of Eurasia is proceeding apace. They have come to meet Prachanda.

Nepal's new leader tells his guests: 'You are the biggest foreign tax payer in this fucking country and you are the biggest FDI investor in this country.* How is your experience?'†

The emissaries from TeliaSonera profess themselves 'very happy with the growth' but 'explained that these are the challenges we're facing'. Prachanda (via Amersi, some thirteen years on, amid Carter-Ruck's biscuits and the fizzy water and the egg painting) says: 'One way for you to think, you don't have to do it, but to think about solving this problem, is to do a combination with one of the other three operators that operate in Nepal.'

In other words, buy one of the other mobile phone companies. And that's what they do. They buy the one Ajeya Sumargi owns.

———————

Sumargi has been swift, after the dethroning of King Gyanendra in 2006, to befriend the Maoists. In 2009, Prachanda makes a ceremonial phone call to launch Sumargi's mobile phone network. The licence was issued under the first

---

* FDI = 'foreign direct investment'. In other words, the biggest investor in Nepal that isn't from Nepal.

† One source who knows Prachanda well describes him as a consummate flatterer, with a Clintonian gift for charm. The man has a Tom Selleck moustache above an equally Sellecky smile, the sort typically referred to as 'winning'. I therefore suspect that Amersi's recollection of his words, while it may be accurate in gist, can't be said with certainty to capture the Fierce One's cadence.

Maoist communications minister. Ajeya is accused of enriching this minister. The allegation is not proven, though a parliamentary committee concludes that licences have been doled out questionably, costing the state hundreds of millions of dollars.

Even as he envelops the highest in the land, Sumargi never forgets the little guys. He takes it upon himself to bring the information age to his immiserated compatriots. His new service, Hello Nepal, will provide 'no frills' mobile telephony to 'villagers' in western Nepal, the Maoists' heartlands. The villagers' pockets are shallower than their liberators'. In Hello Nepal's first two years, only eighty-nine thousand have signed up for Hello Nepal, less than 1 per cent of the market. Even if you add in the value of the airwaves it's been granted rights to, Hello Nepal is worth no more than sixty million dollars.

And yet TeliaSonera is offering four times that. Because Ajeya Sumargi is also selling something far more valuable.

'It was a pleasure to meet you in Kathmandu,' begins the email from Mohamed Amersi, after another trip. 'And thank you for arranging the meeting with Mr Prachanda.' Amersi sends Sumargi a list of questions about Hello Nepal. He forwards the answers to TeliaSonera people including the Eurasia team – the ones he's just worked with on the Uzbek payment.

Mohamed is of the view that 'with Mr Sumargi (with his political contacts and backing) on our side, TeliaSonera would be in better position to defend Ncell in the future'.

Ncell, TeliaSonera's mobile network in Nepal, is growing into the country's biggest, worth a billion dollars. If they don't buy his company, 'Mr Sumargi might turn against us and start lobbying against Ncell.' Amersi's working closely on the deal with the head of Eurasia, Tero Kivisaari, who agrees. In a presentation, Tero calls Sumargi 'a well-established Nepali businessman with close Maoist connections'. One who has 'an immediate need of $30m'.

Thirty million dollars of TeliaSonera's money promptly flows to the opaque British Virgin Islands company where Ajeya stores his wealth in the comfort of secrecy. The following month, in July 2011, Sumargi's wife writes a cheque to her sister for three quarters of a million dollars. The next day, the Nepali press will report, Sumargi's wife's sister becomes the named owner of a plum Kathmandu property. The house, painted a majestic red, is uptown, in Lazimpat. It's not for her to live in, though. It's for Prachanda.

A few months later, Sumargi receives even more of TeliaSonera's money. For forty-four million dollars, the Scandinavians buy a further stake in Hello Nepal, adding to the one the first thirty got them. Already, they've paid him more than their own bankers calculate Hello Nepal is worth. And yet still greater riches are on offer – as long as Ajeya can deliver his end of the bargain. Those 'challenges' that Amersi and the TeliaSonera executives discussed with Prachanda when the Maoist leader suggested they might like to buy a company – this one or that one or, perhaps, Ajeya Sumargi's one. If Sumargi can somehow persuade the Nepali authorities to make these obstacles evaporate, he's on for almost another two hundred million of TeliaSonera's dollars.

Sumargi opens the doors of power for the Scandinavians. There he is, round features lit up, as Lars Nyberg meets the mighty. It's Mohamed Amersi who Ajeya's partner emails with the itinerary for one visit in 2011, in case he has suggestions. The schedule's as rarefied as the one Amersi will soon receive from Ben Elliot's people for his rendezvous with Charles in Scotland. Arrive Kathmandu 10 a.m. At 11.30, meet the prime minister. That's not currently Prachanda – though he remains the potentate, chairman of the Maoists, who hold the majority in parliament. The TeliaSonera party will be seeing him later, along with other boss Maoists and the civil servant who runs the Nepal Telecommunications Authority, over lunch at Sumargi's place. After that – Nepali politics, like politics everywhere, can be fickle, so it's wise to keep a wide circle of friends – a visit to the chairman of the opposition party. Then it's Prachanda again, this time at his residence.

But I'm on the wrong track. I have wandered from the right path.

'Don't rely on bullshit,' Mohamed counsels me. 'Which is what you have done.' He mentions some journalists and some private intelligence types. 'I know you met them or corresponded with them. So fuck off.'

'Sorry, you know what?'

'You met them and you corresponded with them. And they feed you this bullshit. Okay, everybody knows it. Let's move on, forget about it.'

'You know I met them – sorry, who are we talking about?'

'I'm not going to comment any more,' Amersi says. 'My sources are my sources, I'm keeping them confidential, as I have to. But that's it, finished, I don't want to talk about this, move on.'

'It seems like you're telling me you've been trying to find out what I'm up to.'

'Nobody's trying to find out. People talk because you leave your fingerprints everywhere.'

'I'm just going about reporting, yes, it's nothing deeply secret—'

'They all know you have a warped mind and a warped agenda.'

'Sorry, who do?'

'Forget about it. Write your book and you'll see what happens to it.'

He turns to the binder in front of him. I have a matching one. Inside are hundreds of pages of documents. Many of them are TeliaSonera documents, many are marked confidential. They contain some important points, which he will elucidate for me, because 'your head does not understand this, this is your problem'.

'You have not understood,' he proceeds, 'what benefits already accrued to Ncell by this partnership.' The partnership with Sumargi. I need to understand why that was good for Ncell, TeliaSonera's huge mobile phone operation in Nepal.

Amersi explains, and the documents accord perfectly with what he says. That Sumargi's side of the deal was to prevail on the authorities to renew Ncell's licence, let TeliaSonera spread the fee for it, interest free, over several years, then renew it again, this time for free, and chuck in the right to use the latest technology, 3G. The bankers' valuation among Amersi's files does not record the losses caused to the Nepalis' national budget (shortly to be further depleted by the massive earthquake that will obliterate much of Kathmandu, flattening rickety dwellings and ending nine thousand lives). Neither does it, nor any of the other documents, explore how Sumargi is to go about procuring these blessings.* The bankers do, though, calculate what said blessings are worth to TeliaSonera: one hundred and ninety-eight million dollars, payable to Ajeya Sumargi.

Sumargi, Amersi tells me, delivered almost everything. And Amersi should know. One of the documents he's showing me has the heading: 'Issues to be solved in Nepal – with info update from Mohamed.' There's a list of the concessions to be extracted from the Nepali state. Against

---

* Indeed, one of the documents Amersi showed me was a memo by law firm K&L Gates for TeliaSonera. Of the acquisition of Sumargi's Hello Nepal, the lawyers wrote that, based on what they'd been shown, 'the level of legal and financial due diligence appears very light'.

many of them, it says 'to be followed up by Mohamed/
Sumargi'.

Then I say: 'There's another way of looking at that, isn't
there?'

'Which way?'

'Well, another way of looking at that is that it mirrors
very closely what TeliaSonera did with Gulnara Karimova in
Uzbekistan. Which is that you enter a deal to enrich
someone who is part of the regime—'

'That is your fucking head telling you.'

'—and you're given various benefits.'

I am, once more, mistaken. The Nepal
Telecommunications Authority 'is an independent body. I
will show you paperwork here. It's not under the control of
anyone.' He adds: 'Forget about it, it's in your fucking head.'

But in this thick blue binder, alongside the TeliaSonera
delegation's itinerary during which the head of the Nepal
Telecommunications Authority is to join Prachanda and
various Maoist ministers at Ajeya Sumargi's lunch table, is a
report by a committee of Nepali MPs. They investigated the
award of telecoms rights. Airwaves are, the MPs write,
'national property', a limited natural resource that should be
bestowed judiciously, maximising revenues to the state.
'The tendency,' they write, 'has been to give frequency as per
the demand of service provider and wish of the
government.' Sometimes the Nepal Telecommunications
Authority takes decisions, sometimes the communications
ministry. The MPs record that they asked the telecoms

minister (not a Maoist himself, but serving under one) to postpone authorising fresh allocations while they conducted their inquiry. The minister (whom a court would soon jail for corruption committed during an earlier term in office) did not do so. A mobile network was given 3G rights, apparently before anyone had even managed to fill in the Nepal Telecommunications Authority paperwork authorising it. The mobile network was Ncell and the 3G rights were among those TeliaSonera was paying Ajeya Sumargi to get.

'I'm just putting to you an alternative explanation,' I say.

'No,' says Amersi, 'because your agenda is biased against me, and so you are looking for skeletons.'

———————

While Ajeya Sumargi is awaiting his third payment from TeliaSonera – the big one, the two-hundred-million-dollar jackpot – another of the company's Eurasian allies is on the run, his suitcase full of skeletons.

After Bekhzod Akhmedov flees Uzbekistan, two of the Princess's minions show up at her Swiss bank. They ask about an account that, according to the bankers' paperwork, is linked to Bekhzod. Since Gulnara turned on him, Bekhzod has been declared a criminal in Uzbekistan. At the country's request, Interpol has issued an alert on him. This feels too dicey, even for Swiss bankers. They alert the authorities. A Swiss newspaper prints the story. Reporters at Swedish TV's crack investigative team have been digging into TeliaSonera for a while. They spot the Swiss article. From there they establish a link between the Gibraltar company to which TeliaSonera has paid hundreds of millions of dollars and the Uzbek despot's daughter.

At the 2012 annual meeting in Stockholm, straight-shooting Lars Nyberg doesn't dodge the tough questions. 'The allegations directed at TeliaSonera about our operations in Uzbekistan are serious,' the chief executive tells his assembled shareholders. 'So let me state clearly. There is zero tolerance of corruption and bribery at TeliaSonera. It is extremely important to me and something we pay attention to every single day. I've said it before and I would like to repeat it: TeliaSonera did not bribe anyone. TeliaSonera did not participate in money laundering.'

Here, Lars says, is the truth.

> Five years ago, we invested in a license in Uzbekistan
> to provide telecom services. Why did we do that? A
> key reason was to create growth and generate value
> for our shareholders. But it's not just that. At
> TeliaSonera we believe that telecommunication is a
> force for good. Anyone who has watched the
> extraordinary developments during the Arab Spring
> must be aware of this. It is an undeniable fact that
> modern telecommunications speed up a country's
> long journey towards democracy. It is also undeniable
> that telecommunications help eradicate human rights

abuses. We believe that our presence in Central Asia contributes to the advancement of democracy and human rights in the long term.

If you doubt him, look at the impoverished outcropping next to India.

Nepal is a great example of what telecommunications can do to help a country develop. I have been to Nepal six times. When I go there I have two objectives – to meet our employees and talk to politicians. Our decision to invest there was a risky one. The country was in a period of major political change, aiming to build a true democracy after a seven-year period of civil war. Nepal is one of the poorest countries in the world.

Since TeliaSonera arrived, Lars says,

mobile coverage in Nepal has increased from 40 per cent to 90 per cent of the population – in one of the world's most mountainous countries – and more than 60 per cent of the population use a mobile phone every day. It has also turned out to be a great investment for us, which generates an annual return on capital of 30 per cent. But for us it is not just about business. Every year, hundreds of thousands of Nepalis leave the country in pursuit of a better life.

Too many find themselves victims of human
trafficking or appalling work conditions. TeliaSonera
is creating opportunities for these people at home.

Three months later, Lars Nyberg resigns. The new management wants to know more about the local partners in
TeliaSonera's other Eurasian operations. In Nepal, investigators from Control Risks – private spooks like Kroll – are
hired. Their brief is to undertake 'discreet source enquiries'
into Ajeya Sumargi.

The Control Risks operatives have already done a check of
the Nepali media, which has yielded some disquieting findings. Now they talk to 'well-placed contacts' who know
Sumargi or know about him. They report back that these
sources 'were able to provide reliable and well-informed
insights into Ajeya, his reputation, his connections and his
business dealings in Nepal'. The sources say his connections
extend across the ruling class, across political parties, from the
old royals to the Maoists. When power shifts, he adjusts his
allegiances accordingly. 'Ajeya is not afraid to leverage these
connections,' the spies' contacts say.

The Control Risks spooks ask their sources about media
reports that Sumargi 'has invested the unaccounted money of
the Maoist party in business ventures across the country'. Is
that true? 'All the sources that we contacted including three
respected Nepalese businessmen, senior journalists, serving
government officials, Nepalese army sources and political
analysts corroborated these assertions.'

Sumargi is closest of all to Prachanda. The spooks checked the property records and, yes, a swish house he lived in was registered to Sumargi's wife's sister. When the press found out, Prachanda offered an explanation, claiming he was renting the place. The spooks say they're unable to establish whether this is true, but their sources are agreed that Sumargi was involved. The investigators report that Prachanda is believed to have owned a stake in Sumargi's Hello Nepal – the company TeliaSonera has paid tens of millions to buy. Even if Prachanda doesn't have a direct interest in Sumargi's company, the meaning of the Control Risks report is clear. If you've been paying Ajeya Sumargi, there could be grounds to ask whether you've been buying political favour.

———————

'Fuck Control Risks.' Read it carefully, Amersi tells me, and 'if you are intelligent, you will realise that this is a two-hundred-and fifty-thousand-dollar report and says nothing, nothing of any real substance or significance. So, learn, if you haven't already, how to dissect this report for what is true and what is crap.'

I've just got back from Nepal. Several sources I met corroborated Control Risks' findings. One had direct knowledge of an attempt by Prachanda to influence a government minister on Sumargi's behalf. A senior media executive said they understood the key to Sumargi's power to be paying money to Maoists. Another senior media executive, who has worked with Ajeya, understood Prachanda to have channelled the Maoists' illicit funds through him. A long-time associate of Sumargi's said: 'He registered Prachanda's properties in his own name. He was able to influence Prachanda and use his money.' And another former minister said of Sumargi: 'He's the heart of the kleptocracy. He uses the system to make money. And he thinks he's doing the right thing – he's there to make money. If by influencing them with his wealth he can get things done, then you do it.'*

But they're wrong, every one, according to Mohamed. Look, for instance, at Sumargi's diplomatic endorsements. He is no less than an honorary consul of Belarus. 'Under the Vienna Convention for consular representation,' Amersi says, 'the host and the guest country have to diligence somebody's fit for purpose and appropriateness to hold that public position.'

'But Belarus is a corrupt dictatorship, isn't it?'

'What the fuck I care?'

'It sounds like you're trying to say that this is a badge of approval.'

'It is a seal of approval. You may not have it in your head. For you, everything is corrupt. Your whole life is corrupt. Spend your time doing better things in life. It's not how it is

---

* I tried again and again to speak to Sumargi himself, through various of his associates, but he never replied. Nor did he respond to the questions I repeatedly emailed him seeking his own version of events.

just because some bloody transparency report says it's corrupt and this fucking index, which they prepared. The world is changing.'*

But Mohamed, I point out, you yourself are a sworn enemy of corruption.†

'I'm telling you that in any emerging-market transaction, any local person will never tick every single box of honesty, transparency, cleanliness. It just does not exist. You have to make value judgements on whether this is reputationally harming or this is what you would expect anyway in a country like this, when you diligence how people make their money, full stop.'‡

'So, you have to tolerate a certain level of—'

'It's not tolerate. It's making value judgements,' The volume goes up again. 'As I said to your head before, either you come here and you provide the service to poor people or you say fuck them all, let them all die without any telephony.

'That is where you are wrong because you have a problem in your head. On the one hand, you want freedom of press, freedom of information and all this. And then when you go to a tough country to afford that to people,

* This is apparently a reference to the annual Transparency International corruption perceptions index, which ranks countries based on how corrupt their citizens think they are. In the 2022 index, Nepal was ranked 110 out of 180 countries.

† Dear reader, we'll get to that. That's an evening in Oxford we've yet to witness.

‡ Emerging market = country where lots of poor people live.

you say corruption. Make up your fucking mind. Do you want people to have access to telephony or do you want to fight corruption? If you want to fight corruption, these people will be completely cut off from information highway for the rest of their lives, okay, full stop. Make up your mind.'

'With a case like Sumargi, you have to tolerate a certain level of corruption?'

'You have to tolerate, in every emerging market country, local partners, local conditions that have those type of issues. It is well recognised by the Serious Fraud Office, by the Department of Justice. Otherwise, we would not be selling arms to all these countries, so piss off.'

'Okay, but the arms dealers—'

'Piss off.'

'The arms dealers are famously corrupt, aren't they?'

'So what? Then don't send it. Tell your government. Go there and protest outside parliament. Don't waste my fucking time. Do you want to give these people the right to have information or not? Do you want to or not? Answer that, yes or no?'

'It doesn't really matter what I think on that one.'

'Sorry? Answer yes or no. If you had a choice to either starve them from information, starve them from knowledge of the world or allowing them to operate the stuff they operate in their own country, in their own fucking way. Who are you? Are you a global policeman? Are you a moral right wanker? What are you? A little journalist. Fuck off.'

His voice is echoing off the walls.

'There are twenty million people who are dying to have access to information, dying to have access to the internet.* Dying to be able to send money to each other because there are no fucking banks in villages. You want to deny them all that because of your moral high ground? Who will fucking care about you? You understand?'

'I think I do, yes.'

'You don't understand shit.'

When Lars Nyberg resigns over the Uzbek scandal, TeliaSonera's directors appoint a team of English lawyers from a global firm, Norton Rose Fulbright, to scrutinise the rest of the company's dealings in Eurasia. They start with Nepal. After going through emails, contracts, invoices, they recommend the 'reversal' of the deal with Sumargi. The TeliaSonera directors agree. But the dealmaker objects.

'The decision,' Amersi emails TeliaSonera's executives, 'was taken primarily on the basis of the Control Risks reports, the substance of which has not been verified and is probably unverifiable.' He continues: 'If this is the case, it is highly irresponsible!'

* I'm not sure which twenty million people he has in mind. Maybe in Nepal, where there are thirty million people, a fair few of whom are presumably too young, too old, or too busy with other matters to be craving access to the internet as fervently as Mohamed describes.

Better, Amersi suggests, to listen to those, such as himself, 'who have intimate familiarity with the Nepali situation'. You could end up being sued by your own shareholders, Mohamed warns, for value destruction, undue interference, dereliction of your duties as managers. As he's been cautioning them, forgo Sumargi's friendship and you could find yourself plagued with 'constant problems in operations such as customs, strikes, demonstrations, Central Bank blocks on money transfers, etc'. Pay the man, Amersi urges.

Clearly aghast that Amersi has been committing his views to email, the head of finance replies: 'I do not like that you have these discussion in this large group internally within TeliaSonera. Please call if you need to discuss.'

Amersi forwards this to Tero Kivisaari and his colleagues in the TeliaSonera Eurasia team. 'What's this supposed to mean????? What am I supposed to do?????'

No one knows what to do. The Uzbek scandal is getting worse; Swedish prosecutors have opened a criminal corruption investigation. The directors reach a decision, of sorts: they don't want to be friends with Sumargi, and they don't want to be enemies either. A way must be found to pay him off, again.

'Legal opinions have been collected,' a memo records, 'on the issue of whether it is possible to pay any amount in a settlement to Mr Sumargi or his companies without violating applicable anti-corruption laws.' It is possible, the lawyers say, but only if the amount is commercially justifiable. You could, for instance, pay him to save the money you stood to lose if he sued you.

Sumargi himself agrees with Amersi. He too is outraged. He sends TeliaSonera's management a letter. The way you have backed out of this deal, he writes, it discredits me. It insinuates that I am corrupt. If there are allegations, put them to me. Have I been convicted of corruption in a court? No. Even charged with corruption by a prosecutor? No. On July 31, 2013, in London, Ajeya meets TeliaSonera's representatives: two executives and Mohamed Amersi. His customary bonhomie has gone. I'm going to sue, he says. He will have the government of Nepal ensure that Ncell, TeliaSonera's valuable network in Nepal, suffers.

In the end, friendship prevails. TeliaSonera's stake in Hello Nepal is sold back to Sumargi on terms that leave him with a profit of sixty million dollars. The announcement cites 'regulatory reasons' for TeliaSonera's divestment from Hello Nepal.

Nonetheless, a succession of problems, including denial of permission to send profits back to Sweden, befall TeliaSonera's Nepal operation after the break-up with Sumargi. 'We wonder,' one investor writes in a letter to the new management, 'if this hasty divestiture is related to the company's difficulties repatriating cash from Nepal.'

The new management have shut down another scandal before it broke, following the advice of the English lawyers from Norton Rose to get rid of Sumargi. That still leaves their other recommendation. When they report their initial findings to TeliaSonera's directors, the English lawyers write in code. 'Throughout its dealings in Nepal, and from as early as 2007,' they say, TeliaSonera 'appears to have relied greatly upon the services of a consultant referred to here as Mr XY, to guide it in relation to strategy, the details of transactions, and relationship management – ie liaison with local partners, the authorities and senior political figures.' Get rid of Mr XY too, they advise.

Having promised to publish the English lawyers' findings, the new management opts instead to bury them. But eventually, nearly a year after the Control Risks report, the new chair, Maria Ehrling, announces: 'Agreements with an external adviser who since 2007 worked closely with the former management regarding certain transactions in Eurasia have been terminated.'

'The silly cow.' Mohamed was not impressed by this new chair.

The TeliaSonera management that took over after Lars Nyberg resigned didn't sever relations with Amersi then?

'Bullshit. They continued to work with me.'

They did. For all the irritating attention of journalists, TeliaSonera's business in Nepal was undoubtedly, to use Mohamed's phrase, 'win–win'. The TeliaSonera executives won: the ones who bought into Eurasia, and the ones who sold off Eurasia, all were handsomely paid. Ajeya Sumargi won. Was Prachanda a winner too? Whether any of the riches Mohamed Amersi helped to guide towards Sumargi were shared with the Fierce One and the other Maoist leaders, I cannot definitively say. I asked a long-time associate of Sumargi's, one who has detailed knowledge of his business activities. 'There are no official records,' he said. 'Would leaders do that?'

Amersi says: 'To what extent is there absolutely cast-iron evidence that there is a quid pro quo that is tangible, identifiable, and all of that?' Of Sumargi, he goes on: 'There was rumours that he was managing Maoist money or whatever, fuck it. Show me the fucking bank account where he had a signature, right, or a Maoist account. Show it to me, don't write nonsense.'

'The only reason,' I ask, 'not to do business with someone is if there is 100 per cent categorical proof of corruption?'

'Absolutely. Because otherwise, every single person in these markets will have the same tainting. Their heads of state will have it, their businesspeople elite will have it, everybody will have it. Because that is their system, that is their way of doing business, that's a way of living. You're not going to change them.'

And Amersi himself, he was a winner too. By the time he left in 2013, TeliaSonera had paid him sixty-three million dollars over six years. That's Goldman Sachs-style money, only for one man, not a whole Wall Street bank. It's not far off what Steven Gerrard, then captain of the England football team, made annually, or fifty times David Cameron's salary for being prime minister.

And the poor, of course. They also won. Ajeya and Mohamed's roles in advancing the Scandinavian noble vocation to spread democracy through commerce may have come to an end, but neither of them had any intention of ceasing to transform the world. Some of TeliaSonera's millions was to do yet more good, it seemed – the millions paid to these budding philanthropists. When Mohamed Amersi wrote the business plan for his Inclusive Ventures, he named a generous backer, Ajeya Sumargi.

Eight

Making sense

'Great. Well. Good evening.'

The dean of Oxford's school of government welcomes the audience. The lecture theatre is done out in black metal, grey plastic, white screens for slides. What a pleasure, the dean says, to gather tonight, March 8, 2017, for the launch of a new book by two of her fellow academics. She brandishes a copy. On the cover are shifty suits holding brown envelopes. The title is *Making Sense of Corruption*.

The dean introduces the two authors. A pair of Swedish academics. Each will speak for five minutes, she says. After that it'll be an electoral commissioner from Nigeria. 'And then,' says the dean, smiling and extending an arm of welcome to the fourth panellist, who smiles back at her, 'last but certainly not least, a great supporter of the school.' He's given money. Not as much as Sir Leonard Blavatnik, the Russia-made billionaire who endowed this school of government. But enough to earn gratitude. 'Mohamed Amersi,' says the dean, reading from a sheet of paper, who over his long years in business around the world 'has acquired a deep sense of the practical problem of corruption up close and has a commitment to combatting corruption'.

This commitment is apparent from the speech Mohamed goes around making. Soon the lucky youngsters gathered at the One Young World Summit in Colombia will have the privilege to be present when Amersi (blue with pink dots tie and pocket square combo) personally unveils his Ten Corporate Commandments. Alongside his ordinances to defend human dignity, eliminate all forms of modern slavery, embed environmental sustainability in core business models, end negative externalities, and set executive pay based on factors such as respect for the law, there will be an injunction against taking bribes, offering bribes, or engaging in any kind of financial corruption or malfeasance, on pain of what must become stronger criminal penalties.

This is the life he leads today, four years on from the Dumfries dinner with Prince Charles, his inspiration for a life of philanthropy. Amersi's plan for doing good took shape a short stroll across Oxford at the Saïd Business School (named after its benefactor, Wafic Saïd, a wealthy Syrian whose achievements include brokering the UK's biggest arms deal with Saudi Arabia). There Mohamed conceived Inclusive Ventures, an undertaking that knows no borders. There is support for schools where teachers read carefully prepared scripts and fees can be paid using a modern cashless system (fellow backers of this project include Bill Gates and Mark Zuckerberg). Supplying the Chinese with things like cooking oil and detergent through their post offices. Recycling Armenian e-waste.

It was while Amersi was gestating Inclusive Ventures that Ajeya Sumargi visited Oxford on a trip to choose a university for his son's master's degree. Mindful of children with fewer opportunities, Ajeya and Mohamed got to talking. They resolved to bring the business processes outsourcing revolution to the villages of Sumargi's homeland. To equip Nepal's rural youths for the information age. Sumargi may even reward youths who excel with jobs. Mohamed joined him in Nepal to explain the venture to the local press. And Sumargi, Amersi's business plan records, agreed to make a contribution of two and a half million dollars to Inclusive Ventures.

That very sum, as it happens, is what Amersi had in mind for another Inclusive Ventures project. For why should only the unskilled youths of Nepal benefit? Remember what Mohamed says: 'Muslims and Hindus and Jews and Christians – end of the day, we all have the same red blood.' In the Scottish lowlands are there not unskilled youths as deserving of salvation as their cousins on Nepal's hillsides? A project is under way to train them in gardening, cooking, plumbing, carpentry and dry-stone walling. But these are the skills of the past, for the jobs of the past. Mohamed Amersi's Inclusive Ventures can add an IT education facility, so that these youths might aspire, one day, to positions in the business processes outsourcing industry.

Sadly for the youths of both Nepal and Scotland, Amersi and Sumargi found themselves unable to make these dreams reality. In the end, none of Sumargi's millions pass into Mohamed's Inclusive Ventures. Undeterred, Amersi has found the funds to install high-speed broadband across the entire estate where the lowland youngsters were being shown dry-stone walling. The estate is Dumfries.

Amersi has been back to Charles's Scottish retreat again and again. You are, Kenneth Dunsmuir of the Dumfries Trust tells him, 'one of our most regular and treasured guests'. He adds: 'Somehow or other, an event is not quite the same without you!'

Lots of Ben Elliot's Quintessentially clients are at the events. But Amersi can feel sure he makes a special impression. 'Dear Mohamed,' Ben emails one day. 'Hope you are well. I saw the Prince of Wales this morning and he spoke highly of you.' Amersi has been appointed a trustee of the Prince's Trust International. Unsurprising, then, that when the dean of Oxford's Blavatnik School of Government introduces him tonight, it is with evident esteem.

The Swedish academics present *Making Sense of Corruption*. The Nigerian electoral commissioner speaks. His name is Attahiru Jega. Why is there 'mind-boggling corruption' in his country? Because of the two moralities, he says. For the public at large, you put your hand in the till, you are punished. For the governing class, you put your hand in the till, it is condoned.

'Mohamed,' says the dean.

'Let me start,' Amersi says, 'by thanking you for inviting me here.' He sits cross-legged in a grey suit, at his ease. Today the tie and the pocket square are salmon.

'As you know, this is a topic which is quite close to my heart.' He swivels towards the academics. 'I unfortunately was only given a copy of the book this evening. So I haven't read the book.' The authors adopt magnanimous grimaces. They have no idea who he is. The school put him on the panel. It does that for donors.

Amersi turns to the audience. 'But let me just talk from my own experience as a practitioner. I've had the privilege of working in more corrupt areas than a lot of other people. Mainly in the developing world but also in the developed world. And I will explain what I mean in terms of the experiences that I have gained.

'I think it's very important to understand what are the underlying causes of corruption. Because once we have an understanding of the cause, then we can define the problem, then we can define the definition that needs to be applied to it. Then a lot of things flow from it.' This is what matters most: who gets to decide what words mean.

'So Transparency International describe the single biggest cause of corruption today, is inequality. It's the difference between the rich and the poor. And that gap is getting wider and wider.'

Amersi warms to his discourse. The dean diligently takes notes. Mohamed turns again to the two authors of the book. He smiles at them.

'I'm very happy that Bo and, um' – he forgets the woman's name, spins round to read it from the cover – 'Aiysha are here.

They're both from Sweden. And there is one particular case that I will touch on a little bit.'

There are a few copies of the book in a pile on the table beside where Mohamed is sitting. He rests his left elbow on them and proceeds.

'There is a case involving one of Sweden's largest telecom groups: TeliaSonera.' No need for the audience to know his own part of this story. Just to have the benefit of his expertise on what scandals like TeliaSonera mean to the trained eye. 'These cases have exposed what is potentially billions of dollars of corrupt deals. But then you go to the heart of it. And you see, well, what's the definition of corruption? Has bribery actually taken place? Was there a wrongdoing that took place?'

While Mohamed Amersi speaks in Oxford, in Stockholm TeliaSonera's new management is preparing to pay the biggest fine ever levied for corruption.

Because TeliaSonera sold shares in the US, it falls under the jurisdiction of the US Foreign Corrupt Practices Act. Prosecutors use this statute to bring in fines in such quantities they would cover the entire budget of the FBI. Each settlement is accompanied by what's called a 'criminal information': the story. TeliaSonera's is nearly ready. It will tell how the payments to its local partner in Uzbekistan were in fact bribes to the dictator's daughter. Multinational corporation that it is, TeliaSonera will also confess and pay up in the Netherlands, where it keeps a subsidiary that handled Eurasian matters. All told, the fine will be a billion dollars. The company's representatives will give the Americans – the most formidable law enforcement operation that there is – commitments. To maintain 'a rigorous anti-corruption programme'. And to report any allegations of further conduct that might violate US anti-corruption law.

Which is why, back at headquarters, a question has arisen. It's about the millions of TeliaSonera's dollars that Mohamed Amersi promised to a woman in Kazakhstan, the last big province of its Eurasian operations from which the company is yet to depart. The question might seem a simple one but it's proving hard to answer. The question is: Is it a bribe?

As Josef Stalin adds slivers of Scandinavia to the European territory that a pact with Hitler has bought for the Soviet empire, at the far end of his domain the latest in a long line of nomadic herders enters the world. A bright lad full of ambition, Nursultan Nazarbayev leaves the Kazakh grasslands for the steelworks. If becoming a Buddhist would afford opportunity for advancement, a Buddhist he would become. But advancement is reserved for communists. Nursultan joins the Party's youth wing, bearing the red flag through the streets. His first taste of fame comes when his gleaming smile appears in a piece of *Pravda* propaganda for the steelworks.

Thirty years later, while Vladimir Putin is still an obscure spy shovelling secrets into the KGB furnace in Dresden,

Nazarbayev is already a boss, the Party's man in Kazakhstan. But the Soviet order is ending. The path to advancement stops being communism and becomes nationalism. The career apparatchik chameleons himself into the figurehead of Kazakhs' struggle for freedom. His closest comrades call him Papa.

When the transition comes, Papa takes the new position of president. He is commander of the armed forces. He heads the Supreme Economic Council, midwife to what is called a 'market economy'. To Papa's cronies, the council issues money-spinning permits to trade raw materials abroad, like ones Putin dispenses up in St Petersburg. The presidency absorbs the Party. To ensure troublemakers do not foment unrest, Papa takes the chair of a new Security Council too. Local Soviets are replaced with regional governors. These are appointed by the president. So are members of the upper house of parliament, the prime minister, the rest of the cabinet, ambassadors, electoral commissioners, three of the seven constitutional justices including the chief, the central bank governor, the attorney general.

On the outside, all these bodies look like institutions designed to provide what institutions provide – checks and balances on power. On the inside, they are the opposite: tools of that power. But the west, yearning to see its image reflected back at it in these new free capitalist democracies rising from the ashes of the enemy empire, welcomes Papa into the nest.

Official results record that 80 per cent of Kazakhs vote for him in the 2000 elections. In 2005 it is 91 per cent. In 2011,

95 per cent. Parliament gives Papa a further title: Father of the Nation.

Sometimes a father must discipline his children. Agitators are tortured, dissidents assassinated. Proper respect for the ruler is maintained. Until the FBI arrests an American middleman who got Mobil of Virginia rights to the reservoir of oil under the Caspian Sea. This middleman has put millions he'd received from the oilmen into Papa's Swiss accounts. American prosecutors' criminal corruption case against the middleman unravels when it turns out he was thick with the CIA all along. But Papa loses those millions in the Swiss account. And soon more secrets threaten to escape. His own son-in-law has gone rogue.

You could have nicknamed Rakhat Aliyev all manner of things. He was a qualified doctor with a psychotic cackle. But it was Sugar that stuck, after one of the industries he seized for himself after he married Nazarbayev's daughter. Sugar once adored his father-in-law. Then he began to think of succeeding him. Exiled, forcibly divorced from the first daughter and accused of crimes ranging from fraud to murder, he took to styling Kazakhstan's president as a mafia don, a godfather. Sugar was awaiting a verdict on extradition from Austria when his prison guards discovered his body, a noose around the neck.

Before his arrest, Sugar had spoken to a reporter from the *Wall Street Journal*. The article was headlined 'Kazakhstan corruption: Exile alleges new details'. Sugar, corroborated by 'others with knowledge of Nazarbayev family finances', identified those who 'manage offshore assets of the Nazarbayev clan'. One of them was Aigul Nuriyeva. The woman Mohamed Amersi has promised millions.

Just as there are two Jeff Galmonds, two Bekhzod Akhmedovs and two Ajeya Sumargis, so there are two Aigul Nuriyevas.

Both Aiguls are Kazakh women, with an oval face and chestnut hair. Both are born in 1974 to a renowned Kazakh economist, each entering adulthood as the Soviet Union ends. They study finance before being favoured with one of the presidential grants given to inculcate the nation's youth with the western, democratic values Papa so cherishes by sending them to American universities. Aigul and Aigul emerge with MBAs in 1997 and take positions at a Swiss bank. Then their paths diverge. One is named by Sugar as a custodian for his tyrannical ex-father-in-law's corrupt wealth. The other smiles out from a Forbes list: the fifty most influential businesspeople of the Republic of Kazakhstan. The list appears in 2012: Aigul's not yet forty. Her name's next to a large number: three-quarters of a billion dollars, a fortune the size of J. K. Rowling's. The source of her wealth is given as telecommunications. That year, she's struck deals to sell fibre and frequencies to one of the world's biggest telecoms companies, TeliaSonera.

Days after these deals are completed, the Uzbek bribery scandal forces Lars Nyberg to resign as TeliaSonera's chief executive. The rest of his team leave too, or are fired. The new bosses want to get out of Eurasia. Mohamed Amersi's retainer has been terminated. Before he leaves, three senior executives from the new management visit him in London. They dine at the Wolseley, over the road from the Ritz. Amersi tells them: You have unfinished business in Kazakhstan.

How right Mohamed is. Through her people, the demand encoded behind the names of shell companies, Aigul sends word to the Scandinavians: Where's my eighty million dollars? This she has been promised, her people say, by Amersi himself. It's a perfectly legitimate business transaction, they explain, to sell cables for TeliaSonera's Kazakh mobile phone network.

Since the Uzbek scandal, the new TeliaSonera management has created an ethics department. As the settlement with the American prosecutors draws near, the ethics team submits an assessment of Aigul's claim. They've gone back to the inquiries the English lawyers from Norton Rose made into the Eurasia operation. The lawyers reported that a few years ago the Kazakh authorities turned nasty. TeliaSonera's mobile network in Kazakhstan – the country's biggest – was raided by the labour department and the migration police, subjected to an unplanned tax audit, and visited by the fire service.

An initial report by the lawyers sketched out what they believed to have been TeliaSonera's response. 'To address a hostile environment in Kazakhstan,' they wrote, TeliaSonera 'pursued a strategy of active relationship management which went beyond acceptable or conventional lobbying.' In this strategy, the company 'relied heavily upon one particular adviser'. It was Mr XY: Mohamed Amersi. Amersi brokered deals with Aigul. These deals, the English lawyers suggested, were designed, in part, 'to incentivise politically connected individuals'.

One of the deals was to acquire a company owning subterranean fibre-optic cables that carry data. Aigul's people say Mohamed pledged that TeliaSonera would buy her stake in this company. The valuation provided by the Swiss bank UBS for Amersi's deal justified a price of eighty million dollars for Aigul's stake. There was a warning from TeliaSonera's commercial lawyers, though: the company's ownership of the cables looks iffy. Now a second lot of bankers has conducted another valuation. Of its 3,500 kilometres of fibre-optic cables, the company has registered ownership of 186 kilometres. Only five metres in every hundred. By these numbers, Aigul's stake can only be worth a fraction of what Amersi promised her for it.

In Stockholm they agonise: is part of the payment Aigul is demanding actually protection money, like those millions paid to the Uzbek Princess? Aigul, like Galmond and Gulnara and Sumargi, likes to wear a cloak of anonymity, moving money through opaque offshore companies. That makes it all the harder to discern the truth, to establish where she ends and the regime begins. This is how the Kazakh boss class operates. Papa himself regards the power he wields in the name of the Kazakh people as his private affair. Once, when he holds a meeting with Putin at a functionary's home, curious locals approach to try to catch a glimpse of the two rulers. Papa rebukes his functionary for electing to live in a building that is accessible to the public. 'If you want to receive my guests again next time, you'll have to move. Understood?' The functionary puts his house up for sale and commences construction of a new one, elsewhere. Another time, Papa's security forces shoot up a public square filled with striking oil workers. He shuts down the internet, turns off the phone networks, and the survivors are tortured until they are ready to confess at show trials.

TeliaSonera has hired corporate intelligence agencies to fathom the mystery of Aigul. The private spies of Kroll point to her perceived links to the Kazakh elite. Another analyst's sources are unanimous that Aigul Nuriyeva was a protégé of Karim Massimov. Massimov, who has served Papa as prime minister and chief of staff, is one of the regime's most powerful figures. The sources say there is something missing from Aigul's CV online: that she had been Karim Massimov's assistant when, before Papa appointed him to the government, he ran a Kazakh bank. They say assets officially owned by Aigul aren't really hers: she keeps them for the benefit of Massimov and his boss – Papa himself. They say her job is to administer investments and launder money, to make the proceeds of corruption look like the proceeds of clean business. The sources can't enumerate which assets and which money could be said to belong to Papa, Massimov, or Aigul herself, but say that if the Nazarbayev clan ever deemed her disloyal, they could remove her from her positions overnight.

Kazakhstan is a place of shadows, of whispers. Another Nordic telecom company that has invested there, Tele2, has also taken Aigul Nuriyeva as its local partner. After some uncomfortable press reports about this arrangement, Tele2's bosses have published an inquiry into Aigul.

'All of the sources we consulted stressed that the system whereby Kazakh politicians use trusted representatives to hold their assets in name was prevalent in Kazakhstan,' write the private investigators Tele2 hired. They add that 'documentary evidence confirming Nuriyeva's alleged involvement in such arrangement is sparse'; they 'identified no specific allegations of corruption, or other irregularities, relating to her or her business activities during the course of their investigation'.

Nonetheless, the investigators found several business connections between Nuriyeva and Papa's main man, Massimov. 'While it cannot be confirmed, taken in conjunction with the strong speculation from the sources we consulted concerning the existence of "trusted representative" relationship between the two, we assess that this constitutes circumstantial evidence that such an agreement is likely to be in place between Nuriyeva and Massimov.'

If these investigations are correct, to pay Aigul is to pay the kleptocrats who rule Kazakhstan. But ask Aigul herself, and she is having none of it.

'I deny any suggestion,' she says, 'that I was involved in any corruption, illegality, or misconduct, whether directly, via any of the companies I owned or worked for, or on behalf of any other individual.' What's more: 'I have never had any improper or illegal relationship with Karim Massimov,

Nursultan Nazarbayev (or any member of his family), or Mohamed Amersi.'

As for those deals Amersi brokered, Aigul says 'each transaction was heavily negotiated, conducted on arm's length terms, and involved experienced commercial parties represented on both sides by legal and financial advisers'. She says she 'was not aware of or involved in any illegal or improper conduct in relation to these transactions'.

'Did you get a sense of Aigul's relationship with Massimov?' I ask Amersi as we sit across the table at Carter-Ruck. He's told me that he himself attended meetings with Papa's lieutenant on TeliaSonera business.

'They were friends for a very long time,' Mohamed says. She became 'one of the trusted interlocutors in Kazakhstan.'

'What's a trusted interlocutor?'

'Again, don't ask me, do your work.'

'What do you mean by that term?'

'In most of these countries, emerging market, there is an understanding that certain business people will have the right to engage in certain business because they develop expertise.' He mentions the oligarchs who dominate Kazakh mining (backers of Papa), and the ones who dominate Kazakh oil (relatives of Papa).

'On the telecoms side, Aigul Nuriyeva. Any foreigner

coming in there who meets with the government is told that if you want to have a good understanding of how the telecoms space works and who's doing what, where, when, talk to these people because they are invested in telecoms in the country.' The Miss Telecoms of Kazakhstan: that's what Mohamed calls Aigul.

I shouldn't listen to 'rumours' about her, Amersi tells me. But it's not just rumours. Massimov himself told American diplomats that he'd set up a company in Singapore with Aigul. I push Mohamed: there is evidence that links Aigul to the regime.

It's like our first interview, he says.

'When we talked about Galmond?'

When we talked about the man Galmond was said to be a front for: Leonid Reiman, Putin's Mr Telecoms. Amersi says, 'I said: "Who is going to tell me in Russia, to say here's the cupboard, inside there's some paperwork that will show that Reiman is the owner?" Nobody would fucking tell me this and nobody will tell anybody fucking that. So it's only conjecture.'

Amersi's temperature is rising once more. The value of the fibre company was swiftly reduced in TeliaSonera's accounts after the acquisition. Doesn't that suggest the money was buying something else, like political credit?

'No, fuck it, nonsense. Forget this, no.' He expands. TeliaSonera needed fibre cables to run its mobile network. 'We diligenced five projects, which I will show you, so please, fuck off, don't go there. It's a waste of time.' He shows me some paperwork, a list of various fibre companies in Kazakhstan that TeliaSonera could have bought, with the relative merits of each. They selected Aigul's, but 'not because she was an interlocutor and we had to find ways to give her money, it's fucking crap'.

He asks me: 'Do you know how long it took?'

'I don't know.'

'How long?'

'Why don't you tell me.'

'One year, one week, one day, how long?'

'I have no idea.'

'It was such a corrupt deal that you don't know how long it took. You are bullshit completely. You don't know what you're doing.'

'Why don't you explain what your point is.'

'It took eighteen fucking months of painstaking work with the regulators, with the lawyers, with the political establishment, with the shareholders to get bloody approval for this. And if it was a corrupt deal it would have been done in one week, so fuck off, all of you. Fuck off, okay, before you think of what you're saying. Absolute bloody nonsense.'

He reminds me why I'm here. 'I will prove to you all afternoon that everything you've written is ninety-five per cent bullshit, lies and bias. Ninety-five per cent of it. I hope your publishers are going to view this tape recording, so they know before they publish shit what it is.' I'm put on notice: 'If this was to go to court, this matter between us, believe me, there will be a hundred thousand pieces of paper I will provide.* Emails, all, I have nothing to hide here.'

---

* In 2000, the *Sun* ran a story with the headline 'Nurse is probed over 18 deaths'. The nurse, Elaine Chase, sued. Pondering what the printed words meant, a judge wrote: 'The sting of a libel may be capable of meaning that a claimant has in fact committed some serious act, such as murder. Alternatively it may be suggested that the words mean that there are reasonable grounds to suspect that he/she has committed such an act. A third possibility is that they may mean that there are grounds for investigating whether he/she has been responsible for such an act.'

When someone sues for defamation, one of the first things the judge does is decide what has actually been said or written. Not the words themselves – that should be pretty clear – but what these words would mean to an ordinary, reasonable person who heard or read them. 'Chase level meanings', as they have been known since the nurse's case, are the categories judges usually use.

So if Amersi, as he keeps threatening, sues over this book and claims defamation, we would expect the judge who takes the case to rule on the meaning. I can't know which particular passages he might choose to sue on, but I reckon these are the book's central meanings. That there are grounds to investigate whether some of the money paid in business deals Amersi helped to set up amounted to buying the authorities' favour. And there are grounds to investigate whether Amersi knew as much, or should have. (There are also grounds to investigate whether he broke electoral law, and whether he misled a court, though we haven't got to those bits yet.)

Before a journalist prints anything, after taking care to protect sources, there is one crucial question: is it in the public interest to publish this? Especially if publishing might harm someone's reputation or reveal confidential information. Is it in the public interest to publish *Cuckooland*? You're reading about enormous, questionable business deals in countries where corruption condemns generation after generation to penury and strife; about relationships between multinational corporations and authoritarian regimes that crush dissent; about flaws in the policing

TeliaSonera's bosses are in talks with the American prosecutors over the Uzbek bribery case as the letters from Aigul's people come in. They are written in business-speak. There's a lot about how TeliaSonera is engaging in 'value destruction' by mismanaging the fibre operation in which her offshore company still controls a stake. They demand that TeliaSonera 'complete its purchase'. Between the lines of jargon, a veiled threat might be detectable. 'Continued indecision,' Aigul's people inform TeliaSonera's bosses, 'has raised eyebrows at various governmental agencies' in Kazakhstan. It was 'government agencies' that visited havoc on TeliaSonera's Kazakh operation. Might spurning Aigul trigger more attacks?

Notice of legal proceedings follows. The forum is to be the London Court of International Arbitration. Aigul Nuriyeva's name appears nowhere in the claim. The demand is for payment of the promised millions to a company she controls. Even the legal process itself is secret. A private tribunal, where the rich address delicate matters, unhindered by the principle of open justice.

The court is told a story. TeliaSonera, this lamentable multinational, is known to have engaged in 'corruption, money laundering and other serious wrongdoing in connec-

of international bribery; soon – and I do hope you stick with this story – you'll be reading about whether anyone is checking the origins of donations that shape the course of British democracy, about how wealth secures access to elected rulers, about how courts are used to stifle free speech, and about more besides. I'll leave it to you to judge if writing this – and, more importantly, reading it – is in the public interest.

tion with its questionable business activities in Eurasia'. So much so that there have been 'criminal and regulatory investigations in a variety of jurisdictions'. The reneging on promised payments in Kazakhstan 'is entirely consistent with the corporate culture' at TeliaSonera.

A senior TeliaSonera manager sends a proposed response to the board. 'Estimating the probability and magnitude of loss in proceedings such as this is speculative,' goes the memo. The lawyers are saying the company has 'very strong legal defences'. But TeliaSonera lacks witnesses to contest Aigul's account – everyone from those days has either been sacked or resigned. And she does have a witness, one who validates her version of reality.

Yes, the witness's signed statement says, TeliaSonera did promise to pay the eighty million. Yes, bosses from the corporation met Aigul's people to talk it all over. In a skyscraper that climbs towards the mountaintops ringing Kazakhstan's commercial capital, Almaty, and again at a Mayfair members' club called the George. Yes, TeliaSonera suffered an 'institutional memory lapse' regarding the money Aigul's company was owed when the board cleared out Lars Nyberg and his team amid the Uzbek corruption scandal. Yes, Aigul's team was left 'shocked and upset' by the failure of their Scandinavian partners to help develop this tremendous fibre business.

Yes, I promised this money, says the witness who signs his name in Dubai on November 11, 2016: Mohamed Amersi.

Once more, everyone wins. Aigul gets fifteen million. Not eighty, but plenty for a stake the value of which TeliaSonera's assessment has questioned. It's a payout from legal proceedings: nothing improper about this, she says if anyone asks. The ethics department's position demanded, at a minimum, that Aigul be named in a TeliaSonera press release announcing the settlement. Instead, it refers only to her opaque company. TeliaSonera's bosses win as well. The year of the payment to Aigul, the top eleven of them split eleven million dollars.

––––––––––

It matters a great deal to Mohamed that his account of what went down in Kazakhstan prevails. After all, the fee for the Aigul deals – five million dollars – that he received from TeliaSonera in the last days of Lars Nyberg's reign was wired to his Swiss bank, from which less than a month later issued forth his first donation to Dumfries House.

Amersi is showing me his witness statement. He asks if I've read it. I have.

'You first have to be honest with me. I will be honest with you. Because you have no idea what you know, what you don't know. And mostly you don't know. That's the fact.'

'I'm sure, yeah. That's generally my starting position—'

'And you will not admit it because your pride will not allow you to admit that you've done bum research. That's your problem. And it is very bum research you've done. I expected more, to be honest. But I can see it's hopeless. You know nothing, you've read nothing, you've got no

underlying paperwork, no underlying understanding of
Kazakhstan, Nepal or anything. It's just bullshit in the head.'
He turns to the latest binder. 'This is my witness statement.'

When the dispute over whether Aigul was to be paid
began, TeliaSonera's lawyers called me, Mohamed says. 'We
spent three hours on the phone, where they asked me for my
understanding of the whole background, start to finish.' The
plot thickened. Amersi says someone inside TeliaSonera – a
'very senior person in the new management' – called him to
say there were moves afoot to 'distort' his account, in order
to use it in the legal battle with Aigul. 'If you want to make
sure that you come out of it clean,' Mohamed recalls this
Deep Throat advising him, 'you should definitely find a way
to say your side of the story. Otherwise it will be like Norton
Rose, finding a scapegoat, who did this and did that, all this.
I said fuck that.' Mohamed called Aigul's right-hand man
and said: 'I'm going to get fucked in this arbitration because
you guys have not been able to settle your shit. Do you mind
that I issue a witness statement?'

'How were they going to distort it, in what way?'

'Like Norton Rose did in their report. Like that wanker
Galmond did, "I was threatened to be put in bamboo cells ..."'

'But what's the allegation?'

'Forget it. I am going to protect my fucking name and I
said I want to be having in the court my record of what
actually happened. If people like it, good. If they don't like
it, fuck them. And that's what I did. I produced a witness
statement narrating my account of what actually happened.'

No, Mohamed would be no one's scapegoat. Not for him the part of the villain. 'The Norton Rose guys were wankers,' he tells me. The English lawyers who wrote the Mr XY report and recommended TeliaSonera terminate Amersi's retainer. He gave them an interview and they twisted his words. Like their fellow wanker Mr Justice Smith all those years ago, these Norton Rose lawyers simply cannot grasp the realities of the high life. They said he spent loads on entertainment, including for the 'politically exposed', a term lawyers use for those who wield power. Au contraire, says Mohamed: all his guests were quite proper, and anyway it was scarcely two hundred thousand dollars a year. Don't these people know that a simple trip to the motor racing alone costs a hundred grand? Formula One trackside hospitality tickets, flights, transfers, hotels, meals and cars …

Apart from the English wankers, Amersi has given interviews to the Swedish lawyers who investigated the Uzbek deal, to the American prosecutors on the Gulnara bribery case, plus the Swedish and Swiss ones and the Dutch. No one has charged him with anything. He says he told them what he's telling me: that finding out who were the true beneficiaries of these fabulously lucrative deals was not his job; that was for the lawyers, the bankers.

'So fuck off. Don't put anything on my hands and my head here.'

Treasured companion to the highest in the land he may be, but Mohamed Amersi still speaks truth to power. Who better than a son of the British empire to call out the west's hypocrisy, and where better than here, at Oxford, this temple to the truth. Before his audience at the Blavatnik School of Government, he draws ever deeper from the well of his experience.

'There is then, I find, in countries like India, in Nepal, there is legislation that requires, more often than not, that a local partner has to become a part of any business enterprise that you engage in,' he says. 'And that is a licence for problems. It's a licence for state officials, it's a licence for public officials, to basically make money. Because these local partners can end up, through fronting structures, fronting for people in power.'

Before his western audience can tut smug disapproval, he goes on.

'At the end of it, we have to accept that it's the west that have, by and large, created a number of these structures. We have created the whole notion of having trusts. And having, you know, situations where the ultimate beneficial ownership of an asset can be hidden.'

How right he is: Leonid Reiman's shell company in the Isle of Man, Jeff Galmond's in Bermuda and the one Amersi set up for him in the Cayman Islands, Gulnara Karimova's in Gibraltar, Ajeya Sumargi's in the British Virgin Islands – every one of them registered in the UK's empire of corporate secrecy.

'Now we are moving towards more of a transparency age. But there are still structures everywhere. We saw what happened in the Panama leaks. We saw what happened in the

Bermuda leaks. We are the people who have invented this. Our lawyers have invented it. Our private wealth managers practise it. And then when the west was dealing with this type of structures, it was very fine. Now when the developing world has started to make money, and then they engage in wanting to create foundations and trusts, suddenly the whole game is over and we start to complain.'

When he finishes, the dean leads the applause.

'Thank you very much, Mohamed.' She says she is delighted to have heard fantastic comments 'about where corruption actually occurs and hits the ground'. The dean points to a man in the audience who has raised his hand.

'Hi,' comes a mellifluous Scottish voice, 'I'm John Lloyd.' Lloyd is a venerable journalist, formerly of the *Financial Times*. In conversation with young reporters from around the world, Lloyd says, he has discerned a troubling trend. In India, in Africa, even in China, journalists believe they are getting better at holding power to account. And yet corruption is getting worse. 'Do you think,' Lloyd asks the panellists, 'that journalism does hold power to account?'

Mohamed Amersi is a great believer in the power of journalism. He leans forward in his chair to answer Lloyd's question. Look, he says, at the 1MDB affair. Malaysia's rulers looted billions from the state. This, Mohamed points out, was revealed by journalists.

'And then my favourite one: TeliaSonera. It was Swedish investigative journalism that exposed this.' Amersi continues. 'So I think that it's very good for investigative journalism to

bring this out and be able to expose it. But that's not the issue.'
The issue is the meaning of a word, namely corruption.

'Has bribery actually taken place? Was there a wrongdoing
that took place?'

The Swedish prosecutor who opened a criminal investigation after the exposé about TeliaSonera is discovering precisely
this. His case is terminally flawed from the outset. Gulnara is
the Uzbek despot's daughter. Her former minions describe
her marshalling institutions of state in a campaign of looting.
But as she is not formally a government official overseeing the
telecoms industry, Swedish law doesn't consider it a bribe to
pay her off. Swiss judges concur; the Princess herself likes to
cite their ruling when she insists she was not party to corruption. Helpful precedents, as astute analysts of kleptocracy
note, for 'shadow elites' to evade anti-corruption laws because
they 'on paper hold no formal office'.

'The journalists do their job,' Mohamed laments, 'but the
governments and the enforcement agencies are powerless to
do anything about it.'

It is time for me to face reality.

'That's how the system works. Who are you, Tom Burgis,
to impose on them how they should live their fucking lives
and operate their country? Who are you? Who is the
fucking UK? Fuck them all.'

'It's not me so much as it's the law.'

'What fucking law?'*

'It's the UK law.'

'Fuck the UK law. What application does it have in Nepal? What?'

---

* At one point, Amersi asked me for my definition of corruption. I said it's 'the abuse of public trust for private gain', a common, simple definition that gets to the heart of it. But that's an ethical definition, not a legal one. Anti-corruption law varies from state to state. It was not long ago that bribes were tax-deductible in France. Only in 2010 did the UK gain a tough anti-corruption law to update the archaic and unwieldy statutes enacted a century earlier. Post-Soviet Russia has a patchwork of legislation, with a specific anti-corruption law not passed until 2008, long after the free-for-all of the 1990s. And this is before you get to questions of whether the rule of law actually applies or whether in, say, Saudi Arabia or China, corruption prosecutions are often just political vendettas in disguise.

Perhaps the best effort at a consensus is the one arrived at by the club of rich nations called the Organisation for Economic Co-operation and Development, as far as bribing a foreign official is concerned. Its anti-bribery convention says it should be an offence 'for any person intentionally to offer, promise or give any undue pecuniary or other advantage, whether directly or through intermediaries, to a foreign public official, for that official or for a third party, in order that the official act or refrain from acting in relation to the performance of official duties, in order to obtain or retain business or other improper advantage in the conduct of international business'.

The UK's bribery law adopts the OECD standard on bribery of foreign public officials. They're defined as 'an individual holding legislative, administrative or judicial posts or anyone carrying out a public function for a foreign country or the country's public agencies'. To break the law, you must either commit a crime inside the UK, or do something abroad that would have constituted a crime if you'd done it back home. An offer or promise of financial advantage to a foreign public official is as much a crime as making a payment. Senior officers or directors in a company that commits a general bribery offence can be liable too.

'You're a British citizen.'

'If you don't want to operate there, don't operate.'

'But as a British citizen, you're bound by UK law, aren't you?'

'No, I'm not. Not when I'm operating in that country. If I conduct myself in a corrupt way and if the Serious Fraud Office finds out, yes, I will have to respond to it, of course.'

'That's my point.'

'Fuck off.'

He suggests I invite law firms such as the ones who worked on the TeliaSonera deals to refrain from such employment. 'Go to Carter-Ruck and tell them to stop working. Go to everybody, stop working. They'll tell you to fuck off, okay. Don't waste time, talk sense.'

With apologies, I tell him I don't follow what he's trying to say about these law firms.

'You cannot impose your way, your behaviour, your nonsensical approach to countries which have a different way of behaving and operating. You are denying their citizens the right to telephony by behaving in the way you are.'

I try to come back to the facts. The TeliaSonera deals in Uzbekistan, Nepal, Kazakhstan. 'These deals were done, so it seems to be what you're saying is that they were done with an allowance for corruption.'

'No, I have no fucking idea whether there was corruption or not. No fucking idea. I have no fucking idea because nobody gave me paperwork to say he bribed them, he bribed her, he took this, he bought houses. What the fuck? I don't know. Do I want to be there or not? That's the headline question. That's it. Nothing more to it.'

———————

Part II

'Want to make your life easy for you'

Nine

Two scenes from a park in lockdown

The sun rises at eleven minutes before seven. This much we know. In Coronation Gardens, the temperature climbs towards 15.3 degrees Celsius.

It is September 25, 2020. The entrepreneur, philanthropist and thought leader Mohamed Amersi, friend and counsellor to presidents and princes, to prime ministers and chief executives, prepares to meet Charlotte Leslie, the malicious woman who will try to destroy him.

Drops of rain fall. The sky clears. On the radio, a newsreader announces the latest allocations of resources and status. Less of the British public's money is to be given to those who must not work lest they spread the virus. Shopkeepers in Birmingham describe their dismay. Two people – Harry and Meghan – received a large sum of the public's money to travel across the world. A few hundred other people, who were profitably selling chemicals prohibited by law, have been raided by the police. A musician will be given a prize. Food might cost more soon.

'Cheating,' tweets Donald Trump, in regard to the coming US election, 'is against the law. We are closely watching!'

Mohamed moves through London.

The headline on the front of today's *Daily Mail*: 'Now it's time to live without fear'. But the coronavirus rules say meetings must still be outside. And Leslie has been shielding. Pulmonary embolism four years back. 'Out of safety for you,' Amersi tells her, 'I will be driving.'

The location is six miles south, across the river, from his house in Mayfair. The Party has asked him to meet her; she has chosen the place.

Along the edge of Coronation Gardens, an avenue of horse chestnuts. The granite fountain has become a bath for birds.

Leslie sends him a message: I am loitering at the gate in a suspicious-looking macintosh!

Amersi is running late. He replies: Current eta 1.06.

Leslie: Great! I might adjourn to a bench near the entrance!

He arrives. There she is: the failed MP. Spiteful. Sees him as a threat to her schemes. She has taken control of the organisation that maintains Conservative relationships in the Middle East. Turned it into her tool for making money in exchange for access to power.

She has bought him a coffee and a roll from Tesco. The coffee has gone cold. He declines both. Nearby is a Marks & Spencer. They go there. He buys crisps, nuts and sandwiches.

For two hours, they walk around the park and speak. She complains that the Party should have given her an honour when she lost her seat. She tells him that if he even wants to be considered as her organisation's next chair, he must start by giving it fifty thousand pounds. For that, he can host the annual lunch with the prime minister.

After they part, Charlotte Leslie creates a false Mohamed Amersi, an Amersi who Mohamed doesn't recognise. To preserve the truth, to avoid this hijacking of reality, she will have to be silenced.

The sun also rises at eleven minutes before seven the second time September 25, 2020 takes place. The temperature in Coronation Gardens once again approaches 15.3 degrees Celsius.

The former Member of Parliament Charlotte Leslie prepares to meet Mohamed Amersi, the rich man who will try to destroy her.

The drops of rain fall. The sky clears.

On the radio, the latest allocations of resources and status are unchanged. Less of the British public's money is indeed to be given to those who must not work lest they spread the virus. Shopkeepers in Birmingham are constant in their dismay. Harry and Meghan have still travelled the world, the public has still paid their way. The few hundred sellers of proscribed profitable chemicals did not evade the raid. The musician will be given the prize. Food is likely to get pricier.

For a man who deals in alternative facts, the tweet that appears on Donald Trump's feed is perfectly consistent with the one he posted the previous time September 25, 2020 unfolded. He continues to watch closely for cheats.

Charlotte Leslie moves through London. She has floppy blonde hair, same as back in those old *Baywatch* photos from her lifeguard days, the ones the tabloids got hold of.

The *Daily Mail*'s headline writers have still gone for: 'Now it's time to live without fear'. The rules have not flinched: if you must meet, do it outside. The pulmonary embolism four years back was no illusion. Leslie has been shielding.

In the WhatsApp he sends her at 10.47 a.m., Amersi does not say what he thinks. He does not say: Vexingly, not only I am having to travel to meet this Charlotte Leslie, I am having to drive myself, the pandemic having robbed me of my drivers. He says: 'Out of safety for you, I will be driving.'

The park is not far from where she lives in Southfields. The Party has asked her to meet him; she picked the spot. The Coronation Gardens that exists in Amersi's world is identical to the one in her own. The avenue of horse chestnuts along the edge, the granite bird bath that once was a fountain.

She strikes the same merry note: I am loitering at the gate in a suspicious-looking macintosh!

He's still running late, eta 1.06.

Leslie: Great! I might adjourn to a bench near the entrance!

She waits for Mohamed Amersi. This character who's after an honour. She has bought him a coffee and a roll from Tesco's. The coffee is going cold. When he arrives, he declines both coffee and roll. Nearby is a Marks & Spencer. They go there. He buys two packets of crisps.

For two hours, they walk around the park and speak. He has given the Party a lot of money, he says, and now he wants recognition. An honour, for one thing. Also, he wishes to buy the chairmanship of the organisation she leads, the one that maintains the Conservatives' relationships in the Middle East. The Party, he says, have told me I can have this. She politely lets him down. It's a post for an elected representative, not a donor. He can sponsor the gala dinner with the PM if he likes, though.

Ten

Cakeism

Cucumber, potato and olive salad, cashew-nut cream, nasturtium leaf pesto and potato ash, followed by red mullet with salsa verde, artichoke and heritage carrots, then a selection of pudding canapés. The accompanying white burgundy has citrus, grilled nuts and ripe apple on the nose, orchard fruits and wet pebbles on the palate, and a citrus-tinged finish.

The menu for the Winter Party is agreed. The chefs are at work. There are only hours left before the fundraising event of the year begins. It is February 25, 2020. The fateful afternoon in Coronation Gardens is months away. Mohamed Amersi is blossoming into the Mohamed Amersi he wants to be. Today, he will be seated among the highest in the land.

At 10:35 a.m., an email goes round the Conservatives' fundraising team. Subject: Amersi.

> Can we arrange for Amersi to get a table-swing by
> and name check from the PM?

Initially Amersi wanted a shout out from stage but it's too public and not fair on others. In short he is starting a Friends of the Middle East and North Africa which to be fair, would have some of the best group fund raising potential if done right. He wants someone to say this guy is behind a new and very promising concept – Friends of MENA.

If ever there was a PM with the vim for a memorable table swing-by, it is Boris. He's been taking good care of himself lately. A holiday on Mustique, staying at a lovely villa arranged by one of tonight's guests, the boss of Carphone Warehouse. And this past fortnight he's been at Chevening, the grace-and-favour prime-ministerial getaway in Kent. A well-earned rest, now he's Got Brexit Done. Sure, he's missed a few meetings of the Cobra security committee discussing this coronavirus thing. But other urgent matters must be attended to. There's his second wife to divorce and the pregnancy of his future third to announce. He's dashed back to London for the fundraising bash.

All is arranged. Amersi prepares to receive Boris's favour. As Mohamed himself told an audience in Oxford during a recent disquisition on corruption: 'Political donors are not philanthropists. They expect something in return.'

It starts with an invitation to London's most secretive club. 'I am sure you will find it a most enjoyable and informative evening,' Ben Elliot tells Mohamed in an email, before moving on to the suggested donation size.

It is 2015. Elliot's insertion of his good Quintessentially client Amersi into royal circles is proceeding apace; now begins the entrée to real power. Mohamed has banked his last millions from TeliaSonera. His project now is himself.

The club, 5 Hertford Street, is only a five-minute walk across Mayfair from Amersi's London townhouse. Beyond the doorman lies a place that is distinct from the one where stodgier Tories gather, the Carlton Club over in St James's. At 5 Hertford Street, they've mixed in the new elite: the celebrities. Here it's not just your politicos but your Clooneys, your Jaggers, your Neymars and your Lupita Nyong'os, your Leonardo DiCaprios and Cara Delevingnes, as well as those who span the genres, your young royals like William, the heir to the heir to the throne. Which is not to say that the future of the country is neglected by the punters at 5 Hertford Street. The instigators of Brexit gather here. Nigel Farage, Arron Banks, Michael Gove – the owner Robin Birley is a Leave man, and glad to have them in.

It is Gove, clever and gawky former journalist serving as David Cameron's chief whip, to whom Amersi has the pleasure of listening during the intimate fundraiser in a 5 Hertford Street dining room. Before long, the Brexiteers have deposed Cameron. Theresa May succeeds him as prime minister. As she negotiates departure terms with the EU, May reads polls suggesting she could increase the Conservative majority in Parliament. During a long walk in Wales, she resolves to call a snap election and crush Jeremy Corbyn's Labour. The vote is set for June 8, 2017. For the campaign, her aides initially present her as Agent of Change. Then they switch to Strong and Stable Leader. One who calls a spade a spade and Brexit Brexit. Then the Strong and Stable Leader reverses the main policy in her manifesto, a new way to pay for social care, after the prospect of parting with a little of the 'family treasure' to fund everyone's longer lives enrages Tory voters. Announcing the U-turn, May calls a press conference and declares: 'Nothing has changed.' The journalists laugh. Karate-chopping the air in frustration, she repeats: 'Nothing. Has. Changed.'

The polls tighten. Even before this shambles, May has never been much of a fundraiser. She's always in danger of donors defecting further to the right if they deem her insufficiently committed to leaving the EU. Staggering from one mortification to the next, her campaign needs money. With just days to go to polling day, Mohamed Amersi offers to make his first political donation. Two hundred thousand pounds. But there's a hitch. He's a non-dom – a tax status available to wealthy UK residents who say their main home is elsewhere and so pay fewer dues in Britain – and after all these years based in Dubai, Amersi's not on the British electoral roll.

Amersi hastily applies to register as a voter and emails a Party fundraiser, copying in Ben Elliot. 'Can I now send the funds in my name or should Nadia do it?'

Nadia's been dazzling on Mohamed's arm as he tours the philanthropy circuit. London society has embraced her. There she is, just a few months ago in November 2016, rotating for the cameras in a backless black gown and red heels at the entrance to a fundraising fashion show just across Green Park from Buckingham Palace. Beside her, Amersi in a slick suit. Nadia has helped to put on the night. Jacques Azagury dresses the models. Jewellery by House of Garrard. All sorts of names there: the designer Nicky Haslam, the personality Pinkietessa. It's to raise funds for Camilla's osteoporosis charity. (A cause that matters to Ben's aunt, the future queen: her mother suffered so badly with it that a hug once broke her rib.) Nadia is a creative in her own right, of course, even if Mohamed himself is the source of almost all the income at her interior design venture, English Story.

'I have just checked with compliance,' a Conservative functionary replies to Mohamed's question, 'and you will not actually come onto the Electoral Roll until 1st June, so we cannot accept a donation from you until then.' And therefore: 'The donation must please come from Nadia's account.' Important, this. Not being on the roll, Amersi is what you call an 'impermissible donor'. Accepting a donation from an impermissible donor could violate electoral law. And yet the email to arrange the payment does not begin 'Dear Nadia ...' It begins:

Dear Mr Amersi
Thank you so much for the extremely generous donation of £200k from Nadia. Please find below our bank details for the transfer.

And the bank receipt for the payment is sent not to Nadia Rodicheva, but to Mohamed Amersi. What's more, if this receipt is supposed to be proof that the money was Nadia's – as it must be under electoral law, given that it is her name the Conservatives declare as the donor – that's not what it appears to show. The account is at Union Bancaire Privée in Geneva, the bank that's taken over Coutts' Swiss operation. There are no human beings named, just a string of numbers and letters that identifies the bank's address. The same address that appears elsewhere in an invoice for Mohamed's personal foundation. If there is anyone who seems to control this anonymous Swiss bank account from which enough money to help swing a close election is being injected into the UK's democracy, it is Mohamed Amersi – a man prohibited by law from donating.

None of this concerns the Party. What concerns the Party is the materialising prospect that it might be about to cease doing the thing it exists to do – rule. The treasurer, a mining mogul called Mick Davis, emails Mohamed and Nadia.

Thank you again for your recent extremely generous donation for the General Election Fighting Fund of £200,000. Your financial support has been exemplary.

Your commitment is really very much appreciated, especially for this crucial Election. I guess every Party Treasurer has claimed that their campaign is era defining, well I feel our one next week really is just that. The outcome of course will not just effect Brexit negotiations but determine whether Corbyn's socialist agenda can be killed off for another generation.

You will have seen that the polls have tightened and the fight is most definitely on.

So much so that, even as he thanks Mohamed and Nadia, the treasurer asks for more. The donation has already covered almost the whole cost of helicopter and private jet flights, or half what the Party spent hiring one of Barack Obama's election strategists. Lynton Crosby, the Tories' Australian election guru, has a shopping list for the final week: half a million for Facebook videos, more for ads that wrap over the front pages of newspapers. Could you manage another fifteen thousand? Half a year's wages for the average Brit. For Mohamed, it's less than a day's worth of the fees his consultancy used to charge TeliaSonera.

'We are in Madagascar and slightly out of touch with events,' Amersi replies twenty minutes later. 'It's a pity about the tightening but at least complacency will not set in. We are happy to contribute a further £15,000.' Once more, the name entered in the donor registry is Nadia's.

The Conservatives retain power. But they lose their majority. Eight ministers are defeated, as well as a Bristol MP recently named backbencher of the year for exposing a cover-up by hospital bosses, Charlotte Leslie. For a while, May clings on in Downing Street. She is still prime minister when a new star on the Conservative scene called Mohamed Amersi hosts the annual Carlton Club Dinner (this year held, conveniently for Mohamed, at the Dorchester, round the back of his Mayfair townhouse).

By now Amersi is on the electoral roll and able to donate in his own increasingly illustrious name. He breezes through the Party's vetting. The Conservatives conclude that Mohamed Amersi is what he says he is: 'a well-connected worldwide man'. And why wouldn't they? He's an open book. His websites explain his charitable philosophy. His work with the Prince of Wales. The time the Royal Agricultural University welcomed him alongside that other noted philanthropist, Mr Ajeya Sumargi of Nepal. Just as he opted for Global Elite membership of Ben Elliot's Quintessentially service, Mohamed purchases membership of the Conservatives' Leaders Group. Fifty grand a year buys you monthly lunches with ministers.

Mohamed and his chequebook attend the Party's 2019 Black and White Ball in Battersea. Lots of police to protect this elite gathering. Theresa May zooms in from Brexit negotiations in Northern Ireland to be present when an evening with her at the Proms, then a set of campaign posters bearing her autograph, are auctioned for the price of a medium-sized house. You could pay to go to Michael Gove's home and be cooked a meal. Or for a cheese-tasting session with Liz Truss, a minor minister known only for a speech in which she denounced the 'disgrace' of Britain importing most of its cheese. Amersi parts with fifty grand for two lots. Dinner with the foreign secretary, Jeremy Hunt. And a magic lesson, to be taught by international development secretary and former illusionist's assistant Penny Mordaunt.

Eventually the Conservatives' Brexit frenzy consumes May and she tearfully announces her resignation in May 2019. When she arrives at Oxford, a few months later, a relaxed smile has returned. After extending her gratitude for the invitation to be here at this very special event tonight at Brasenose, she reminds her audience that she grew up nearby, studied at the university and met her husband here.

'So I've got quite a lot to thank Oxford for. But of course today, we're here to give our thanks to Mohamed Amersi and the Amersi Foundation for financing the amazing refurbishment and provision of this lecture room.'

It means so much to Mohamed to be able to advance what he calls the Three Es – education, engagement and empowerment – by funding the refurbishment of Lecture Room XI at Brasenose College. Or as it is now known, the Amersi Foundation Lecture Room. When it opens in December 2019, Amersi moves closer to his dream: to see his name upon the Clarendon Arch. The hallowed stone lists Oxford University's top donors: Henry VIII, Charles I, Oppenheimer, Rhodes. And what a lecture room it is. The architects have skilfully matched the original Victorian timberwork. The panelling is offset by the freshest shades of beige on the painted walls above. The room boasts state-of-the-art technology too. The sixty-five-inch touchscreen has a built-in Windows PC and whiteboard functionality. There is climate control.

'Your generosity has made this incredible facility possible,' May says. 'You've been clear about the social responsibility that business has to the communities they operate in and the societies they serve. And I think you put it yourself with very great force when you said: "Business has to understand that the privilege of being allowed to make money comes at a price. And the price is: it has to be responsible." And those sound like words that politicians say.' Hearty chuckles. 'I may have said them myself,' May hoots. 'But dare I say it, when someone who has succeeded in business says it, actually it can't be ignored. It has much, much greater force.'

Mohamed Amersi rises. His gown is red with black trim. Through his spectacles, his eyes sparkle with delight. Tell a dream, lose a reader, Henry James said. But Amersi's audience is captive. He's the money.

'A few nights ago I had a dream,' he says. 'A dream about Oxford. The city of dreaming spires itself. But an Oxford half a century after Brexit. And an Oxford subtly changed. As I often do in dreams, I began in the air.'

Amersi relates his dream. He is flying balletically between the city's landmarks, each of them now renamed to feature starring characters from Brexit. 'I finally came down to Earth outside All Souls as a strange yet familiar figure emerged in a velvet-coloured tan overcoat and fruitcake-flecked tie puffing heavily on the Union Jack cigarette, a figure who somehow by some mystery I knew to be the Regius Professor of Brexit' – he can barely contain his laughter at this wit – 'then it was past the Radcliffe Camera, now the Faculty of Brexit, through sea upon measureless sea of tourists and into the Bodleian, now the Brexit Library, past the Sheldonian Theatre, now the

Graduate School of Business Studies' – corrects himself – 'Brexit Studies, and on to Blackswells, er Blackwell's bookshop miraculously still with its apostrophe s. There in the sunless caverns of its Brexit wing I found myself leafing through the Greater Brexit Dictionary' – turns to Theresa, humorous straightface – 'a hundred and fifty-seven volumes but still not quite at the end of the letter N, nobody-wanted-to-be-poor was there and No Deal and Northern Ireland and Norway dear neglected Norway was still to have its moment in the sun.'

He takes a breath.

'So this is how it all finishes, I said to myself, an all-conquering all-consuming academic hydra, a fiendishly tricky academic discipline with which to mould and torture vulnerable young minds, a whole new academic industry giving employment to thousands. Oh dear, I thought' – drops his script (there is a script), lurches to catch it, bangs the microphone – 'it's the Schleswig-Holstein Question Mark Two and I remembered the words of Lord Palmerston, the Schez – the Schleswig-Holstein Question is so complicated only three men in Europe have ever understood it: one was Prince Albert who is dead, the second was a German professor who became mad, and I am the third and I have forgotten all about it.'

Some in the audience laugh, perhaps less out of amusement than to avoid being mistaken for one who does not understand the Schleswig-Holstein Question.

'No, history does not repeat itself but yes, it sure does rhyme. With that, I jumped awake. And then I thought of something else.

'When future generations of dons and of students take their chewed pens and freshly sharpened scalpels to our time, tell your story' – nod to Theresa – 'and mine, puzzle over the people and wonder over the dramas of Brexit, the political drama, the cultural drama, the human drama, one of the places they will do so will be none other than the Amersi Foundation Lecture Theatre here. I believe I am therefore entitled to give these generations a message.'

He has prepared this message, reads it carefully.

'When you study us, do so with your hearts as well as your heads. And note that there was reason as well as passion and plain good sense and dreams of a better, more generous, more unified and in every sense more democratic world on all sides of the Brexit argument. Before and after and during the referendum. And that there are reasons to admire as well as pity or condemn us.

'Secondly, before you toast our passing in champagne, remember that vision without action is a daydream, and action without vision is' – eyebrows to Theresa – 'a nightmare. And that we were there and you were not. And that choosing between Boris and Brussels, sovereignty and safety, autonomy and affluence, Brexit, No Brexit and BrINO' – such is the extent to which the nature of one of Britain's diplomatic relationships has consumed public discourse that terms such as Brexit in Name Only now have acronyms – 'was more difficult than it might look to you now. And that far from being deranged we were just earlier versions of you. Which means in turn that to understand us – and to any people of the past, or indeed of the present – and above all to avoid falling into the trap of condescension, or arrogance, or inhumanity, you need first to understand a thing or two about yourselves.'

Having thus established that he is not deranged, Amersi concludes. He's grateful to Theresa for being here, especially because we are, once again, in an election campaign.

When May fell, Amersi spread his largesse among the candidates: ten thousand apiece for Gove, Hunt, and the Brexiteers' champion, Boris Johnson, a gifted rhetorician and career fibster who promised the British people three hundred and fifty million pounds a week for their health service, plus the repulsion of dusky hordes massing to immigrate, if they voted Leave, the side in the referendum that he had, at the last minute, chosen to front. In a moment of confusion and foreboding, Johnson's cakeism – an ideology of having your confectionery and also eating it, a seductive rejection of the most basic tenets of reality – triumphs. So breakfast with him is the most desirable lot at the next Carlton Club Dinner. Amersi wins the bidding with a hundred thousand. Peanuts in Amersiworld, equivalent to a solitary trip to the Grand Prix for half a dozen influential types. But plenty in British politics, where a little money goes a long way.

Johnson says only he can Get Brexit Done. In a few days, he will regain the majority May lost. On average a constituency costs about two hundred thousand pounds to win. By that measure, the half million Amersi's given since the last election would get you two and a half seats. Not bad when the

Conservative gain of forty-eight has given Boris a commanding hold on power. Now it's on to the Winter Party (renamed this year – 'Black and White Ball' is not a great look during a culture war). A time to reward friends.

Amersi emails the outreach team at Conservative headquarters the day before the Winter Party.

'From my side I have spoken to many Mid-East Ambassadors about this and they are hugely supportive. Indeed some of them will be on my table on Tuesday.' He's also discussed his plan with Boris's new Party chairman, and with the member of the government who will host Amersi's table: James Cleverly, the minister in the Foreign Office for the Middle East and North Africa. 'They both expressed huge support!'

If he can get it approved, Amersi's Conservative Friends of the Middle East and North Africa, or Comena, will join the Tories' legion of friends. Conservative Friends of India: it's said they can deliver forty seats. Conservative Friends of Israel is better funded and better connected than any other lobbying operation at Westminster, with four in five Tory MPs as members. Conservative Friends of Russia was embarrassing – the jolly to Moscow, the liaising with the son of a KGB officer – but there are dozens of others that manage not to cause a fuss. It's hard to tell who funds the Friends groups. But Amersi is clear where the money for his Comena will come from – himself. He'll put up a quarter of a million, with the same again from Mohamed Mansour, an Egyptian tractor tycoon who served as a minister in Hosni Mubarak's despotic regime before turning to British politics and handing a slice of his fortune to the Conservatives.

To the money Amersi will add his own conspicuous talents. What he displays, apart from his wealth, is that remarkable ability to be on everyone's side. He's the dealmaker. He gets on with Dave, he gets on with Theresa, he gets on with Boris. He gets on in Tel Aviv and he gets on in Tehran. One day he's WhatsApping with Lord Polak, stalwart of Conservative Friends of Israel. Another, he's persuading the Iranians to let his foundation make a documentary there.

Amersi has placed Nadia to his left. To his right, Cleverly. Then the ambassadors of the United Arab Emirates, Kuwait, Lebanon and Iraq. Envoys from the region so pivotal to British interests: supplier of oil, buyer of arms, gatherer of counter-terrorism intelligence.

Few relationships could be more vital to the UK than that with the Middle East. And it is into this relationship that Amersi has decided he must be slotted. He's lived in the Gulf, between the Swiss years and coming back to London. Name a telco from the Arab world, Mohamed's worked for it, like those gigs in Uzbekistan for the Qataris and the Emiratis. As he has honoured the region with his wealth, the region has honoured him back. Amersi's foundation received the ruler of Dubai's Knowledge Award, bestowed on pioneers who 'create new ways to spread knowledge around the world'.

The auction lots at the Winter Party are delectable. Whisky tasting with Truss. Dinner in Mayfair with Michael Gove or at the Carlton Club with the health secretary, Matt Hancock, who is in the meantime supposedly getting to grips with this new virus. Eighty grand gets you into a box at Lord's to watch cricket with the chancellor, Rishi Sunak. A game of tennis with Boris goes for forty-five thousand.

The mega-donors have their own tables. There's Lubov Chernukhin, wife of one of Putin's old ministers. Tends to splash the cash at these events. Last year she bought a 'girls' night out' with vicar's daughter Theresa May; before that it was tennis with David Cameron.

The prime minister already knows about Mohamed's plans for the Middle East. Amersi chatted it over with him when they sat next to each other at a dinner some months ago. It was clear to Amersi from their conversation that Boris was intrigued by his knowledge of the region. Last month, in January 2020, he saw Boris again. Over dinner, Mohamed talked once more about his idea. 'Go for it': that was the signal he took from Johnson. There is no door that will stay closed to Mohamed: Boris even offered an introduction to Mike Pompeo, President Trump's secretary of state.

Amersi senses he is needed in the vanguard of the new Global Britain. Less than a month ago, at 11 p.m. on January 31, 2020 the UK formally withdrew from the European Union. No three hundred and fifty million pounds has succoured the health services, this week or any other. The dusky Turkish hordes were never coming anyway. But Boris is rampant. He has proclaimed: 'The doubters, the doomsters, the gloomsters, they are going to get it wrong again.'

And now Johnson draws near. He's working the room. At Amersi's table he shakes hands with the ambassadors. Then, in full view of the diplomatic corps, not to mention a cabinet member and whoever else in this estimable gathering may be watching, the prime minister singles out Mohamed for a compliment.

The boy from Mombasa is where he belongs. Here, in the elite. How rich the cashew-nut cream must taste, how sumptuous the mullet. There's now just the formality of letting that ex-MP who's doing Middle East stuff for the Conservatives know about Amersi's vision. A week after the Winter Party, a senior official at Conservative headquarters sends an email introducing Mohamed to Charlotte Leslie.

By declining to give Amersi the shout-out he wanted, the Conservatives missed a strategic opportunity. Not just for Comena, his Conservative Friends of the Middle East and North Africa – for the nation. 'It would have helped the cause of showing the attending Arab ambassadors that Comena and UK soft power was alive and had merit,' Mohamed tells me in written answers to the questions I've sent him. Observe what's happened in the Middle East in Comena's absence: Russia and China have stepped into the vacuum. 'Comena was about meritocracy and helping the

UK government, the Party and the UK people but you and Leslie regrettably saw otherwise.'*

He means the articles I wrote about him in the *Financial Times*. Sitting here in Carter-Ruck's offices, I say: 'You know I'm not at the *FT* anymore.'

'You got fired.'

'I didn't get fired.'†

'I know that. Say it, it's fine: you people get fired all the time.'

'Do you think I got fired? Do you really think so?'

'One hundred per cent. People told me. Senior people inside the firm.'

---

* The point about meritocracy may seem obscure until we recall that one of Comena's stated aims was to recruit people of Middle Eastern origin into British public service. An email (sent the day before the Winter Party) disclosed in Amersi's defamation proceedings against Charlotte Leslie sets this out.

From [redacted]@conservatives.com
Sent: 24 February 2020 11:46
To [redacted]@conservatives.com
Subject: MENA MA

My good friend Mohamed Amersi will be leading a Friends of the Middle East and North Africa group. Friends of MENA will work alongside [the Conservative Middle East Council] in building better relations with countries in the region and seek to attract the best talent from these communities into public life in the UK, as well as doing what Mohamed is passionate about – filling up our coffers.

† I resigned, as it happens, to go and write this book. Then, I got an offer to join the *Guardian* staff as a member of its investigations team, which I accepted.

'Senior people in the *FT*?'

'Yes.'

'Can I ask who?'

'Are you crazy? I would reveal my source? Senior people.'

'It's your position that senior people in the *Financial Times* had told you that I was fired?'

'Yes.'

'Could you tell me what I was fired for?'

'I don't want to say any more. Finished, let it go. Incompetence.'

'Over what?'

'I have no idea. I couldn't care less.'

'Well, you seem to be taking an interest in it.'

'I'm not. I couldn't care less. You're interested in my case; I'm not interested in your case. I couldn't care less.'

'Can I just let you know, I mean I don't know if you really care, but I wasn't fired, I resigned and I got a job somewhere else.'

'Yes, that's what everybody does, they jump ship before they're booted, so fine.'

'So you don't think I was fired?'

'I thought you were fired, but they would have a little respect for you to say either you jump ship or we let you go, take your choice. And most people in that situation would jump ship before they're booted out. It's fine, that's how life works. Be proud, don't be upset with that, be proud.'

'I couldn't be less upset.'

'Be proud. A fifteen-year journalist with the *FT*, head of Africa, head of kleptocracy, shown the door, it's fine.'

'I was never head of Africa.'*

'So go and find the job back there again, if it was you who left. Go find it, I challenge you.'

'But I've got a job somewhere else now.'

'Sorry?'

'I work somewhere else now.'

'Where?'

'I work at the *Guardian* now.'

'No, you are a columnist at the *Guardian*. You're not a full-time employee.'

'Sorry?'

'Come on, Tom, let's get real. Don't bullshit me. I'm not interested in bullshit. It's fine, I also have friends at the *Guardian* who tell me what happened.'

'And they're telling you that I'm not on the staff?'

'You're an independent columnist.'

'An independent columnist?'

'Yes. That's what was described to me by senior people. But it's fine, that's how they see you.'

'You might notice, I haven't written any columns.'†

---

* And there's no such position as 'head of kleptocracy', though it sounds a great job.

† I'd published a column in the *Guardian* years earlier, about dirty money, and a bit on Putin when he invaded Ukraine, but months before this meeting with Amersi my appointment to the staff had been announced and I'd started writing news stories.

'I have no idea what you do. I don't care. You can do what you like.'

'I'm just telling you that these sources are mistaken.'

'I don't give a shit. Yours are not mistaken, yours are all pristine and beautiful and believable. Whenever my sources say something, they are not believable. See how you feel. You're on the receiving end of two comments and already you've gone crazy. And you have used a hundred fucking sources on me.'

'Mohamed, I'm not going crazy in any way, I'm simply trying to—'

'You are, look at you. If this was a video call, people would see your face. It's red and it's bothered.'

'Mohamed, I'm amused.'

'You're not amused, you're upset. But it's your emotions, you can feel whatever you want.'

Eleven

The boxer

They have a particular aroma, sweaty boxing gloves. Not the same as, say, sweaty feet. A unique smell that Charlotte Leslie still loves. It takes her back to the rickety barn, on a farm in the West Country across the fields from her parents' home, that housed a rudimentary boxing gym. There were rings for sparring, mirrors, men with scars and pasts, and the bags. Charlotte's bag would become teachers who tried to squash her. She had every advantage – a loving family, a private school – but there was something about the gym that felt, when she discovered it in her early teens, like coming home. Here, with her shaved head, her broad shoulders from swimming training, she belonged.

Had it not been for the parents, the education and the boxing, Charlotte reckons she could have ended up in prison. People like her are hugely over-represented there: dyslexics. It's the humiliation. That turns to anger, and anger can lead to trouble. The seven years as an MP were a chance to spar again. She loved the Bristol constituents who wanted her to take on some fight or other. Her skin, already tough, thickened further. Thanks to social media, even the laziest misanthropes, misogynists and megalomaniacs found that abusing elected representatives no longer even required turning up at their surgeries. Towards the end of Charlotte's second and final term, during the Brexit referendum campaign, a neo-Nazi in Yorkshire approached his MP, a mother of two called Jo Cox, outside a library. He drew a sawn-off rifle and shot her in the head, then dragged her by the hair into the road, stabbed her repeatedly with a dagger, and left her to die.

If you count all the campaigning to get elected in the first place, by the time she lost her seat in Theresa May's 2017 snap election, Charlotte had given ten years to the Conservatives. She was pushing forty and suddenly had to find a job. The one that came up was running the Conservative Middle East Council. She knew the region – a fascination that had begun when the 9/11 attacks jolted her to abandon a planned master's on Ovid and attend instead to current affairs. Margaret Thatcher oversaw CMEC's creation to tilt the debate among Conservatives to include some consideration of the Palestinian cause. Heavyweight parliamentarians serve as its chair, the prime minister addresses the annual lunch, and there could be no grander grandee than its current honorary president, Churchill's grandson Sir Nicholas Soames.

It was only supposed to be for a few months. After the intense years in Parliament, Charlotte has had enough. She's been sick: pulmonary embolism. It was thrilling at the start, this political life, this public life. At one Conservative conference in Blackpool when she was starting out, she was touched by the kindness of a star politician who complimented her speech and whisked her off to a donors' reception, merrily quoting the *Iliad* (in the Greek) in the taxi. Today she scarcely recognises the Boris Johnson who has just become prime minister. The Party has changed into something else, too.

So when she hears that the rich donor who's been trying to become CMEC chairman is now setting up some rival Middle East organisation for the Conservatives, she feels an exhausted urge to let him do whatever he wants. As she remembered it, when they met at Coronation Gardens, after she disabused him of the idea he could acquire the CMEC chair with a donation, Amersi told her he'd let her know if he decided to go ahead with his Comena plan. Instead she's heard about it from a colleague. For fuck's sake, she says, the two-faced creep.

She's sitting in the kitchen at her partner Andy's place near Coronation Gardens, absently googling someone she's heard Amersi has lined up for Comena. The name is unfamiliar: Dr Ilma Bogdan. Leslie opens her LinkedIn profile and looks upon a young, glamorous woman who records her most recent appointment as 'Head of Administration' at Amersi's Comena, seemingly the equivalent to Charlotte's position at CMEC. Leslie reads Ilma's CV: studied at Cambridge and Harvard, speaks Arabic. She's younger and brighter than me, Leslie thinks. And I'm tired. Just let her do it. For me, time for a change.

Leslie scrolls down. Dr Bogdan doesn't seem to have had much by way of paid employment but she's evidently put in time at the Party. She lists posts at a couple of Conservative organisations. Then Charlotte comes to education, and realises: this woman is Russian. A Russian who attended the Moscow State Institute of International Relations. Leslie reads it again. Some call this place the cradle of the KGB. But it's also produced plenty of high-flying non-spook graduates. Still, Amersi having picked a Russian to run Comena has sparked Leslie's attention.

Charlotte thinks back to the inquiry by Parliament's intelligence committee into Russian influence in the UK. Boris Johnson – an avid consumer of rich Russians' hospitality who has recently ennobled one of his generous hosts, the son of a KGB officer – held up publication of the report for months. Only after an independent-minded Conservative MP snatched the chairmanship of the committee was it made public six months ago. 'The UK welcomed Russian money,' the inquiry found, 'and few questions – if any – were asked about the provenance of this considerable wealth.'

> It appears that the UK Government at the time held
> the belief (more perhaps in hope than expectation)
> that developing links with major Russian companies
> would promote good governance by encouraging
> ethical and transparent practices, and the adoption of
> a law-based commercial environment. What is now
> clear is that it was in fact counter-productive, in that

it offered ideal mechanisms by which illicit finance could be recycled through what has been referred to as the London 'laundromat'. The money was also invested in extending patronage and building influence across a wide sphere of the British establishment – PR firms, charities, political interests, academia and cultural institutions were all willing beneficiaries of Russian money, contributing to a 'reputation laundering' process. In brief, Russian influence in the UK is 'the new normal', and there are a lot of Russians with very close links to Putin who are well integrated into the UK business and social scene, and accepted because of their wealth.

And, the MPs wrote after hearing evidence from the UK's intelligence agencies, it's not just the oligarchs. 'The arrival of Russian money resulted in a growth industry of enablers – individuals and organisations who manage and lobby for the Russian elite in the UK. Lawyers, accountants, estate agents and PR professionals have played a role, wittingly or unwittingly, in the extension of Russian influence which is often linked to promoting the nefarious interests of the Russian state.'

In Andy's kitchen, Leslie googles some more. This time Mohamed himself. He too, she reads, has some Russia in his past. There's a Forbes piece from 2006 that mentions 'a mysterious figure named Mohamed Amersi' who's doing St Petersburg telecoms deals. Vladimir Putin's minister of communications, Leonid Reiman, is quoted dismissing allegations that he's the secret beneficiary. Charlotte reads that Amersi once sat on the board of MegaFon, one of Russia's biggest mobile phone networks. And there's a blogger who's found a link between him and the oligarch Mikhail Fridman.

At CMEC Charlotte has taken delegations of Tories to meet Mohamed bin Salman, the Saudi crown prince; Abbas in Palestine; Sisi, the Egyptian strongman. Sometimes there's intrigue. Like when a general from a Gulf state approached her, apparently seeking a channel to pass information to British intelligence. What if it will now be Amersi in those rooms instead of her, Amersi receiving those secrets? Were these traces of Russia cause for concern?

Charlotte knew she lacked the experience or expertise to judge. There aren't many people you can ask about this sort of thing. But through her work on the Middle East, she has a trusted contact who's worked in national security. It might be nothing to worry about, the contact tells her when she calls, but it has hallmarks of a Russian influence operation.

Over Christmas, Charlotte gathers what more she can find on Amersi into a memo. There is nothing to finger Amersi as some sort of Russian agent. Rather, he appears to be something harder to define. He seems to share with Boris, with Putin, with Trump a belief that reality is his to command. What really worries Leslie is the gap between what she seems to be discovering about Amersi and his public image. She sends her memo to some MPs, some diplomats, some more intelligence people. And to Julian Lewis, the MP who'd taken control of the intelligence committee and published the Russia report, so he can pass it on to the spooks. But first she sends a basic version to Sir Nicholas Soames, the Tory grandee who's her honorary president at CMEC, recounting her contacts with Amersi, how he seemed to be angling for an honour, how he wanted to be CMEC's chairman but has now decided to form his own organisation, to be run by a Russian. Soames forwards her message to the Party chairman.

'Charlotte Leslie who is the director got in touch with me just before Christmas about this issue and it seems to me is serious enough to warrant urgent attention at the highest levels of the party organisation,' Soames writes. He adds: 'In view of the seriousness of this I asked Charlotte Leslie to lay out in detail the background and further some information on the players concerned. I leave this to you but Charlotte will of course be very happy to provide you with any further and more detailed information.'

Soames sends the email to the chairman's address: Ben@ quintessentially.com.

Twelve

The libel factory

P eter seizes the haddock and runs.

It is Sunday morning in the Carter-Ruck household. Peter and his sister Peggy have been awaiting breakfast. Their father is a disciplinarian and the young boy is deemed to have committed some infraction. In Peter's six-year-old breast there stirs a righteous passion. The allegation is false yet the sentence has been imposed: no haddock for him. This injustice will not stand. He snatches the fish from its dish. Gripping it by the tail, he runs. Out of the door, into the garden.

'Well Peggy shall not have any either!' he declares. And so the spirit of the law is upheld.

After a war spent shooting down German bombers, it is in the law that Peter Carter-Ruck makes his stellar career. He qualifies as a solicitor and is assigned to a firm's defamation department. He enjoys the urgency of this work. For a while, he defends newspapers. But they start to hire their own in-house lawyers. So Carter-Ruck takes on plaintiffs as clients.

Twenty-four hours a day, seven days a week, he makes himself available to them – to all who have had their good names tarnished. His ammunition is the threatening letter. Not for him the politesse with which other solicitors write their correspondence. Carter-Ruck's letters say what he wants and when he wants it. The retraction, the apology, damages.

Some of the most valuable reputations in the land are entrusted to his protection. Robert Maxwell's, Sir James Goldsmith's, Lucian Freud's, Laurence Olivier's. The country's perennial rulers, the Conservatives, turn to him. Nigel Lawson, Neil Hamilton, Normans Lamont and Tebbit, Edwina Currie, Cecil Parkinson, Michael Heseltine. When that incorrigible rag *Private Eye* in 1963 prints a cartoon of Randolph Churchill of which the son of the great Winston disapproves, Carter-Ruck extracts three thousand pounds in damages and a full-page apology in the *Evening Standard*. In the *Eye*'s pages, he becomes Carter-Fuck (and when he asks for this to be corrected, Farter-Fuck).

But while those *Private Eye* hacks scratch around in Soho, Peter can live as his clients do. Four homes. A BMW, a Rolls-Royce Silver Shadow. A succession of yachts, each called *Fair Judgment*. Randolph Churchill once took a taxi straight from court to Cartier to buy his invaluable solicitor an inscribed cigarette box in gold and silver. He's no rich mark, though. Won't have his wealth leeched away by the undeserving. When he deems the caterers have poured too much champagne at his daughter's wedding, Peter refuses to pay the full bill.

Carter-Ruck can discern a libel where lesser lawyers see none. The author of a book about Peter Sellers retains him because the *Sunday Telegraph*'s review, with its lurid insinuations about the star of *The Pink Panther* and his director Blake Edwards, cannot be allowed to stand. Carter-Ruck fires off a letter. 'It is *untrue* that Peter Sellers and/or Blake Edwards talked to our client excitedly of a new penis-enlarging ointment.' The tale about the Copenhagen mail-order address and the tub of rancid garlic butter is likewise a monstrous falsehood.

Such talent earns reward. When the tears are flowing, he says, that's the moment to bill a client. Half a day in court: the fee is twenty thousand pounds. His costs for the Ugandan politician Princess Elizabeth of Toro's successful proceedings in the 1970s over a sex smear story amount to a quarter of her forty thousand pounds in damages. When Neil Hamilton extracts twenty grand from the BBC, Carter-Ruck's costs are twelve times as much. This man is a chancer out for the maximum fee, one of his partners concludes. He's doing for freedom of speech what the Boston Strangler did for door-to-door salesmen. The libel factory he's building is paid for by the media, through its legal bills and insurance premiums.

The influence of the firm Carter-Ruck founds swells to match that of a Fleet Street editor. Its mercilessness consumes Peter himself, who departs saddened by the perfidy of the colleagues who pushed him out. 'I've put a very great store on loyalty and playing the game and I think, perhaps, some of the younger generation hadn't had the advantages I'd had because I had served in the army, where loyalty came before your life.'

There is nonetheless a partner at Carter-Ruck who Peter sees as something of an heir. 'He's a very good lawyer. He's intelligent and he's got some quite remarkable results. It's rather presumptuous of me to say he's following in my footsteps, but some people think that.'

When the Russian state oil company run by Vladimir Putin's closest crony needs a lawyer to fight for the truth, it's Nigel Tait who's hired.

What joys have befallen Igor Sechin since St Petersburg. No longer just the veteran of the KGB's Angolan campaign serving as gatekeeper to Deputy Mayor Putin. Now he is the don of Russian oil. Few dare to challenge him. But a petite woman from the north of England has. Catherine Belton is her name. She needs to be taught a lesson.

Belton used to be a *Financial Times* correspondent in Moscow. Lives in London now, from where she's published a book: *Putin's People*. There's plenty about Sechin in it. He's known as Russia's Darth Vader, Belton writes, 'for his ruthless propensity for plots'. She says he 'had overseen and propelled the legal attack on Khodorkovsky since its start'. Khodorkovsky: the richest Russian back in the 1990s when Putin and his crew came to the Kremlin. They'd had to knock his political ambitions out of him. Send him to the gulag and dismember his oil company, Yukos. Some of Yukos's most valuable operations ended up in the state oil company,

Rosneft. The billionaire Igor Sechin is Rosneft's chief executive.

Sechin's at the heart of the *siloviki*, the KGB cabal who control Russia. It was the takedown of Khodorkovsky that demonstrated their control over that most powerful weapon, the law. That's what this Belton says. 'The pressure Sechin had brought to bear on the judges, the speed of the appeal process, the lack of substance to the charges, had brought the court system irrevocably under the *siloviki*. If, previously, the judges' pitifully low wages had left them open to bribery by powerful oligarchs, now the Kremlin was taking over.'

To be sure, come 2021 there's plenty more for Sechin to celebrate. Russia is feared again; traitors like Sergei Skripal can run as far as Salisbury but they'll still get a dose of nerve agent. No one likes Covid but it is at least helping to spread corruption around the west through crooked contracts to cronies of the ruling classes. And four years after Putin's regime helped him win the White House, Donald Trump is bringing the United States to the brink of collapse. But this damn book is an irritation. The insufferable Alexei Navalny waves a copy in his new video on Putin's palace. It's maddeningly effective, the way this lawyer exposes kleptocracy. He's being taught a lesson or two in the gulag. For Catherine Belton, they'll need different techniques.

Nigel Tait gets his kicks from 'suppressing free speech'. He's risen to head Carter-Ruck's defamation and media law department. Sometimes they act for broadcasters and publishers defending a case. What they're known for is shutting down journalism (even though, they say, they do not 'set out improperly or unreasonably to censor the media').

Tait and his colleagues have helped to pioneer the super-injunction: a court order that certain information, including the existence of the order, must remain secret. Unfortunately, there are those who trample on the rights of the rich. Like that MP who unmasked one of Carter-Ruck's super-injunction clients as the multinational commodities corporation Trafigura. Back in 2009 a *Guardian* reporter got hold of a confidential Trafigura report about the dumping of toxic waste in Africa. A judge granted a gagging order, stipulating that his ruling must not be revealed in the media because it could be seen as an attempt by the company 'improperly to muzzle the press'. Paul Farrelly MP tabled a motion in the House of Commons naming Trafigura and revealing the gag order. That meant the *Guardian* could circumvent the super-injunction using the legal privilege that protects reporting of anything said in Parliament from a defamation claim. Carter-Ruck wrote to the *Guardian*: print your story and you'll be in contempt of court. A subversion of the rule of law, that's what Nigel Tait calls it. Whereas Peter Carter-Ruck just had to have books pulped and newspapers shredded, these days there's the whole of the internet to censor. The Trafigura super-injunction crumbled partly because Twitter users defied it.

Since then, comfortingly, lawyers have learned to police online speech. Three years ago, in 2018, Carter-Ruck won a landmark case. A businessman had served six months in jail for conspiracy to intercept communications a decade earlier. He now wished this fact to be excised from the internet. Invoking a new 'right to be forgotten', he demanded Google scrub references to his crime from its search results. Google's bosses refused. The judge sided with Carter-Ruck, even after Google's lawyer warned that the businessman was being granted a 'right to rewrite history'.

This is what Carter-Ruck do. They win. They make the public record say what their clients want it to say, or, more frequently, not say.

Sometimes the press must be kept in order even when it's hard to see that much harm's been done. Take the time in 2001 when the tabloids printed a picture showing a pair of pert young buttocks on display in Ibiza. This shapely rear, they reported, belonged to a gentleman romping on a beach with Mick Jagger's daughter Jade. None other than the twentysomething nephew of Camilla Parker Bowles who founded that new concierge service, Quintessentially. But the reports were wrong: these buttocks were not Ben Elliot's. He hired Carter-Ruck, won an apology and damages – then got with Jade Jagger anyway.

And don't the papers screech when they lose. 'The day free speech drowned in a paddling pool of olive-oil,' the *Sun* once bleated. A judge had granted an injunction on a story about two of Nigel Tait's celebrity clients: a man who had enjoyed a threesome lubricated with said condiment, and this frolicker's rich, famous spouse. Rupert Murdoch's paper went to the

Supreme Court and lost. The judge ordered the *Sun* to pay the celebrities' legal costs.

Costs. Nigel Tait's most powerful weapon. Judges don't tend to award damages above a hundred thousand, so the real terror for the media and their insurers is lawyers' fees. Defy Tait and lose and you're on the hook not just for your own but his. He charges five hundred pounds an hour. Every time he reads an article or watches a news report about his client, that's another hundred. The cost of a UK libel trial starts at about half a million pounds.

Well might an editor quickly agree that Tait's letter makes a really rather compelling case, and cave. The shift of advertising online has gutted the newspapers' business model. There's barely enough money to pay what remains of the journalism staff, let alone hiring lawyers to fight a complaint or for the excess on defamation insurance if you end up in court. Meanwhile, the financial resources of those who bend the media to their will have grown almost limitless. Especially a new type of client, one that emerged as the old order of the Cold War gave way to something new, something richer: the oligarchs.

It took Catherine Belton seven years to write *Putin's People*. When the book appeared in 2020, the reviews were superb. *The Times* judged it 'the best and most important on modern Russia'. What the reviewers were missing, as Nigel Tait explains in the letter he sends to Belton on May 28, 2021, is the parade of untruths in her pages.

Tait begins with the usual formalities. He represents

Rosneft. It is a Russian company. But it has every right to bring legal proceedings in Britain. Some of its stock is listed on the London exchange. On Rosneft's international board sit the chief executive of BP and his predecessor. Tait explains that he knows which law firm to write to because they're representing Belton and her publishers at HarperCollins in the other claims already brought against the book. This is true. The defence solicitor for Belton and HarperCollins has never seen a legal attack of such scale and intensity, brought by the cream of London's reputation-management law firms. Roman Abramovich, Russian oligarch and Chelsea FC owner, is suing. Mikhail Fridman is suing, and so is his business partner. All told, defending the book could cost five million pounds.

The publisher's proprietor, Rupert Murdoch, is rich, but not as rich as Putin's kleptocracy and the oligarchs who feed off it. Draining amounts like that from a publishing house, even a big one with good insurance, would mean books that otherwise would have been published won't be. And the costs always exceed the insurance: even if you win, you lose.

A judge has set a date for a preliminary hearing of the oligarchs' claims by the time Nigel Tait sends his letter. Curiously, the claimant is not Igor Sechin, the billionaire Putin crony Belton's written about at great length, but Rosneft, the state oil company he runs.

At the foot of the first page of Nigel Tait's letter are logos of the top-rank awards that Legal 500 and the Chambers guide have bestowed on Carter-Ruck. Over the next eleven, he makes his case. It is outrageous to claim that Rosneft paid an enormous kickback to Putin and his KGB associates. Mikhail Khodorkovsky? He's a crook. The Russian authorities simply took various enforcement actions against him and his oil company for fraud and tax-dodging. These investigations were properly conducted, and he was convicted in accordance with the relevant Russian laws. The Russian judiciary took instructions from the Kremlin? A baseless allegation. And there was no 'murky deal' by which Rosneft acquired Khodorkovsky's oilfields. It was all perfectly proper. The aspersions Belton casts on Rosneft's London flotation are misplaced. Look at the banks that worked on it: JP Morgan, Rothschild, Morgan Stanley and the rest. And what Rosneft's bosses did with the money they raised was entirely normal. As for the bit about a plan to channel millions to the Italian far-right using sales of Rosneft's oil, the company was not represented at any such negotiations. The harm that Belton has done to Rosneft's reputation is serious. Not just that, she has harmed a whole nation. 'The false information published in the book has resulted in lower investor trust in the Russian investment climate.'

Nigel Tait and his clients are ready to go to court. If Belton and her publishers wish to avoid this fate, they must urgently recall and destroy every unsold copy of *Putin's People*. They must delete the offending passages from the audiobook and the ebook. They must publish a retraction and an apology in all future editions. They must then read in court a statement agreed with representatives, including Nigel Tait, of the Kremlin's oil arm. They must undertake not to repeat these allegations. They must pay damages to Rosneft – this company that Putin's closest ally runs. And they must reimburse this tool of the Russian regime for the sums it has spent retaining Carter-Ruck.

Belton is stunned. What she wrote about Rosneft taking over Khodorkovsky's oilfields – it's been said countless times before in the press, and in an international court ruling in The Hague. She declines Tait's invitation to censor herself, so they go to court. A judge rules that all but one of the passages in *Putin's People* that Tait's complained about fail to meet the basic threshold of libel proceedings: they don't defame the claimant. They might defame Igor Sechin, but he hasn't sued. Instead, the claim's been brought by Rosneft, a company run by Sechin and owned by the Russian state that Putin controls. That shields Sechin from submitting to personal discovery, cross-examination or any other such awkwardness that human beings undergo in a court but corporations do not.

This has not been lost on Mrs Justice Tipples. 'A corporate libel claim might represent an abuse of the court's process,' she's written in her High Court judgment, 'if the reality is that the company has been "put up" by individuals who are seeking to use it indirectly to vindicate their personal reputations or obtain compensation.' Belton's barrister has called this case a put-up job. If he's right, then this claim has deployed Rosneft as a front so that Igor Sechin, even Putin himself, can hijack the British legal system. There's a word for this, for manipulating an institution for sinister purposes: cuckooing.

But this is just a preliminary hearing, and Mrs Justice Tipples says it's not the time to decide that question. It never will be the time, because after she delivers her decision, and once Belton has made a minor tweak to her text to insert a denial by the company, what remains of Rosneft's case is withdrawn.

Yet even when Nigel Tait loses, he wins. On the face of it, this one is an ignominious defeat. But to gauge Carter-Ruck's success on what happens in court is to misunderstand the service it gives clients. Sure, the Rosneft claim has ceased early. But what will happen the next time a journalist considers writing about the company? Or about Igor Sechin. Or Trafigura. Or all those other clients Carter-Ruck's known to represent, from the African mining bosses to Tesco and Liam Gallagher. The journalist, their editor or the newspaper's lawyer will pause. Better, they may well conclude, to do a story about someone else.

And Tait has a new client to be getting on with. One with a reputation to defend as a thought leader, philanthropist, ambassador for Global Britain and pioneer of the information age.

Thirteen

Reputation hit

December 31, 2020, 16:42:24 Ben Elliot
Happy new year my dear

December 31, 2020, 16:43:09 Mohamed Amersi
Same to you and your family my dear friend!!!

New Year is less happy than we were all hoping it might be. Another lockdown is coming. Infections are surging again. Boris Johnson, voluble lover of freedom, has baned Christmas parties in London because the virus is rife. So his hardworking staffers in Downing Street have had to enjoy their booze and food and Secret Santa at a festive gathering that did not take place.

At midnight, the Brexit transition period will end. And how did Brexit get done? With the money that Ben Elliot brought in. Boris picked his fellow Old Etonian, this maestro of favour trading, as Conservative chairman, in charge of Party money-making. Boris's majority of eighty, the majority that slammed Brexit past the treacherous Remoaners – the Conservatives won it after record fundraising. Ben's ramped up the Quintessentially model: pay your fees, join the club. Donate a quarter of a million and you get membership of the secret Advisory Board, pretty much unlimited access to anyone from Boris down.

'Ben has opened every cheque book across Mayfair,' a Tory source purrs in the press. 'Boris acknowledges the important role he is playing.'

As ever, Quintessentially is there to meet the unique needs of the upper echelons. Proximity to their remarkable clientele has given the company's top-end concierges an insight into what really matters in the Covid era.

'Everything has changed,' they've concluded. 'And yet, nothing has. The human need to feel connected to people, places, experiences, things and oneself remains, stronger than ever.' What do the clients want now? To be away from cities, those epicentres of disease. A home office installed at their country residence. To fly by private plane to a private island. To look after their nearest and dearest with a champagne Zoom party or a virtual nanny. To give.

'Philanthropy,' the Quintessentially concierges write of their wealthy clients, 'signals values and enhances their sense of impact and ownership for a future they can help to build.' They give to mental health charities, to foodbanks. Thermometers and masks and financial modelling and data science – all this and more they give.

Quintessentially clients also like to unwind a little. The

1 per cent are humans too. From the comfort of your own home, you can have a celebrity chef teach you to cook, a master blender guide your whisky tasting, a famed conjurer perform magic tricks for your delight. Of course, the pandemic can sometimes cause delays. One top-tier client's magic show is overdue. And he's already paid for it. Ben Elliot has personally been trying to get this sorted. He writes to his underlings at Conservative headquarters: 'Mohamed has 3 outstanding requests for breakfast/lunch/magic show with Pm/Hunt and Mordaunt.' I know this is unlikely to happen until full lockdown is over, he concedes, but can you ensure this is coordinated?

Then there's the Middle East role Amersi wants. The chairmanship of Charlotte Leslie's Conservative Middle East Council might have worked. But Leslie wouldn't agree – something about it being a position for someone who's been elected to public life rather than buying in. So Amersi's ditched this idea and instead wants to proceed with setting up his Conservative Friends of Middle East and North Africa. Could be a good ruse, this Comena, as Ben realises. Closer to the Party than Leslie's operation. Money-wise much better too: potentially a sterling funnel for donations.

Three weeks back, on December 7, Ben sent an email that delighted his Quintessentially client. Comena sounds good, he wrote. 'Let's get going.' Now it's just a case of having the Party board grant Comena affiliation.

Amersi responded: 'Thank you very much. I am deeply honoured and appreciate the trust that you have placed in me.'

January 2, 2021, 15:03:19 Mohamed Amersi
Happy new year my friend. I know you said I
shouldn't disturb you before the 4th but this is out
there. Not causing any damage but obviously a little
awkward. Let me if and when you want to chat about
it; otherwise, we now have 130 supporters, 100
needed and going very strong!!!

He sends Ben Elliot two documents.

The first is a letter seeking support for Amersi's Comena. 'As you may know,' Mohamed writes, 'I am a member of the Leader's Group of the Party.' It is time for the Conservatives to ditch Charlotte Leslie's CMEC, which has drifted too far from the Party, and embrace a new and utterly loyal body, Comena. 'Senior officers of the Party and I believe that this presents a timely and an immensely important opportunity for a truly Global Britain, post-Brexit, to exercise its unrivalled influence and soft power to bring economic prosperity, peace and stability to the region.' Money will be made too: Comena can 'assist, post-Brexit, in opening efficient bilateral trade channels' between the UK and the region. At the bottom of the letter Amersi has listed Comena's exalted supporters. MPs, peers. Theresa May as patron. Mohamed Amersi as chairman. The management team isn't sorted yet but there's a named administrative director, a young woman called Ilma Bogdan who's been active in Tory circles.

With regret, though, Mohamed feels he must also share

with Ben a second document: Charlotte Leslie's memo. It was being passed between Arab diplomats. A copy reached Mohamed Mansour, who sent it to Amersi. It has made him exceedingly angry.

Elliot doesn't reply. Two days pass. Now it's January 4 – officially fine to start disturbing Ben again.

> January 4, 2021, 16:16:46 Mohamed Amersi
> Call when you can! 5 mins only! Want to make your life easy for you ... 🙏 😄

Evening comes. Boris addresses the nation. The new variant of the virus is more transmissible. Deaths are rising. The NHS cannot cope. The prime minister knows how tough it is once more to be ordered to stay at home. 'But now more than ever, we must pull together.'

> January 4, 2021, 20:59:16 Mohamed Amersi
> I am sure you have more important things on your mind but just to let you know I have instructed reputation/litigation counsel to write as appropriate to charlotte Leslie but keeping the party and comena out of it.

Ben must be warned: Charlotte Leslie is, he says, breaking the law. Using CMEC for illegal lobbying.

At just gone nine o'clock, Ben replies. 'I am busy on other stuff. Can speak later in the week.'

Ben has a lot on. As if filling the Party's coffers isn't enough, there's also the fraught matter of filling Boris's. When the refurbishment of the prime minister's Downing Street flat got preposterously out of hand, Party funds had to cover fifty-eight thousand pounds' worth of bills. Prime ministers are required to declare such financial assistance, but you don't exactly want it known that donors' cash is going on designer wallpaper for the boss. The solution took the form of an ex-policeman from Slough who'd made money from a recruitment business, given a load of it to the Tories and been created a lord. Two months back, on October 20, Lord Brownlow emailed Ben to confirm he would donate fifty-eight grand to a new Downing Street Trust, thus filling the hole. His donation should have been declared too, but wasn't.

And Quintessentially's been losing money even faster than Boris. A few million a year. So much so that some of the dividends paid out to the owners are illegal. Happily, there's been public money to keep the wolf from the door. A government contract worth more than a million pounds, awarded in 2016, to create 'a sense of excitement about what the UK has to offer' by showing ultra-wealthy visitors around in the hope they bring some of their lucre to Britain.

January 4, 2021, 21:07:03 Mohamed Amersi
I don't care about her or CMEC. I just want us to be affiliated and get going. Can you accelerate our affiliation approval! 🙏 🙏 🙏 🙏 🙏
We have satisfied all requirements

And she and CMEC and the party can then do what
they all want
Sorry to bother you with this 🙏 🥀
PLEASE

Global Elite members are surely entitled to more attentive
service than this. Fifteen grand year after year after year
Mohamed's paid in Quintessentially fees. A minute passes.
Consider, Amersi exhorts Ben, the interests of Her Majesty's
Government.

January 4, 2021, 21:10:07 Mohamed Amersi
This is good for HMG, the Party and of course me ...
And I know with all on your plate your bandwidth
and concentration on this will not exceed 30 secs

January 4, 2021, 21:11:48 Ben Elliot
Will be discussed as agreed in next board meeting.
Pls leave it with me till then

January 4, 2021, 21:12:07 Mohamed Amersi

Good luck with all else
When is the board?
I have taken a huge reputation hit just for helping the
party and HMG
And spending money!
Not important but understand how I feel

Thirteen minutes elapse. Elsewhere, Covid patients suffocate alone.

Clearly, Ben is underestimating Comena's potential. Look at what Jared Kushner's been achieving, Mohamed writes. Trump's son-in-law has been devoting himself to building bridges in the Middle East. The rapprochement between the Qataris, the Saudis, the Emirates, Bahrain and Egypt. This is what they could do! Amersi's new organisation, alongside the Foreign Office and Number 10, as opposed to letting Washington take the lead ...

Nothing more from Ben tonight.

January 6, 2021, 19:34:07 Mohamed Amersi
Would you like to see in confidence what my lawyers have drafted as a response they will send out to charlotte tomorrow? Clearly I have kept the Party and comena out of it ...

January 6, 2021, 19:53:41 Ben Elliot
No

January 6, 2021, 20:22:19 Mohamed Amersi
Ok
So you and Amanda will receive it officially tomorrow by way of bcc

Amanda Milling, Ben Elliot's co-chair of the Conservatives. She's been on Amersi's emails about getting Comena started. Important that she's in the loop about his efforts to counter the smear campaign against him.

Less than an hour ago, Dominic Pezzola has smashed a window of the US Capitol using a policeman's shield. Known as Spaz, this former Marine is a member of an all-male fascist street gang called the Proud Boys. He enters the building and is joined by Oath Keepers, QAnon adherents (the resistance to the Satanist paedophile elites who control politics and the media), the InfoWars fabulist Alex Jones and others determined to Stop the Steal.

Spaz and his comrades are hoping to encounter someone they can murder. Ideally the vice president, Mike Pence, who is proceeding with ratification of the presidential election in which Donald Trump has been defeated.

Trump has responded with a tweet.

> Mike Pence didn't have the courage to do what should have been done to protect our Country and our Constitution, giving states a chance to certify a corrected set of facts, not the fraudulent or inaccurate ones which they were asked to previously certify. USA demands the truth!

January 6, 2021, 20:23:13 Mohamed Amersi
And when can we speak?
Do I still have backing for this or not?

January 6, 2021, 20:26:58 Mohamed Amersi
Why can't you just call me?

Finally, Ben replies. Says he's getting phoned up every day by big guns in the Party who've been dragged into this unnecessary spat.

January 6, 2021, 20:27:49 Ben Elliot
I am not calling you as I have many other things
which are currently more of a priority and i will when
I get to it.

This is the last thing Ben needs. Another fuss involving donors. The press is writing about a Tory chumocracy. VIP lanes for Covid contracts. Cash for favours. Elliot himself is becoming the story. It was he who arranged that Carlton Club fundraising dinner at the Savoy. The one where Amersi bought a breakfast with Boris. The one where the housing secretary, Robert Jenrick, was put on a table next to a porn-baron (and donor) who wanted him to overrule officials and approve the porn-baron's property development, which the minister proceeded to do.

'The new regime has a significantly lower tolerance for this sort of thing,' an unnamed Party figure has intoned in the media. 'Ben Elliot's an idiot and desperate to prove to Boris he can raise lots of money.' Ben has been hauled before backbench MPs to grovel. But then there were more stories. About Hawthorn, the lobbying company he co-founded. He still owns shares in it, even if they're in trust, and the papers keep writing about its clients. Huawei, for one, which despite extensive image-management continues to be known as the communications arm of the Chinese Communist Party. Others are Party donors, such as the family business empire of Mohamed Mansour, former minister to a Cairo generalissimo and now backer of Amersi's Comena.

It used to be that every piece on Ben Elliot talked about the Madonna teabags or the Sydney Harbour Bridge stunt. Now they dig out that quote when he called himself a 'relentless bossy fucker'.

January 6, 2021, 20:30:03 Mohamed Amersi
The spat was not my fault. I did not wring!!!
She attacked me
Nothing wrong!!

January 6, 2021, 20:33:09 Ben Elliot
Am sure

January 6, 2021, 20:35:24 Mohamed Amersi
Ok

January 8, 2021, 17:45:34 Mohamed Amersi
Shall we have a quick chat now or is that pushing you … if you want me to drop this, please say so to me! I am at least owed that! Friendships usually outlast positions in my humble experience …

I know you hate confrontation. I hate it too! I didn't start this mess. Charlotte Leslie did!

January 8, 2021, 18:20:22 Ben Elliot
!!!
I am being bombarded. I do not mind confrontation. Have a meeting with team next week on all this.

January 8, 2021, 18:31:39 Mohamed Amersi
On this stuff or other stuff? Hear me out mate. You will benefit and be better informed. I will be objective. I now know about everything on everyone and it will benefit you! But up to you! 🐿️

Half an hour goes by. Another locked-down Friday night.

January 8, 2021, 19:06:09 Mohamed Amersi
You take everyone's call but mine! Somebody who by Charlotte's own admission has given the party £750k! 🐿️

The figure includes the money that was declared as a donation from Nadia Rodicheva while Amersi was an impermissible donor. If this total is correct, if it was actually Mohamed who gave the money, then that would seem to be a crime. But this is not the topic to which the chairman is addressing his energies.

January 8, 2021, 19:53:13 Ben Elliot
I know what to do. Do not need to be instructed

January 8, 2021, 20:00:25 Mohamed Amersi
Ok buddy

Amersi makes sure Ben knows how much this is all costing.

January 8, 2021, 21:49:49 Mohamed Amersi
David Burnside wants me to pay him £20k for
potential media management if charlotte goes to the
press! I have already incurred £25k of legal costs.
Money that could have gone to the party instead of
this BS!! Waste of time and money because of ...
indecision!

Burnside's a former Ulster Unionist MP. 'I can go to cabinet
ministers, former prime ministers,' he says of the services he
can offer. 'I've been dealing with them for 25 years, through
PR in-house or through consultancy work, which I've been
doing since the mid 1990s.' Not cheap, these services. Though
the kind of clients who seek him out aren't exactly poor: a
Ukrainian oligarch, an old judo partner of Putin's.

In the morning the Saturday front pages report the highest
daily death toll of the pandemic: one thousand, three
hundred and twenty-five.

January 9, 2021, 08:15:16 Ben Elliot
It will not go to the press. And nothing to do with
indecision.
There has been no board meetings Mohammed. Pls!

January 9, 2021, 08:36:58 Mohamed Amersi
Ok thank god!!!

Within a week Amersi's donated another fifty thousand
pounds.

Fourteen

A world of pain

On January 7, 2021, Charlotte Leslie's life changes irrevocably. Nicholas Soames calls her in a state of alarm. A letter has arrived from Mishcon de Reya. Charlotte says: Who?

Like Carter-Ruck, Mishcon de Reya's reputation-management lawyers tend to the very finest, the most precious reputations.

When a reporter in London – me – prints stories about a corrupt tycoon's African mining deal, a Mishcon lawyer writes to my publisher with the revelation that I am corrupt: I have enjoyed an all-expenses trip to South Africa's picturesque Kruger National Park, paid for by an ally of the Guinean president who wants to bring this put-upon billionaire down. The slippery Burgis wriggles out of it – regrettably I've never been to the Kruger National Park – but at least his editors have been alerted that he is a suspect fellow.

A journalist in Malta looks into a company that helps the dubiously rich buy citizenship there. A Mishcon lawyer writes to threaten legal proceedings not in the Maltese courts but the English ones, with their terrifying costs. In the end no further correspondence with Daphne Caruana Galizia is necessary. Some other target of her reporting takes a more direct route to silencing her: a car bomb.

> Dear Ms Leslie
> We write to you on behalf of our client Mohamed Amersi.
> Our client has been passed a memo, which appears to have been authored and widely circulated by you, including to members of the Arab diplomatic corps in London.
> The memo constitutes an extraordinary and inexplicable defamatory attack on our client's reputation.

Charlotte reads on. Her dyslexia means she focuses carefully on each word, one after another. She is, she learns, guilty of a 'plainly malicious attempt' to 'sabotage' Amersi's Comena plan 'by disseminating false and misleading information to damage our client's personal and professional reputation'. Our client's organisation and yours could co-exist. But you have chosen a different path. Our client was disappointed to learn this.

> He was also shocked that he should have been subjected to such an outrageous and baseless attack on his character and integrity.

We have had the opportunity to take detailed
instructions and review pertinent correspondence.
The impropriety and malice in the memo is patent.
The scurrilous, misleading and untrue allegations
against our client cannot be left unaddressed.

These untruths are catalogued. Not just one or two untruths.
There are nine untruths. That he's after an honour (in truth
official Party approval for his Middle East project will be satis-
factory); that he enjoys networks of influence in Iran (in truth
he has simply been involved in dialogue with officials there);
that his main business is abroad (in truth he is committed to
contributing to British business and the UK economy, expects
to pay a significant seven-figure sum in UK taxes this year, and
the principal focus of his energies is now on his philanthropic
work, predominantly in the UK). On and on the untruths go.

This is what you must do, Charlotte Leslie. This is what our
client wants you to give him: 'an unqualified retraction of the
allegations and an apology' for the memo, 'together with a list
of all those to whom it has been circulated'. Pending your
response, Mohamed Amersi's position is expressly reserved.
In other words, if you do not give him what he wants, he's
ready to sue you.

Leslie, through a lawyer, replies to say there really isn't any
need for this fuss. The stuff that's said about him in the memo
is hardly all that bad.

The Mishcon lawyers have discovered they have a conflict
of interest in dealing with Soames. So Amersi has hired a

replacement. Nigel Tait of Carter-Ruck. And Nigel Tait doesn't see it like that. Leslie's toxic lies have now circulated for weeks, he says in his first letter. Her campaign to do irreparable damage to Mohamed Amersi's reputation goes on. Tait wants to know – pronto – how she intends to declare in public that she won't stand in Amersi's way. How she intends to help Amersi's Middle East ambitions come to fruition. It is perhaps testament to Tait's power that not only is he the scourge of free speech but he can now dictate to his client's foes how they should wield their political influence for the client's benefit.

If she refuses, she could lose everything. Her job, her flat. She could be disgraced, defaced. It's Dorian Gray in reverse: she will be shut away in silence while a grotesque portrait of her is unveiled. No longer the champion swimmer, muscles searing with pain as she makes the turn for the final length, the roar from the crowd reaching her ears through the rush of the water. No longer the MP. No longer the backbencher of the year. No, just a creature of malice and spite.

But there is still hope. With supplication, she can still save herself.

Carl Stephen Patrick Hunter OBE BA Hon DSc (Dunelm) FRINA FIMarEST AFNI MRAeS apologises for ringing later than he'd said he would. He's been on another call, you see. 'And it overran and I hadn't had a bite to eat so I raced down to make myself a quick sandwich.' His voice is full of refined ebullience.

'Oh by all means, if you want a bit more time,' says Charlotte, 'I'm here all afternoon—'

'No I don't. I want to do this because it concerns me greatly.'

Charlotte gives a sigh of relief. It's been nearly a month since the letter that threatened her with ruin.

He adopts a comedy military bark. 'I've had my sandwich, Leslie! I'm a soldier! I can eat quickly.'

Hunter is a purveyor of maritime technology, Queen's Award for Enterprise laureate, Mayfair address. I don't know whether you know, he says, but I was in the Green Jackets. With Tobias Ellwood, the senior Tory MP who has, Hunter says, asked him to intervene. And he's been a donor for some time. 'I do a lot for the Party.'

It seems there's a chance to bring this unpleasantness to an end. Hunter says he can talk to Amersi. 'Don't roll your eyes but I happen to have sat down next to him at numerous lunch tables at one of my clubs. Don't judge me, please Charlotte. And obviously in the last three or four years we've rubbed shoulders at a number of Conservative party donor events.'

Hunter explains that Amersi's recently asked him to support Comena. Then today he spoke with Mohamed about this dispute. You're in this horrible position, he tells Charlotte. 'I wouldn't like to be up against the wallet of the person you are involved with.' He continues. 'If you're not careful, this will keep you up at night. Will monopolise your life for as long as it lasts.'

Charlotte says she'd be happy just to put the whole thing behind her. 'If Mr Amersi is upset about things, I don't have much pride and I will happily apologise to him if I have upset him. I don't think we have actually done anything wrong to be honest. But I don't like people being upset. I prefer to be friends.'

Hunter asks: Has there been any besmirching of your own name?

I'm not very offendable, says Leslie. 'You don't go through life being an MP having a thin skin.' Yet she's worried about accusations that she herself is part of the influence industry. 'We do not do lobbying,' she says. Amersi's putting that about. What she would like is for these lies to stop.

Hunter says there is a peace to be made.

'Lovely,' says Leslie. 'Carl, it's really very good of you. And here's to getting a good, common sense, calm, harmonious solution.'

Hunter rings off. He calls Amersi. Charlotte walks the dog. Hunter phones back. The refined ebullience has given way to refined foreboding. 'Please think of yourself in what I'm about to say first. All of us are decent and always want to think of others.'

Charlotte listens.

'There are times when one is alone. And I just think, in this case, you could be alone.' But there is good news. Give an apology and a retraction to Mr Amersi and he might yet spare you. 'I have had a private assurance that no costs will be sought from Mohamed Amersi's side, and that all possibility of going further into this' – the dog barks – 'and into a really gruesome stage, which would cost, I believe, more than you may imagine – then I think it would all finish.'

This could end in bankruptcy, Hunter says. Best if you write a draft apology and let me see it and tell you whether it's likely to pass muster.

I will get cracking, says Charlotte.

That evening Chris Whitty, the chief medical officer, announces that the UK is past the peak of this second Covid wave. The next day at noon Charlotte sends Hunter the text of a grovelling apology. But she doesn't want Carter-Ruck picking over the words. That would just mean more fees. 'There is only so far I will bend to apologise for something I haven't done because someone has a lot of money and is upset,' she tells Hunter.

Hunter says he's speaking to her as a political friend. 'I feel what I am doing is trying to save you from the world of pain that I think could come your way.'

'If he wants to take me out,' says Leslie, 'it's not difficult for a man like him to stamp on someone like me.'

Amersi wants to neutralise the memo, Hunter says. He reads from an email he says he's sent Amersi, reporting that he's spoken to Charlotte, and that the hurt Amersi has felt may soon be relieved. 'All I would ask, Mohamed, is that once it is, that you restrain your power with the humility and grace that it deserves.'

Hunter feels he has to set Leslie straight. We're talking about someone who pays seven figures in tax and has given not much less to the Party. 'That is a person that is different from us.' You have to look at him in the way that you as a politician would look at the President of the United States.

Leslie's recalcitrance is irritating Hunter. I'm doing all of this to help you and all the while I've got my thirty-five employees who depend on me and I've created a new instrument for the NHS and I put my hand in my own pocket for that and I'm doing fourteen-hour days, just ask my wife, and I innovate and do science and I've got seventy per cent women in my company and I am so far behind in my work because I am trying to help you. 'I don't want to see you photographed in some tabloid, with you standing on the steps of somewhere explaining your position.'

And by the way, he tells her, 'You won't find another man in this country that told Mohamed Amersi to behave himself and not abuse his power.'

Mohamed rejects the apology Leslie offers. She thinks: What he wants is to humiliate me, to destroy me. She knows about humiliation, and not just from the dyslexia. She's seen how it goes: a woman called stupid, called a slut, and thinking, Yes, I'm stupid, yes, I'm a slut. Losing the ability to tell what's real. Becoming whatever he says you are.

For a while that Lily Allen song was stuck in her head. The one about not knowing what's real any more. ''Cause I'm being taken over by the fear ...'

Only she isn't. Not all of her. A defiance is returning. She remembers her surfing days. What they used to say. When the wave looks too big, too full of power. That's when you must paddle towards it. Towards your fear.

Maybe she will lose everything: her job, the flat her father proudly helped her buy. Well, then these things will be lost. Amersi and Nigel Tait can drag the doppelgänger Charlotte Leslie that they've conjured – malicious, spiteful, truthless – to the public square and humiliate her. Charlotte will know that that wretched woman is not her. And that is enough.

Which is not to say she's leaving the ring. She wants this fight now. She's found the old High Court judgment, the one where Mr Justice Smith – that fucking imbecile farmer, as Mohamed would have him – found Amersi's evidence unreliable, incredible, extraordinary and generally unsatisfactory. What he wants, Charlotte believes, is the power to decide that two and two equals five. 'If you pretend two and two is five, the whole world falls apart,' she tells an acquaintance. 'You can't communicate with each other because nothing's real. Why should the words I say to you mean to you what they mean to me? Everything falls apart. You have to have some basis of objectivity, otherwise we're just isolated consciousnesses moving around with holes in our face making noises.'

Looking at Mohamed across this Carter-Ruck office, I think back to the first time I spoke to him.

It's July 2021, six months after Charlotte Leslie sent her memos, and I'm about to break the news of this intra-Tory dispute in the *Financial Times*. I've sent Amersi a list of questions. We've arranged a Zoom. As his face appears on the screen, I press record on my dictaphone.

He's in Greece, he's told me, doing philanthropy.

He knows lots of people at the *FT*, he says. I ask about his Russian deals.

'This doesn't have to be confrontational,' he says. 'You are trying to trap me. Don't waste your time because I am in good faith speaking to you. I don't have to speak to you, okay?'

I bring up Charlotte Leslie.

'I personally think – now you have to hear me out, and be patient – you've been completely duped by Charlotte Leslie. She has misled you. And my only reason for talking to you is, I respect your paper and I respect your independent, inquisitive mind. And I don't want you to be misled or duped. It will not do your reputation any good.'

Quickly his temper rises. I put to him some of what I understand about Conservative Friends of the Middle East and North Africa.

'This is Charlotte Leslie's bullshit. And this is why I'm suing her. And I'll sue her to the end. Because this is bullshit.' Amersi tells me Ilma Bogdan, the Russian woman whose involvement aroused Charlotte's concern, was only ever going to have an admin job, and he hasn't hired her at all in the end.

I've got everything backwards, he explains. It's not him who's dodgy – it's Charlotte Leslie. She's been taking cash in exchange for arranging access to the British government. 'It is very serious stuff, Tom. Very, very serious stuff.' Especially, he adds, after the Greensill scandal, when David Cameron was caught lobbying the government on behalf of a calamitous banker who was paying the former prime minister to advance his cause. Charlotte's doing this too, Amersi says. Illegal lobbying. For Middle Eastern interests.

Quite a story, that would be. I ask him to give me his evidence.

'The swamp is full,' he says. 'It has to be drained.' He adds: 'And for the record, and for this conversation, not a penny that I earned in Russia – and you know the amounts I have earned – has even remotely, closely come to being invested in the UK political system.'

I keep asking: Show me the proof that Charlotte Leslie, this well-connected ex-Conservative MP, is funnelling dark money into Westminster. 'That would be serious information,' I tell him. I ask him for documentary evidence that supports what he's saying, anything at all he can give me.

'I'm not saying it's happening. I'm saying it has to be investigated. And maybe if you are lucky, because of your work on plutocracy, you may find that there are some interesting front structures. It's possible. I'm not saying there are. I'm not saying there aren't. I don't know.'

He talks about Leslie's memos. 'It's the worst kind of behaviour. The worst behaviour I've experienced. Not even a Russian in my career has ever behaved in the atrocious, selfish and dishonest way that this woman has behaved.'

He is growing angrier. Already, he says, his legal bills in this dispute with Leslie are three hundred thousand pounds. 'If I have to take her to task for it, I will absolutely do it. Because she has lied and she has made up stories.' Yes, she offered an apology once. But it wasn't enough. 'What, am I a stupid idiot? I'm a child?' He is spitting with rage. 'How dare she insult me.'

The headline on my *Financial Times* story is: 'The donor, the Russian deals and the Conservative money machine.' I report that Amersi made four million dollars buying a St Petersburg telecoms company for Jeff Galmond, and that Galmond was the following year found by a Zurich court of arbitration to be a front for Putin's telecoms minister, Leonid Reiman. I report that Amersi's lawyers have sent threatening legal letters to a former MP called Charlotte Leslie who wrote a memo raising questions about his past. 'He also became a client of Quintessentially,' I write. 'Its founder, Elliot, "connected us to the Prince of Wales", says Amersi.'

Reading this is how Charlotte Leslie discovers that Mohamed Amersi is a paying client of Ben Elliot's Quintessentially. Elliot didn't tell her this when he received her warning about Amersi, after which the Conservative Party he chairs accepted another fifty-thousand-pound donation from Mohamed. And Elliot doesn't tell her this when, after Carl Hunter's intervention failed, he instigates mediation. Via a Tory peer, Lord Hunt, Charlotte and Amersi have been negotiating a possible settlement. If it succeeds, the process will probably lead to Charlotte signing a gagging order – and the good name of Ben's cherished Quintessentially client will be shielded. But Leslie won't yield. Even when Lord Hunt claims Amersi has suggested that an old Russian contact – the oligarch Mikhail Fridman – could join the legal action against her.

On June 29, just after Amersi learns that I've started looking into his past, Nigel Tait files a lawsuit against Leslie at the High Court.

Fifteen

Statements of truth

The sun rises at three minutes past eight. A winter Tuesday in London. Nine degrees Celsius. Mohamed Amersi enters the gothic splendour of the Royal Courts of Justice.

CNN is reporting that although Britons are paying the highest taxes since the war their National Health Service is falling apart. Because it's raining, I discover a hole in the sole of my right shoe. The sock's got soggy on the way here.

It is January 10, 2023. In Brazil, supporters of a politician known as Legend have stormed the presidential palace. They demand a coup to restore Jair Bolsonaro to power. His defeat in the election is the proof they've been waiting for that what he's been saying all along is true – there's been a conspiracy to steal victory from him.

In Ukraine, Yevgeny Prigozhin says his Wagner mercenaries have advanced through territory witnessing such carnage that soldiers call it the meat-grinder. Not long ago, Prigozhin had business before this very court. Rishi Sunak's Treasury granted him special relief from sanctions so he could sue the

British journalist Eliot Higgins of Bellingcat. The defamatory allegation was that this character known as Putin's Chef controlled a private military operation called Wagner. The case was struck out when the British lawyers walked off the case after the invasion, but not before Higgins had spent seventy thousand unrecoverable pounds defending himself.

Through security Amersi goes. Up the stairs to Court Thirteen, with its stone walls and high windows. He sits beside Nigel Tait, hefty, ruddy and wispily bearded. They confer in hushed voices.

When she walks in, Mohamed turns to look at her.

A double knock from within. 'All rise.'

Matthew Nicklin enters. The most senior High Court judge of libel law. Wearing black robes with red trim, Mr Justice Nicklin takes his seat in a leather chair on a dais. We all take our seats on the wooden benches below.

'Yes,' says the judge, 'Mr McCormick.'

William McCormick is the third barrister Mohamed Amersi's hired. His smooth swoosh of hair is turning from grey to white. At the tip of his nose sit a pair of learned spectacles. Half a dozen Carter-Ruck lawyers behind the barrister marshal binders full of documents. In these pages they have made their client's case.

Mohamed Amersi has been harmed. He has been shunned by important people, celebrated people. Ambassadors. Politicians. The rich. He, Mohamed Amersi, who has been lauded by prime ministers and sheikhs and whose chairmanship of Conservatives' Carlton Club Dinner at the Dorchester in 2018 was hailed as a 'resounding success' by a peer of the realm. He whose name adorns the Oxford lecture theatre the opening of which Theresa May graced. He whose name has been written – if matters of this import are ever committed to paper – in the membership list for the Leaders Group of the wisest and worthiest Conservative donors, invited into the drawing room of democracy to help guide our nation's stewards. He who has bestowed his charity on the faithful, the young, the arts, heritage, the enslaved, the poor and the planet, to name but a few. He – as the court can see in the business plan at page one thousand, eight hundred and forty-seven of the hearing bundle – who not only bankrolled an internet connection at Dumfries, the Scottish property saved for the nation by Charles, but secured a two-and-a-half-million-dollar donation towards Inclusive Ventures' mission from the Nepali businessman Ajeya Sumargi. (The disclosures do not record that, alas, Mr Sumargi's largesse was ultimately not forthcoming.)

Who, their name despoiled as Mohamed's has been, would not seek justice? There come times in a life when one must make a stand. Just to pluck one example, this woman has dared to claim he said he wanted an honour for his contribution during the pandemic. To impugn his motives securing, among other things, a consignment of dates – seven tonnes of Emirati dates – for our frontline NHS workers. For this and for all the rest, she cannot go unpunished. Who are the Charlotte Leslies to tell the Mohamed Amersis what can and cannot be true? Who are they to rewrite his story?

So he has retained William McCormick, a King's Counsel (his title now that Charles has been crowned) with an accomplished Northern Irish lilt, to spell out for the judge the many grievous harms Leslie has caused to his reputation. That will clear the path towards the full trial that this wanton case of defamation so clearly deserves.

Take the Conservative Member of Parliament Crispin Blunt. With whom for a few years Leslie shared the Conservative benches in the Commons. Thanks to the efforts of Mohamed Amersi and his first-class legal team, we now know that she sent one of her disgusting memos to Blunt. And we know what Blunt said after he received it. 'It is pretty graphic,' Mr McCormick warns the judge.

Leslie to Blunt, attaching memo:

> Dear Crispin,
> In confidence. There may be no cause for any unease but felt that as much information as possible maybe helpful.

Blunt to Leslie:

> Plainly a total bounder! with some very odd fish for company. More than enough here to kill it off I think.

To kill off Comena. What solace this must have brought to the scheming Leslie, as the prospect of Comena threatening her illicit self-enrichment receded.

Thanks Crispin. Good to know I am not alone in feeling uneasy about this.

Amersi has given a witness statement describing what Blunt said next – perhaps the most graphic of all his filthy language.

> Mr Blunt continues with this derogatory theme in his email to Ms Leslie of 31 December 2020 in which he compares me to the fictional character Augustus Melmotte, who my solicitors have explained to me is a dishonest and corrupt financier with a mysterious past in Anthony Trollope's novel 'The Way We Live Now'. I had never met Mr Blunt before he made these insulting remarks about me, and I therefore infer the obvious conclusion that his view of me was based purely on the contents of the memorandum sent to him by Ms Leslie.

Blunt, in his own witness statement, says he considers it 'touching' that his private opinion of Mohamed's merits 'could have such a devastating impact upon his reputation so as to justify court action'.

Let's just hold on a minute, though. William McCormick, King's Counsel, invites the judge to parse this politician's curious words. Blunt denies amplifying the memo's harm by sending it on. But look more closely. He says he did not discuss Amersi's 'headline traits beyond my conversation with Charlotte'. 'That,' McCormick observes, 'is pointedly well short of the denial that he repeated the content of the documents with others.' McCormick has suggested more than once that witnesses favourable to Charlotte Leslie might be lying when they say her memo didn't make them think ill of Amersi. Now it seems Crispin Blunt could be at it too.

The judge is puzzled. He wants to check: What are we all doing here? 'The purpose of a libel action in relation to the sending of the document to Mr Blunt is to vindicate your client's reputation in the eyes of Mr Blunt?'

Yes, McCormick says: in Blunt's eyes, and in those of the others to whom the Westminster gossip train is likely to have carried the slurs Leslie imparted to him.

'That is a valuable exercise to spend what is likely to be millions of pounds of costs?' the judge asks.

'My Lord,' McCormick replies, 'it is an exercise which my client is entitled to have the court undertake.'

'Right,' declares Mr Justice Nicklin. 'We will reconvene at two o'clock.'

Everyone stands. The judge slips his hands through his robes into his trouser pockets, and vanishes through the door that leads into his private rooms.

Mohamed Amersi goes out into the corridor with his legal team. As the courtroom empties, Nadia Rodicheva remains, alone. Her auburn hair is parted down the middle. She comes with him to these hearings, soothingly stroking his back.

There is news from Russia every hour now. Ever since the first missiles hit Ukraine. During the lunchbreak a hundred and seventy Russian medics publish a letter urging Vladimir Putin to end the abuse of Alexei Navalny in the maximum-security prison where he's held. Oligarchs once fêted in London are under sanctions: Mikhail Fridman, Alisher Usmanov. Igor Sechin too, the boss of Rosneft, on whose behalf Nigel Tait went after Catherine Belton in this court.

Amersi's first go at Leslie was under data-protection law. He claimed she'd breached a legal duty to tell him who her sources were and the identities of those who'd received her memos. He was thwarted, when a judge ruled he and Carter-Ruck had broken procedural rules, and told him to pay most of Leslie's costs. Amersi said he'd revise his approach and go again. But just before the trial, he dropped the case – sued her for libel.

At the initial hearing in the libel case, Nicklin addresses Amersi's barrister: 'What I am interested in, Mr McCormick, is ensuring that litigation sought in these courts is done proportionately.'

'There is no basis for your Lordship's concern that this litigation is being run disproportionately or oppressively, let alone that there is any form of SLAPP suit,' McCormick replies. Strategic Lawsuits Against Public Participation, where the rich use the courts to intimidate those who cross them into silence by sheer force of wealth.

Nicklin evidently wants to put this to the test. One indicator of a SLAPP is when the wealthy party ramps up costs that are daunting to their less affluent opponent. The judge asks what the parties have spent on legal fees so far. Amersi declines to say. That's confidential, he claims.

'Could we have a look at the article that followed from an interview that your client gave to Mr Burgis?' Nicklin asks McCormick. 'Would you help me with how you can maintain a claim of confidentiality when you have given an interview to a newspaper in which you have told the newspaper how much your costs are?'

'Has your Lordship read Mr Amersi's evidence about whether or not what Mr Burgis reported is correct or not?' says McCormick.

Amersi has submitted a witness statement prepared with the help of Nigel Tait and his team at Carter-Ruck. Above Amersi's signature, it says: 'I believe that the facts stated in this Witness Statement are true. I understand that proceedings for contempt of court may be brought against anyone who makes, or causes to be made, a false statement in a document verified by a statement of truth without an honest belief in its truth.'

In his statement, Amersi writes: 'I did not say that my legal costs were approaching £300,000.' For a start, the number he said was lower: £260,000. 'Mr Burgis appears to have taken this out of context to mean costs incurred for the legal action that I have taken against the Defendants.' Actually, Amersi says, this figure also included the legal costs of setting up Comena.

There you have it, McCormick explains: Amersi's never said how much he spent specifically going after Leslie. It's confidential. 'It has not been revealed to Mr Burgis, and therefore has not been revealed by Mr Burgis to anybody else,'

McCormick says, with a glance towards the press box, where I'm sitting. 'All Mr Burgis has revealed – we say inaccurately – is the total of Mr Amersi's legal fees.'

In the press box, I open my laptop to check that I haven't gone mad. I bring up the transcript of our interview. At the part where Amersi's explained what he wants from Charlotte Leslie (apologise, retract, cease and desist, say who you sent the memos to, admit that you wrote them), he says:

> If she had done this in good faith, given me these five points in good faith, I would not want to have sued her for damages. Do you know what my costs are to date? £260,000. I could go there and give it to a Covid charity, which would help people. Instead, I'm wasting my time and wasting my money for absolute nonsense.

Later he says it again: '£260,000 worth of costs, right? Nearly £300,000 now, after the DPA filings.' That's the Data Protection Act, the initial claim against Leslie.

> £300,000 I would have wasted, which I would have given to the party, to the poor, to other people. I have wasted this on this, so it is only fair now that I recoup as much of that, which I will donate to the party.

I beckon Leslie's solicitor over to the press box. The transcript is open on my laptop screen. He takes a photo and goes over to her barrister. David Price is slender and pinstriped. His tone is quieter than McCormick's, understated. When he sees the shot of my screen, he jumps to his feet.

'My Lord, may I just raise one matter?'

The judge doesn't see the need. It's clear enough, he says, that he's not going to be told what Amersi's costs are.

'But you are also not being told the true picture about what Mr Amersi said to the *Financial Times*,' Price says.

Nicklin wants to get back to Leslie's memo. He does not know that weeks before Amersi signed his witness statement, Nigel Tait wrote a long letter to me and my editor at the *Financial Times* about all the 'falsehoods and inaccuracies' I'd been peddling in my articles. On the second of his nine pages, Tait quoted a line from one of my stories, about Amersi having spent '£300,000 on legal disputes with those who raised concerns about his growing influence in the ruling Conservative party'. Then Tait wrote this: 'Notwithstanding that our client is well within his right to use his money to seek redress through legal mechanisms,' Amersi 'has been forced to incur these costs initially (which are now much greater) because of the uncooperative stance that Miss Leslie, regrettably, chose to take in initial efforts to resolve this matter.'

And there is more that Nicklin has not been told. Amersi himself confirmed to a *Private Eye* reporter that he spent £300,000 on legal fees to fight Leslie – before telling the court something different in his witness statement. When I put this to Amersi, he says: 'I cannot now recall the total costs incurred by then and how much were legal costs, but I absolutely dispute that I deliberately lied to the court.' When I put it to Tait that he's misled the court, Carter-Ruck's reply ignores the question.

But these are not the questions before the court, as we return after lunch on January 10, 2023. Whether Carter-Ruck's lawyers, as they claim, 'conduct ourselves in accordance with our professional duties including to the courts, to our professional body and to our client'. Whether Mohamed Amersi made millions facilitating a deal that allowed a Putin crony to expand his illicit business empire: that is not the matter in hand. Nor, whether Amersi may have been complicit in the kleptocracy that blights Uzbekistan and Kazakhstan and Nepal. Might he and Conservatives have broken electoral law by falsely declaring the origin of a donation? Neither is this something the many talented lawyers and journalists in this room are here to examine. The question for today is: has Mr Amersi's good name been harmed, and if so, how badly?

When Mr Justice Nicklin resumes, Charlotte Leslie's barrister puts her case. Amersi's barrister has claimed that Leslie damaged Mohamed's standing in Ben Elliot's eyes. Days after her memo landed – three years after the Tories started accepting his money – emails were flying around Conservative headquarters asking for 'a proper report on Amersi himself as a due and proper person'. But it's not the possibility that dirty money may be pouring into the Party that concerns Elliot, says David Price, KC. It's the possibility that this fight might get out. The possibility of scrutiny.

After Amersi forwards him a copy of the initial letter Mishcon sent to Leslie, Elliot emails a fellow Party official.

They are both as bad as each other
Keen to have neither

Word goes round at headquarters: tell them both to down tools. This Middle East idea of Amersi's is on ice. But neither are there to be any more of these accusations from Charlotte. Price paraphrases: Elliot just wants this nasty spat to go away.

Amersi's money mustn't go away, though. Months after Charlotte's memos raise questions about Amersi's wealth, senior Tory officials are emailing staff at Number 10 about the breakfast with Boris that Amersi's still owed. 'Can you do quite an in depth look into this?' writes one. 'He's a massive donor, just want to know if it's likely to blow up into something if we do a breakfast.'

The Conservative Research Department does a check. 'Nothing bad came back,' the senior Party official assures the prime minister's aide. Let's get that breakfast sorted. Some swish hotel near Downing Street.

But before it can happen, news of his fight with Leslie comes out. Amersi thinks to himself: I would expect somebody senior from the Party to at least have the decency to phone and say, 'Look, Mohamed, I'm sorry that you're having to face all of this. We stand behind you.' They'd release a state-ment: 'Mohamed Amersi is one of our loyal supporters. We have huge respect for him, and for all that he has done, not only for this party, but for so many academic institutions, char-ities.' Yet Conservative headquarters is silent. After all those donations. After all those fees to Ben's firm as an elite Quintessentially client. Not a word of public support for this selfless thought leader.

On the *Sunday Times* front page of August 1, 2021, along-side news that the prime minister and Carrie have another child on the way, the headline reads: 'Tory chairman "peddled access to Charles"'.

'In a video interview from his Mayfair townhouse,' the *Sunday Times*'s crack investigative reporter Gabriel Pogrund writes, 'Amersi's cool demeanour cannot hide how bruised he is by the row, and how let down he feels by Elliot.' Pogrund asks if the Conservative chairman was operating 'a pay-to-play scheme'.

'You call it pay-to-play,' Amersi replies. 'I call it access capi-talism. It's the same point. You get access, you get invitations, you get privileged relationships, if you are part of the set-up, and where you are financially making a contribution to be a part of that set up. Absolutely.'

Like those of many other principled whistle-blowers, Amersi's revelations have a note of sorrow. The sorrow of he who must break up with friends for the greater good.

Charlotte Leslie, in a black jacket and a dark dress, with a gold crucifix on a necklace, closes her eyes, as though in her mind she has gone elsewhere. Day after day, there is this fight over reality, and on many of them there is bleakness to be fought too, and exhaustion. Andy is here next to her. He knows pressure, every journalist does. Iraq and Ukraine for the BBC; almost got locked up in Egypt. But this is the woman he loves. This fight has swallowed his life as well as hers. It was he who said they ought to get some insurance to cover legal bills. Without that, defending the case would be practically impossible.

It's not only Carter-Ruck they're up against. The UK propaganda industry stands ready to assist the disparaged rich in modern communications warfare. The private spies of K2 – offshoot of the legendary Kroll – are looking into Leslie. Lady: that's the codename they choose for her. They write up a profile. 'As a young, photogenic MP in Cameron's government she received largely favourable but fairly low-key coverage.' She plays the flirty Oxford graduate. Clearly a compromised figure: look at that Saudi trip she took, paid for by a benefactor in Riyadh. Or that time when she was an MP and failed to declare thousands in donations. Blamed her dyslexia. Had to apologise. The spies hear that she has former lovers who might have things to say about her.

And Fleet Steet journalists start getting messages from Phil Hall Associates. Messages setting the record straight about Mohamed. Hall used to be the editor of the *News of the World* (before a successor oversaw the mass hacking of phones, got caught, and Rupert Murdoch closed the paper). And of *Hello!* He's left journalism to found a public relations firm. What clients he's had: from celebrity footballers to celebrity chefs to celebrity plastic surgeons. Hall is proud that the finest lawyers hire him to help with their cases. Nigel Tait's son works for him.

Yet there are encouraging signs for Charlotte from the dais above. Mr Justice Nicklin's patience is indubitably thinning. He's been thirty years in the law. A leading barrister himself before his elevation to the judiciary in 2017. Without concealing his impatience, he's been interrupting McCormick to remind him of some legal basics. To bring a libel claim, you must show you've suffered as a result of what's been written about you – suffered serious harm. At the last hearing, Nicklin told Amersi and his lawyers to go away and show how Leslie sending her memos harmed his good name in the eyes of each of those who received them. Amersi's declined to do so. But he still wants his case to proceed. See how his pioneering work in combatting jihadism has been imperilled. He's been warned that he may be removed from the board of the organisation he set up for this task by his co-founders, Kevin and Ian Maxwell. They are committed to this cause – just as they are committed to exposing the wrongs done to their sister Ghislaine over her relationship with Jeffrey Epstein – but say they must have an eye to good governance while Mohamed is the subject of allegations.

Nicklin addresses McCormick. 'You said this morning that the claimant had an entitlement to bring his claims.' But it's not so simple. 'Gone are the days in which the court simply provided a playing field and a referee to allow parties to bring forward whatever claims they brought and the court would not investigate any further and would simply referee the dispute.' Instead, when he rules whether he will let this case go ahead – costing maybe millions, lasting years – Nicklin says he intends to scrutinise the likely benefits, the likely scale and cost, the likely drain on the resources of the defendants and of the court itself.

The last light is draining out through the ornate metalwork of the windows high in the courtroom walls. My sock is still soggy. I look at Amersi. He is tapping away on his phone. Once, as the judge concedes a point to his barrister, Amersi lets out a loud, sardonic laugh.

Nicklin announces that he will not give judgment today. He's off to hear a criminal case in Nottingham. When he gets back, he will let the parties know his decision. Before he goes, he says he will give thought to whether he should enable Amersi to litigate against Charlotte Leslie for her memo when Amersi has been accused of far more serious things. 'The court,' he says, 'must not detach itself from reality.'

Sixteen

The very fabric of this country

Dear Mr Speaker

My name is Mohamed Amersi. I am writing to seek your assistance in relation to the conduct of the Right Honourable David Davis MP, who has engaged in a public campaign of bullying against me since I brought my claim for defamation against his colleague and former MP Charlotte Leslie, for reasons I do not know.

Mohamed lists all the ways this bullying has taken place. 'I have the last 50 years of my life invested in this country in one way or another, and it is deeply hurtful to now be treated with such contempt by the very people who are meant to uphold society and the rule of law.' He invites the Speaker to examine this veteran member's conduct. 'By abusing Parliament's privilege quite wantonly in order to shield his campaign against me, he is undermining the very fabric of this country, its democracy and its institutions.'

Davis has used a speech in the Commons to describe what he calls 'an industry that hides evil in plain sight'. 'There are those,' he says, 'with exceptionally deep pockets and exceptionally questionable ethics' who 'use our justice system to threaten, intimidate and put the fear of God into British journalists, citizens, officials and media organisations. What results is injustice, intimidation, suppression of free speech, the crushing of a free press, bullying and bankruptcy. It results in protection from investigation and gives encouragement to fraudsters, crooks and money launderers. It has turned London into the global capital of dirty money. In extreme cases, it can undermine the security of the state by allowing people to act as extensions of foreign powers.'

He describes a few cases. One involves a donor to his own party. 'Amersi,' Davis tells the Commons, 'has used his wealth and influence to try to bully Charlotte Leslie into silence.'

Soon a letter arrives from Nigel Tait. 'It is iniquitous – and from our client's perspective somewhat revealing – that while you were content to use the Parliamentary chamber to make poorly researched, defamatory and unfounded remarks about our client,' you have not looked into Leslie's sinister past. 'It is simply not the case, as you suggest, that Miss Leslie has been "subject to legal harassment". Our client was, and is, perfectly entitled to seek suitable redress over the wrongs he has suffered.'

Even after Davis's speech, the Conservative cause continues to profit from Mohamed's beneficence. The Party has to refund two hundred thousand for the Johnson breakfast,

Hunt sushi, and Mordaunt magic that never took place and a year's Leaders Group subs. But at a lunchtime auction in May 2022, Amersi gives another sixteen thousand for the 'Thatcher Package' (commemorative plate, autographed bottle of whisky, tea with two of the late Margaret's colleagues) and dinner at a Green Park mansion with 'four guests from the Westminster political scene'.

He is, however, vocal in his disappointment with Ben.

Labour calls on Johnson to sack his chairman for the conflicts of interest between his political and commercial roles that the Amersi affair has exposed. The prime minister declines. A spokesperson for the Party says that Elliot's role at the Party is 'entirely separate from his other interests'. When Boris himself goes, felled by one lie too many in a career of fabrication, Elliot (soon to be knighted in Johnson's resignation honours) goes too. He stands behind his old friend outside the door to Number 10 as Boris gives a valedictory speech quoting a Roman dictator.

'Ben Elliott's resignation as @Conservatives co-chair was long overdue,' Amersi tweets. The clean-up of Conservative headquarters that he has long advocated has begun. 'But the rot doesn't stop there. It goes deeper!' Plus a prophecy: 'Only when the clean up is complete, the process of governing and delivery can begin. And this will be rewarded by more money, cleaner money!'

It's a vital subject, and the topic of an important recent report. 'Losing Our Moral Compass' is Margaret Hodge's account of her long campaign against the UK's enabling of international corruption. It contains expert analysis of how to protect democracy from the march of kleptocracy. But many readers will never read a word of it. Nigel Tait has been in touch with the publisher, King's College London. Among its hundred pages are a couple of brief references to a British political donor who seems to have profited from 'apparently corrupt deals' between a Swedish telecoms company and a member of the Uzbek regime. Tait says his client, Mohamed Amersi, 'cannot allow these damaging misstatements to go uncorrected'. The report is withdrawn.

Tait's written to Chatham House too, the country's most illustrious foreign affairs institute. A recent study by a group of academics – 'The UK's Kleptocracy Problem: How servicing the post-Soviet elite weakens the rule of law' – has appeared on its website, and is due to be printed. It contains a passing mention of Amersi's part in the Uzbek deal, calling him 'the intermediary for payment' from TeliaSonera to the Princess. Tait demands changes. 'These allegations are part of an orchestrated and politically motivated media campaign against our client,' he informs Chatham House's director. The report is all the more unfortunate because Amersi so values his relationship with Chatham House – he's even offered to donate. It's amended to say Amersi 'authorised a payment' to the Princess's offshore company. No, says Tait, it should say Mohamed 'advised, alongside other international advisors, on a payment'. The text is changed again but another letter from Tait in February 2022 says Mohamed 'requires' further changes. In red ink, it shows the lengthy additions Amersi wants. Eventually, the tinkering ends and the report can go to the printers. By now, though, it's too late for anyone who might have benefited from receiving a copy before the invasion of Ukraine a few months ago.

Another letter goes to Michaela Ahlberg, who joined TeliaSonera as head of ethics and compliance in the thick of the Uzbek scandal. She appeared on a *Panorama* about how Tory donors made their money to confirm that Mohamed Amersi is Mr XY, the highly paid Eurasia dealmaker in the Norton Rose report. Tait quotes her contribution: 'It is important that people around him, that trust him, that listen to him, understand the whole context of his career, and wealth ... He has been involved in one of the biggest corruption scandals that we have seen in Sweden in modern times.' These are 'appalling allegations', Tait writes. Ahlberg must retract them. She declines. Her lawyers write back to Tait: 'It is clear that your client has simply targeted our client in an attempt to intimidate her.'

Russian oligarchs have sued Catherine Belton, the Brexit backer Arron Banks is suing the *Observer* journalist Carole Cadwalladr, three Central Asian tycoons are suing me, through a London subsidiary, over my book *Kleptopia*. These cases and others have MPs talking about 'lawfare'. The Ministry of Justice calls for submissions from those with knowledge of how the rule of law is being abused by the powerful. One victim, Mohamed Amersi, duly contributes. He has, he explains, been the target of a 'reverse-Slapp'. A little thought leadership has produced a remedy.

'In light of what I and others have experienced in terms of obstacles being artificially placed in my path to seek justice', Parliament should 'institute a system to deal with so-called investigative journalists who behave irresponsibly by distorting twisting or hiding true facts to suit their own financial or other motives. They should be placed on a register and be initially suspended and ultimately barred from being able to practise their profession and/or be employed in media circles.'

After Davis declines to retract his words, Amersi sends his letter to the Speaker in July 2023. By then, Mr Justice Nicklin has delivered his judgment. Amersi's defamation suit against Charlotte Leslie is dismissed.

'There are several aspects of the conduct of the claimant' that 'give real cause for concern' that Amersi's legal actions might have had some 'collateral purpose', the judge writes. Amersi has shown an 'exorbitant approach to the litigation', first the data claim, then the data claim again, then the libel action. 'Subjecting a person to successive civil claims can be a hallmark of abusive conduct.' Mohamed's media interviews and elements of his witness statements 'strongly suggest that the claimant has treated this libel action as providing him with an opportunity also to seek to embarrass (and possibly to punish) the Conservative party for, as he perceives it, having wronged him. That is not a legitimate purpose of civil proceedings for defamation.'

Seventeen

Reality

We've been here all day. Mohamed has unfurled a flapjack.

Being gaslit for hours is disorienting.

Amersi once WhatsApped me to ask: 'Why are you running this campaign against me?'

'I'm doing no such thing,' I replied. 'I'm reporting on a matter of serious public interest.'

'Well that's how it feels to me, my friends, my family and my associates,' he said. 'You are biased against me ... search your conscience and admit it and one day explain to me why.'

Many people want to believe in Mohamed Amersi. And in Boris Johnson and in Donald Trump. Hearts beating in Vladimir Putin's troops' chests fill with zeal as they march to save their Ukrainian cousins from the genocidal fascists of Kyiv. When they liberate Mariupol, Putin declares it an 'ancient Russian city', ready for enfolding back into the motherland. His evidence – the 'well-known' fact that Peter the Great, the emperor whose image hung in the St

Petersburg deputy mayor's office thirty years ago, founded his first naval flotilla there – is fiction. But the hearts still stir. And even when the heart doesn't stir – the head knows what it's best for your health to believe.

A free society works only when reality itself is free. When the stories by which we live are composed by the many, challenged and tested and adjusted and debated, not imposed by the few. What we are witnessing is the privatisation of reality. The advent of generative artificial intelligence, distributed through social media, is hastening what's been called epistemological bankruptcy. The point at which we'll be unable to tell whether any of the information we encounter is authentic or not.

For something like two centuries – since Darwin, we might say – the pursuit of the truth grew steadily more democratic. Now we risk a return to feudal reality, where the word of the strong, of the rich, is gospel. If that happens, we won't know what we don't know. Like the cuckoo and the poor bird it fools, their power derives from others' ignorance. Ignorance that we, like those dupes, can be so keen to embrace, if it seems to make our lives a little easier.

Surely that's why our parliaments, our courts, our media, scientific inquiry and freedom of speech have evolved: as ways to uphold objective truth against the dupe in each of us, the liar in each of us. They are meant to guard against those who would seize reality by force, or try to buy it. That these institutions are themselves being captured, being sold, is ominous for the truth. Because they protect not some sacred truth but the opposite: the right to dissent, to dispute, to say that no word is ever final.

It looks like Labour will win the coming election in the UK. They may soon have some help with the campaign. Mohamed Amersi has announced he would be happy to donate. Meanwhile, he's busy on the world stage. He's just been appointed a trustee at a distinguished American political think tank. It has listed his accomplishments. 'Mohamed Amersi is also extensively engaged in bringing peace, prosperity and unity to the MENA region through diplomacy and dialogue by advising key stakeholders on foreign policy issues, conflict resolution, inclusion, and tolerance.'

Look at him go. 'What a few days it's been!' he's posted on Twitter, recently renamed X by its new owner, the world's richest man.

Shuttle diplomacy between Istanbul, Beirut, Baghdad, Tehran and now Doha, engaging with senior leadership and addressing the challenges and opportunities that a transforming Middle East is presenting!

Next stop New York to continue the dialogue with senior Middle East leadership in addressing some irretractable conflicts. What Leslie and her merry band of lying 'have beens' tried to stop Comena from doing in the Middle East is happening full swing. I am proud to fly the British flag!

I ask Amersi what he thinks of Mr Justice Nicklin's judgment throwing out his defamation claim against Charlotte Leslie.

'I think, frankly, between you and me the judgment was more of a set of mistakes done by my lawyers rather than me, in many respects. The way they pleaded the libel, the way that they failed to show what harm had been done to me and all of that.'

He has lodged an appeal. Leslie is to remain in the world of pain for a while longer. In November 2023, appeal court judges will finally terminate his defamation claim against her. Charlotte will stand, welling with tears, free but still bound, knowing she must for ever take care not to anger him again, lest she give him a chance to resume the pain.

Mohamed will not be in court for the ruling. 'I have a right to defend and restore my reputation when it has been attacked unfairly,' he will say on X afterwards. 'It is ironic that those who have libelled me are now posing as the victims, but no one should be fooled by their weasel words.' Another account – going by Twittetwist, which does little but like Amersi's tweets, and whose only follower is Mohamed – will offer some support at this difficult moment.

Mr Amersi, EVERYONE KNOWS YOU ARE DEALING WITH PIGS! 🐽🐽🐽 Nothing new … and completely expected …

Amersi's campaign for truth will not stop. In December 2023, Nigel Tait and the team will once more arrive at the High Court. This time Mohamed is suing the BBC, over the *Panorama* documentary examining his role in how nearly a quarter of a billion dollars found its way to the Uzbek dictator's daughter. Carter-Ruck's writ says: 'The Claimant has an established reputation as an anti-corruption campaigner,' which the BBC has 'seriously undermined and damaged'. Perhaps his next target will be this book.

Mohamed Amersi is moving towards the door, leaving this room, its egg painting, its untouched luxury biscuits. The fight for the reality he wants goes on.

'I'm doing this because I have to do it,' he says.

'Why is that?'

'I'd rather get out of all this shit. Go back to my life. It was beautiful.'

NOTES

One: Hard-won truths

5 The Chinese Communist Party: Mara Hvistendahl and Benjamin Mueller, 'Chinese censorship is quietly rewriting the Covid-19 story', *New York Times*, April 23, 2023, nytimes.com/2023/04/23/world/europe/chinese-censorship-covid.html

Two: Take-off

7 private plane: Amersi call with me, July 5, 2021

7 his decency, his warmth … Ben understands: Gabriel Pogrund and Henry Zeffman, 'Access capitalism scandal: A dinner with Prince Charles, then the begging letter arrived', *Sunday Times*, July 31, 2021, thetimes.co.uk/article/access-capitalism-scandal-a-dinner-with-prince-charles-then-the-begging-letter-arrived-kngk0xqfk

7 'Unless you have somebody': Pogrund and Zeffman, 'Access capitalism'

7 nothing Ben can't provide: For example, Elliot's comments about what he's done for clients in Jonathan Moules, 'Business diary: Ben Elliot, Quintessentially', *Financial Times*, August 29, 2011, ft.com/content/37669c60-cff9-11e0-81e2-00144feabdc0

7 airlifted teabags: Guy Adams, 'An Englishman in New York', *Independent on Sunday*, April 15, 2007

7 penguins, false eyelashes … llamas: Tom Leonard, 'A willing
slave to the stars', *Daily Telegraph*, July 20, 2006

8 backstage passes to Beyoncé: Emma Jacobs, '21st-century
butlers', *Financial Times*, December 20, 2010, ft.com/
content/90ba14cc-0709-11e0-94f1-00144feabdc0

8 signed by Lionel Messi: 'Ben Elliot – The interview',
Gentleman's Journal, December 3, 2012,
thegentlemansjournal.com/ben-elliot-the-interview

8 albino peacocks: Adams, 'An Englishman'

8 Sydney Harbour Bridge: Moules, 'Business diary'

8 Shanghai's couture boutiques closed: Jacobs, '21st-century
butlers'

8 party beside pyramids and dine on icebergs … Batcave: Lucy
Barnard, 'Selling class', *Estates Gazette*, January 29, 2011

8 below zero: Data from Time and Date, timeanddate.com/
weather/uk/london/historic?month=1&year=2013

8 forebears: Mohamed Amersi, 'Fighting an asymmetric war',
Citi Private Bank, 2021, web.archive.org/web/
20210515200834/https://www.privatebank.citibank.com/
we-serve/mohamed-amersi. The article appears to have been
published around 2021 and taken down the following year

8 send his son: Amersi interview with me, July 2023

9 adolescent Amersi arrived: 'Obituary – Marhuma Fatma Bai
Amirali Amersi', Council of European Jamaats, January 28,
2022, coej.org/the-council-of-european-jamaats-newswire-
january-edition

9 if he were John Smith: Martin Beckford, 'Tories would not
treat me like this if I was white: Major donor involved in cash-
for-access row claims he was treated badly because of his
background … but insists he still loves the party', *Daily Mail*,
August 2, 2021, dailymail.co.uk/news/article-9853823/
Tories-not-treat-like-white-Major-donor-claims.html

10 premier mergers and acquisitions adviser: 'Mohamed Amersi
utterly rejects the misleading and inaccurate reporting in
articles published today (4 October 2021) by the Guardian
and the BBC', press release sent to journalists by PHA Group
for Mohamed Amersi

10 emailed the itinerary: Pogrund and Zeffman, 'Access capitalism'

10 Gobelin tapestries: 'The story of the Tapestry Room', Dumfries House Trust, published around 2010 and stored on Wayback Machine, web.archive.org/web/20130214002641/ http://dumfries-house.org.uk/tour/tapestry-room

10 peeps like a pearl: Image published by Dumfries House Trust around 2010 and stored on Wayback Machine, web.archive. org/web/20130216033207/http://www.dumfries-house.org. uk/about

Three: A furnace for the past

13 'I will be around': The details of the conversation between James Hatt and Jeffrey Galmond come from a transcript of a recording of their conversation, September 6, 2004. This was entered into evidence in the Zurich Arbitral Tribunal in Ipoc International Growth Fund Ltd v LV Finance Group. Unless otherwise attributed, details of Hatt's life and Russian business dealings come from interviews with me

14 'the newest conqueror': Conal Walsh, 'The acceptable face of Russian capitalism?', *Observer*, September 5, 2004, theguardian.com/business/2004/sep/05/russia

14 'I have been assisted': Jeffrey Galmond's fourth affidavit in Ipoc International Growth Fund v LV Finance Group et al., Eastern Caribbean Supreme Court, July 27, 2004, par 149

15 detached ... furnace bursts: Nataliya Gevorkyan, Natalya Timakova, Andrei Kolesnikov, *First Person*, Public Affairs, 2000, chapters 1–5

16 'You know I'm lying': David K. Shipler, *Russia: Broken Idols, Solemn Dreams*, Times Books, 1983, p. 21

16 Moscow is silent: Catherine Belton, *Putin's People*, William Collins, 2020, p. 43; Max Seddon, 'Vladimir Putin, Russia's resentful leader, takes the world to war', *Financial Times*, February 25, 2022, ft.com/content/c039db89-7201-4875-b31f-b41a511496f1

17 Lyudmila hates the queues ... German neighbours: Gevorkyan et al., *First Person*, p. 87

17 negotiates with them through the night: Belton, *Putin's People*, pp. 48–9
17 Igor Sechin: Gevorkyan et al., *First Person*, p. 202; Belton, *Putin's People*, p. 99
17 Putin chooses: Gevorkyan et al., *First Person*, p. 90
17 the crash: Gevorkyan et al., *First Person*, pp. 104–10
18 falls in love with Moscow: Gevorkyan et al., *First Person*, p. 128
18 I'm married: Gevorkyan et al., *First Person*, p. 138
18 helicopter over Chechnya: Gevorkyan et al., *First Person*, p. 144
18 want him to watch: Gevorkyan et al., *First Person*, p. 155
18 'I found him to be': 'Press Conference by President Bush and Russian Federation President Putin', White House transcript, June 16, 2001, georgewbush-whitehouse.archives.gov/news/releases/2001/06/20010618.html
18 can be unpleasant: Gevorkyan et al., *First Person*, p. 158
18 has his secrets: Gevorkyan et al., *First Person*, p. 149
19 a job at a telecoms venture: Elena Rudneva, Gleb Krampets, Igor Tsukanov and Anna Nikolaeva, 'The Germans attacked the Putins', *Vedemosti*, July 28, 2005, vedomosti.ru/newspaper/articles/2005/07/28/nemcy-napali-na-putinyh (Russian). Ritz transcript, September 6, 2004, p. 44
20 cigars-and-caviar: Ritz transcript
20 waiting in the ten-hour queue: The account of Georgiou's activities in Russia is drawn from his affidavit. First affidavit of Antony Nicholas Georgiou in Ipoc International Growth Fund v LV Finance Group et al. in the Eastern Caribbean Supreme Court, October 19, 2004
22 wired the payment: Tony Georgiou letter to Leonid Reiman, October 12, 1992, in exhibit 1 to Georgiou's affidavit
22 signed his name: Letter from Tony Georgiou to James Hatt, December 14, 1995, in exhibit 3 to Georgiou's affidavit
23 now belongs: Leonid Konick, 'Telecominvest Holding shows its cards', Delovoy Peterburg, 1997, dp.ru/a/2005/07/29/Holding_Telekominvest_r (Russian)
23 Galmond has unmasked: Galmond fourth affidavit, par 142

24 'arrogant': Georgiou affidavit, par 46

24 not a fucking dime: Ritz transcript, p. 64

25 'star': Richard Tromans, 'Jones Day star quits to run fund', *Legal Week*, April 15, 1999

25 He knows God: A person with knowledge of Galmond's view described it to me

25 London and Dubai and St Tropez: Correspondence with Mohamed Amersi, August 2023

25 long seen himself: Amersi confirms this in his written responses to me of August 2023. Regarding the Saab project, he says: 'I was the dealmaker'

25 case was brought: Mr Justice Smith's judgment of December 5, 2002 in Ayoub-Farid Michel Saab and Fadi Michel Saab v Jones Day Reavis & Pogue and Mohamed Amersi at the High Court in London, bailii.org/cgi-bin/format.cgi?doc=/ew/cases/EWHC/Ch/2002/2616.html

28 seniors on the bench found: Judgment in Paul Howell et al. v Marcus Millais et al., Supreme Court, July 4, 2007, bailii.org/ew/cases/EWCA/Civ/2007/720.html

28 'a deeply worrying': Judgment in Janan Harb v Prince Abdul Aziz bin Fahd, Court of Appeal, June 16, 2016, bailii.org/ew/cases/EWCA/Civ/2016/556.html

28 'When making deals': Amersi, 'Fighting an asymmetric war', Citi Private Bank, web.archive.org/web/20210727031920/https://www.privatebank.citibank.com/we-serve/mohamed-amersi

29 'At the outset': Memorandum from Mohamed Amersi to Jeff Galmond, August 1, 2004, given to me by Amersi

30 to become the new corporate vessel: Amersi interview with me, July 2023

30 Industrial Development Corporation: Corporate filings by Industrial Development Corporation are available on the Luxembourg corporate registry. The statutes of Mandolino Holdings SA show it was incorporated on March 6, 2003 in Luxembourg with €31,000 in subscribed capital. Little happened until July 2004, when its name was changed to Industrial Development Corporation SA. Mohamed Amersi

was appointed managing director (so says the paperwork; Amersi in his July 2023 interview with me says he was just a director, and merely a 'placeholder' at that). The record of an Extraordinary General Meeting on December 23, 2004 states that Enigma Fund of the Cayman Islands has a 'claim' against Industrial Development Corporation for $109 million. This filing says Enigma Fund has received Industrial Development Corporation shares against this claim – but has also paid Industrial Development Corporation for these shares, to the tune of $17 million. Industrial Development Corporation's auditors, Ernst & Young, wrote that 'we have no observation to mention on the value' of the Industrial Development Corporation shares that were being exchanged for Enigma Fund's cash. Amersi resigned as managing director of Industrial Development Corporation on January 30, 2006. He was replaced by Felix Paulson. In an affidavit Jeffrey Galmond gave in the MegaFon dispute (August 6, 2004, Ipoc International Growth Fund v LV Finance et al. in the Eastern Caribbean Supreme Court) he calls Felix Paulson the 'financial controller' of his Danish law firm. Amersi told me in 2023 that he set Enigma up as a fund to receive Galmond's and others' telecoms assets but that the plan didn't work out

30 Coutts account: Mohamed Amersi emails with Coutts' Swiss bankers and with Jeffrey Galmond, May 2005

31 student in Moscow: Guy Chazan, 'Lunch with the FT: Mikhail Fridman', *Financial Times*, April 1, 2016, ft.com/content/9527e2be-f5b5-11e5-96db-fc683b5e52db

32 Reiman is growing angry: Ritz transcript, p. 61

34 Mohamed has been negotiating: During his career as a telecoms consultant, Amersi had a company called Emergent Telecom Ventures (ETV). It was ETV that was named on the paperwork for the PeterStar transaction; it was in ETV's name that he later sent invoices to TeliaSonera for his consultancy work. In this book, I sometimes refer to Amersi getting paid for working on a deal when the legal entity that was contracted or received money was ETV. When we first spoke in June 2021, Amersi said of ETV: 'I have been the legal

owner. I am, I was and I have been 100 per cent, yes.' He said there was a co-founder who would have received fees for any deals they brought in, but all the deals described here are Amersi's. In his witness statement in the arbitration over a Kazakh fibre company (see Chapter 8), he describes it like this: 'I was a Senior Advisor to TeliaSonera ... through Emergent Telecom Ventures, a company that I co-founded'

34 'there might be a group': Gregory L. White and Glenn R. Simpson, 'Megafon's fund-raising effort gets complex at critical point', *Wall Street Journal*, November 8, 2004, wsj. com/articles/SB1099866664876666990

34 'Mr Galmond's story': Ben Aris, 'Russian minister faces $1 million telecom claim', *Sunday Business*, November 14, 2004

35 Sberbank: 2005 accounts of First National Holding

35 the PeterStar negotiations: Metromedia International Group 14D-9 filing to the US Securities and Exchange Commission, July 13, 2007, sec.gov/Archives/edgar/data/39547/000095012907003441/h48297sc14d9.htm

35 'an intensifying': Glenn R. Simpson, David Crawford and Gregory L. White, 'Commerzbank is at center of probe', *Wall Street Journal*, July 25, 2005, wsj.com/articles/SB112206586718993673

35 Less than a week later: Metromedia 8-k filing to the US Securities and Exchange Commission, August 3, 2005, sec. gov/Archives/edgar/data/39547/000115752305006922/a4944766.txt. Amersi, in his correspondence with me of August 2023, says the accelerated completion was unrelated to the *Journal* article

35 four million dollars: Mohamed Amersi interview with me, July 2021

37 'unquestionable proof': Amersi correspondence with me, August 2023

38 state of Room 5330: Judgment in New York Criminal Court v Jeffrey Galmond, December 20, 2006

38 'with caution': Second Partial Award of the Zurich Arbitral Tribunal in Ipoc International Growth Fund Ltd v LV Finance Group, May 16, 2006, par 196

38 'intentionally misled': Second Partial Award, par 232. The judgment refers to Galmond not by name but as 'Witness No 4'. That Galmond is the person referred to as 'Witness No 4' is clear from, for instance, this witness being described in the judgment as Ipoc's purported owner (par 2) and as one of the two people in a secret recording made in London, quotations from which (par 402) match the Ritz transcript in which Galmond is identified by name. At par 230 of the judgment, the Zurich Arbitral Tribunal refers to a comment made by 'Witness No 4' in a *Wall Street Journal* article published on January 19, 2006. In that article, the comment is attributed to Galmond. Glenn R. Simpson, Gregory L. White and David Crawford, 'Putin ally may control big mobile-phone stake', *Wall Street Journal*, wsj.com/articles/SB113763657133550478

39 'misappropriate for his personal enrichment': Second Partial Award, par 429. The judgment refers to 'Proposed Witness No. 7'. This is clearly Reiman. For example, at par 230, Reiman is identified in the *Wall Street Journal* article (Simpson et al., 'Putin ally may control') that also identifies Galmond. At par 390, the judgment says: 'In the relevant period (2000–2002), the Proposed Witness No. 7 served as a high-ranking officer of the Russian Federation with the function of coordination and regulation of activity in the sphere of communication of Russia.' Reiman at the time was Putin's minister of communications. And at par 402, the judgment quotes a 'secretly taped conversation' in which 'Proposed Witness No. 7' is described as having the idea to 'create a Pan-Russian Network'. In the Ritz transcript, on p. 7, the person having this idea is Leonid Reiman

39 Galmond can't sleep: Judgment in Jeffrey Galmond v Ministry of Taxation in the Copenhagen City Court, January 22, 2018, p. 52

40 have you locked up: Amended complaint in Ipoc International Growth Fund v Leonid Rozhetskin et al., Southern District of New York, February 7, 2007, par 81

40 bamboo jail: A person with knowledge of Galmond's version of this exchange described it to me

Notes

40 spoke to Fridman ... Galmond ... Reiman: Amersi's correspondence with me, August 2023

42 Putin had been asking Leonid Reiman: Ritz transcript, p. 68

42 highest Swiss court upholds: Decision of the Swiss Federal Tribunal 4P.168/2006, February 19, 2007, jusmundi.com/en/document/pdf/decision/fr-ipoc-international-growth-fund-ltd-v-lv-finance-group-ltd-decision-du-tribunal-federal-suisse-4p-168-2006-monday-19th-february-2007 (French)

42 a letter from their Russian counterparts: David Crawford, 'Germany ends probe implicating Russian corruption', *Wall Street Journal*, April 11, 2012, wsj.com/articles/SB10001424052702304587704577336211193313438

42 forty-five million dollars confiscated: The Queen v Ipoc International Growth Fund and others, Eastern Caribbean Supreme Court, August 20, 2008, www.eccourts.org/wp-content/files_mf/20.08.08thequeenvipocinternational growthfundltdetal.pdf. The date the $45 million was confiscated was May 1, 2008

42 guarded by attack dogs and Kalashnikovs: Patricia Hedelius, *Telia: Alliansregeringen och korruptionen*, Massolit Förlag, 2015, p. 116

42 friend to the Putin Kremlin: Courtney Weaver and Charles Clover, 'Alisher Usmanov: Uzbek eyes a prize listing', *Financial Times*, November 16, 2012, ft.com/content/37720a28-2f1b-11e2-b88b-00144feabdc0

42 buying everyone out: 'Russian tycoon Usmanov buys stake in Megafon-paper', Reuters, May 12, 2008, reuters.com/article/megafon-usmanov-idINL1237627920080512

42 gets five billion dollars: Courtney Weaver and Daniel Thomas, 'Usmanov to control Russia's Megafon', *Financial Times*, April 24, 2012, ft.com/content/0bb38bfc-8e33-11e1-bf8f-00144feab49a

42 far less than it's worth: Copenhagen City Court judgment, p. 23

43 not some front: Copenhagen City Court judgment, pp. 26–33

43 'Finally': Crawford, 'Germany ends probe'

43 Danish tax authorities: Copenhagen City Court judgment

Four: The host

45 Abramovich is a client: George Grylls and Henry Zeffman, 'Conservative co-chairman Ben Elliot boasted of helping billionaires in capital', *The Times*, February 26, 2022, thetimes. co.uk/article/conservative-co-chairman-ben-elliot-boasted-of-helping-billionaires-in-capital-ddc93mdgm

45 Knowing the right people: Moules, 'Business diary'

45 Ben sends Quintessentially clients Charles's way: Ben Elliot declined to answer the detailed questions I sent him. He did say: 'I do not "sell", and have never sold, access either to any UK government minister or to any "British royals", for any fee (large or small)'

45 forking out: 'The Sovereign Grant and Sovereign Grant Reserve Annual Report and Accounts 2012–13', royal.uk/ sites/default/files/media-packs/sovereign_grant_2012-13.pdf

46 fall into ruin ... Pink Dining Room: 'Britain's hidden heritage: Dumfries House', BBC, August 14, 2011, bbc.co.uk/ programmes/b013nh00. Clip on YouTube, 'The Duke of Rothesay and Dumfries House', MyDigitalRealm, youtube. com/watch?v=7CHDJnvktgY

46 his foundation had to borrow: Andy Verity, James Oliver and James Melley, 'The Prince of Wales, the oligarch and the stately home', BBC, March 4, 2019, bbc.co.uk/news/ business-47441114

46 Russia team: 'Ben Elliot', *Gentleman's Journal*

47 Global Elite member: Amersi call with me, July 5, 2021

47 Amersi likes that: Pogrund and Zeffman, 'Access capitalism'

47 Alan Titchmarsh: 'Prince Charles: The Royal Restoration', ITV, May 29, 2012, clip on YouTube, Royal Family, youtube. com/watch?v=a7eF6elT9GQ

47 give back: Second witness statement of Mohamed Amersi, in his defamation claim against Leslie, July 29, 2022, par 8

47 How to bring humanity together: Amersi call with me, July 5, 2021

47 interview with ... Harry: Max Foster and Peter Wilkinson, 'Prince Harry on Vegas nude romp: "I let my family down"',

CNN, January 22, 2013, edition.cnn.com/2013/01/22/
world/europe/harry-vegas-media/index.html

48 used to be headteacher: 'Top director departs Costley &
Costley', *Herald*, July 11, 2006, heraldscotland.
com/default_
content/12432759.top-director-departs-costley-costley

48 'It was a real pleasure': Pogrund and Zeffman, 'Access
capitalism'

48 nineteen thousand pounds: TeliaSonera paid Amersi's
Emerging Telecom Ventures $63 million over six years, an
average of nearly $29,000, or about £19,000 a day

48 Amersi commands: Amersi message to me, July 5, 2021;
Pogrund and Zeffman, 'Access capitalism'

49 'Well done': Pogrund and Zeffman, 'Access capitalism'

Five: Protection

51 Harvard Business School ... martial artist: David Stern, 'Rich
pickings for Uzbek leader's daughter', *Financial Times*, August
18, 2003

51 pop star ... diplomat ... fashionista ... poet: Kristian Lasslett,
Fatima Kanji and Dáire McGill, 'A dance with the cobra',
International State Crime Initiative, 2007, statecrime.org/
data/2017/08/Full-Report-with-Executive-Summary.pdf

51 'You look fine': RealGoogoosha, 'Googoosha – How Dare
(Official Video)', YouTube, December 21, 2012, youtube.
com/watch?v=d3HLFIx8QmU

51 'exotic beauty' ... mezzo-soprano: @realgoogoosha,
Twitter/X, twitter.com/realgoogoosha

51 government minister: 'Gulnora Karimova appointed
deputy minister of foreign affairs for cultural issues', US
diplomatic cable sent February 4, 2008, published by
WikiLeaks, wikileaks.org/plusd/
cables/08TASHKENT153_a.html

51 delegate to the World Economic Forum: 'Uzbekistan takes
part in the "Summer Davos" World Economic Forum',
UzDaily, September 16, 2009, uzdaily.uz/en/post/7056

52 I hope you had: Email from Bekhzod Akhmedov to three
senior TeliaSonera employees, December 26, 2009

52 maintain their ignorance: Mannheimer Swartling report to the directors of TeliaSonera, January 31, 2013, p. 42

52 her own husband: Judgment in Mansur Maqsudi v Gulnara Karimova Maqsudi, Superior Court of New Jersey, September 12, 2002, caselaw.findlaw.com/court/nj-superior-court/1474229.html

52 her nineteenth birthday: Lasslett et al., 'A dance with the cobra', p. 30

53 clan is influential: Lasslett et al., 'A dance with the cobra', p. 31

53 Coca-Cola select him: I asked Coca-Cola's spokesman about this account. He did not dispute it, or answer any of my questions. He just said: 'Across the globe, Coca-Cola follows high standards of ethics, transparency, and compliance to all applicable laws'. Email from Coca-Cola, August 4, 2023

54 Washington propaganda consultants: Complaint in Mansur Maqsudi et al. v Global Options et al. in the US District Court for the District of Columbia, July 11, 2007, storage. courtlistener.com/recap/gov.uscourts.dcd.126479.1.0.pdf. The consultants denied wrongdoing and the case was settled

54 rounded up Mansur's relatives: Maqsudi v Karimova judgment

54 same agency brings legal action: Lasslett, 'A dance with the cobra', p. 36

54 forty dollars a month: Expert opinion of Scott Horton in Mansur Maqsudi et al. v Global Options et al., par 13

54 reviewed, edited: Witness statement of Farhod Inogambaev in Roz Trading at al v Coca-Cola Export Corp, United States District Court for the Northern District of Georgia, August 10, 2007, cdn.occrp.org/projects/corruptistan/documents/uzbekistan/Telecoms_4.pdf?_gl=1*w9qzd5*_ga* MTI4OTAzOTgzMS4xNjY2NzA0MDk4*_ga_ NHCZV5EYYY*MTY2NzI5OTUyNi4yLjEuMTY2Nz MwMTAzMi42MC4wLjA, par 29

54 new local partner: Lasslett et al., 'A dance with the cobra', p. 35–8

55 power into money: For a comprehensive account of the corruption Gulnara Karimova is accused of perpetrating, see Lasslett et al., 'A dance with the cobra'

55 'Why did God create us': 'Uzbek leader gives news conference on Andijon events – full version', BBC Monitoring Central Asia, May 14, 2005

56 puddle of blood: The account of the Andijan massacre and the cover-up are drawn from two Human Rights Watch reports, 'Bullets were falling like rain', June 2005, hrw.org/reports/2005/uzbekistan0605/uzbekistan0605.pdf, and 'Burying the truth', September 2005, hrw.org/report/2005/09/18/burying-truth/uzbekistan-rewrites-story-andijan-massacre

56 'We could tolerate it no longer': Galima Bukharbaeva, 'No requiem for the dead', Institute for War and Peace Reporting, May 16, 2005, iwpr.net/global-voices/no-requiem-dead

58 trained his troops: C.J. Chivers and Thom Shanker, 'Uzbek ministries in crackdown received US aid', *New York Times*, June 18, 2005, nytimes.com/2005/06/18/world/asia/uzbek-ministries-in-crackdown-received-us-aid.html

58 falls apart: Russian interior ministry Department of Investigation record of the interrogation of Bekhzod Akhmedov in Moscow on September 10, 2012; Information filing by the Department of Justice in US v Telia Company AB, Southern District of New York, September 21, 2017, justice.gov/criminal-fraud/file/1009321/download, par 17; 'Coscom cautiously optimistic about future', June 15, 2007, wikileaks.org/plusd/cables/07TASHKENT1140_a.html, which describes the motive for the Uzbek authorities' attacks on the Americans' network, Coscom, as 'simple greed'. Amersi rejects any suggestion that the Qatari bid he worked on was blocked because Gulnara wasn't offered a bribe. He gives an alternative explanation: 'The Qataris were rumoured to be supporting the Muslim Brotherhood and Islamic extremism. The Uzbeks were worried about that and so the bid was rejected'

58 'Dear Sirs': Email from 'Gergiy' to Coscom, February 6, 2007

59 Gulnara has had a hand ... 'notable interlocutor': 'Scandinavian-Turkish firm may buy Coscom and sister companies in Central Asia', US diplomatic cable sent April 27,

2007, published by WikiLeaks, https://wikileaks.org/plusd/cables/07TASHKENT769_a.html

59 'preliminary hand-shake': Mannheimer Swartling report, p. 4

59 described admiringly: Hedelius, *Telia*, p. 59

60 'a strong local group': Dutch Public Prosecution Service statement of facts, p. 4

60 strikes Nyberg: Hedelius, *Telia*, p. 98

61 Tashkent State alumni gather: Akhmedov interrogation record

61 I will destroy: Farhod Inogambaev witness statement, par 20; Akhmedov interrogation record; Simon Ostrovsky, 'MTS pays premium to Uzbek "Princess"', *Moscow Times*, July 19, 2004

62 'When I meet': Mary Dejevsky, 'She is the jet-setting daughter of Uzbekistan's notorious dictator, and married into one of the nation's wealthiest families. But her bitter divorce could derail America's war on terror. Now she tells her story for the first time', *Independent*, January 7, 2004, independent.co.uk/news/world/asia/she-is-the-jetsetting-daughter-of-uzbekistan-s-notorious-dictator-and-married-into-one-of-the-nation-s-wealthiest-families-but-her-bitter-divorce-could-derail-america-s-war-on-terror-now-she-tells-her-story-for-the-84765.html. Karimova is stated to own 'a major share in Uzdunrobita, the country's main mobile-phone company'

62 Russian oligarch buys it: Lasslett, et al., 'A dance with the cobra', pp. 53–5

62 negotiates with TeliaSonera's people: Information filing by the Department of Justice. Bekhzod Akhmedov is not named in this filing, which relates the criminal conduct admitted by Telia. But he is clearly identifiable as Associate B, described at par 12 as the chief executive of a rival Uzbek telecoms company. Akhmedov was at the time chief executive of one such company, Uzdunrobita. The Department of Justice filing also says Associate B represented 'the Foreign Official' (Gulnara Karimova) in dealings with Telia. Akhmedov says so himself in testimony he gave to Russian law enforcement on September 10, 2012, a copy of which I obtained. At par 14

the Department of Justice information says of Associate B: 'Certain TELIA management negotiated the terms of the corrupt partnership with Associate B, who represented the Foreign Official'

62 takes Lars Nyberg: Hedelius, *Telia*, p. 98

63 who he says he is: A TeliaSonera press release, issued before the Zurich arbitration ruling but after the first press coverage of Galmond's alleged fronting for Reiman, stated: 'Jeffrey Galmond is the beneficial owner of First National Holdings.' 'TeliaSonera: MegaFon shareholders unite behind shareholders' agreement,' March 9, 2005, sec.gov/Archives/edgar/data/1169870/000117184305000094/newsrelease. htm

63 Don't compete: Amersi's written responses to me, June 2021

64 retained Amersi: Mohamed Amersi witness statement in Almaty Engineering Company v Sonera Holding says at par 1 that he held this position 'from 2007–2013, first through my position as Senior Banking Advisor at Rothschild in 2007 and then through Emergent Telecom Ventures, a company that I co-founded, from 2008–2013'

64 thirty-million-dollar down payment: Mannheimer Swartling report, p. 31

64 suggests ways: Email from Mohamed Amersi to Tero Kivisaari and other senior TeliaSonera employees, December 30, 2009

64 'Tero': Email from Mohamed Amersi to Tero Kivisaari and other senior TeliaSonera employees, December 31, 2009

64 'Mohamed, thanks': Email from Tero Kivisaari to Mohamed Amersi, December 31, 2009

64 'The discussion was very friendly': Email from Tero Kivisaari to Mohamed Amersi and senior TeliaSonera employees, January 6, 2010

65 give an undertaking: 'Acquisition of 20 percent in U'Cell Uzbekistan', memo to the TeliaSonera board, January 19, 2010

65 incorporated four thousand miles away on Gibraltar: this 'local partner' is Takilant. Dutch Public Prosecution Service statement of facts, page 2, prosecutionservice.nl/documents/

publications/fp/hoge-transacties/feitenrelaas/statement-of-facts-telia-company
65 By keeping this obscure Gibraltar company: 'Acquisition of 20 percent', TeliaSonera memo
66 an invoice: Emerging Telecom Ventures invoice to TeliaSonera UTA Holding BV, March 10, 2010
67 Bekhzod himself: 'during the initial sounding in Uzbekistan ... interest was focused on Bekhzod Akhmedov, who claimed to be a representative of Gulnara Karimova's business group'. Mannheimer Swartling report, p. 49. It goes on: 'In this context, it was important to clarify that Gulnara Karimova was not a politician or a representative of the authorities. Given TeliaSonera's state ownership, the country's reputation and the circumstances behind the local partner, a clear message was conveyed to Bekhzod Akhmedov that it was of fundamental importance that everything be done legally and correctly. On that basis, and given that Ms Karimova could be considered a businesswoman, it was considered that the involvement of Ms Karimova would not be a problem in itself'
67 'thought to be held': 'Information memorandum: MCT Corp', Lazard, February 2006
67 lack of proof: Amersi written responses to me, August 2023
68 saying so for two years: Mannheimer Swartling report, p. 49
69 'peculiar': Mannheimer Swartling report, p. 43
69 'sensitive security': Cafter-Ruck's letter for Mohamed Amersi to Norton Rose Fulbright, March 18, 2022
70 opened the wall safe: Joshua l. Ray, 'The continuing façade of FCPA enforcement: A critical look at the Telia DPA', New York University, *Journal of Law & Business*, Vol. 17, Summer 2021, No. 3
71 bags under his eyes: Interpol alert for Bekhzod Akhmedov (archived) web.archive.org/web/20130515093513/https://www.interpol.int/%C2%B4en/Wanted-Persons/(wanted_id)/2012-312933
71 'Everyone is tired': Akhmedov interrogation record

Notes

Six: The right path

75 'has shown himself': Pogrund and Zeffman, 'Access capitalism'

76 'We now live in a world': Inclusive Ventures business plan. Disclosed in the defamation proceedings Amersi brought in the UK High Court against Leslie

76 lives in Dubai: Claudio Modola Design Studio testimonials, July 2016, claudiomodola.com/wp-content/ uploads/2016/07/Mohamed-Amersi.pdf; witness statement of Mohamed Amersi in Almaty Engineering Company v Sonera Holding, London Court of International Arbitration, November 11, 2016; my correspondence with Amersi, August 2023

76 'a picture-perfect' ... seven million pounds: Penny Churchill, 'A superb Georgian house for sale, set in 38 acres of Cotswolds parkland', *Country Life*, September 27, 2018, countrylife.co.uk/property/supebr-cotswolds-house-sale-set-38-acres-parkland-185110

77 use the barns: 'St Matthew's Church news', *Watershed Magazine*, October 2016, d3hgrlq6yacptf.cloudfront.net/ 5f1183fdb2263/content/pages/documents/1475496523.pdf

77 buying a tract: my correspondence with Amersi, August 2023

77 effusive quote: 'Royal Agricultural University welcomes Rural Shores', Inclusive Ventures, July 30, 2014, inclusiveventures. com/royal-agricultural-university-welcomes-rural-shores

77 transform the world: 'Royal Agricultural University welcomes Rural Shores'

77 To the needy, to the young: 'IVG fuels Rural Shores expansion into Nepal', Inclusive Ventures, August 10, 2014, inclusiveventures.com/ivg-fuels-rural-shores-expansion-into-nepal

77 Sumargi's admirers: Subash Singh Parajuli, 'Sumargi: The right path of living', My Republica, May 18, 2019, myrepublica.nagariknetwork.com/news/sumargi-the-right-path-of-living

Seven: Mr XY

79 by the other chaps: 'Eton's royal connection', BBC, June 2, 2001, news.bbc.co.uk/1/hi/uk/1366105.stm

79 same British lord: 'Dipendra and Devyani', *Jana Aastha*, June 29, 2001, archive.nepalitimes.com/news.php?id=8217

79 But his are living gods: Rebecca Armitage and Lucia Stein, 'A royal massacre: 20 years ago, a lovesick Nepalese prince murdered his family', April 30, 2021, abc.net.au/news/2021-05-01/how-a-lovesick-prince-wiped-out-nepals-royal-family/100056562

80 At nine o'clock: Barry Bearak, 'A witness to massacre in Nepal tells gory details', *New York Times*, June 8, 2001, nytimes.com/2001/06/08/world/a-witness-to-massacre-in-nepal-tells-gory-details.html

80 gun collection: Lisa Mullins and Mary Kay Magistad, 'Why Nepal's crown prince went on a killing spree', *The World*, June 1, 2011, theworld.org/stories/2011-06-01/why-nepals-crown-prince-went-killing-spree

80 'not necessary': Barry Bearak, 'Nepal gives "synopsis" of massacre by drug-addled prince', *New York Times*, June 15, 2001, nytimes.com/2001/06/15/world/nepal-gives-synopsis-of-massacre-by-drug-addled-prince.html

80 one of his cousins thinks ... kicks it: Kunda Dixit, 'Dipendra kicked his father aft er he shot him', *Nepali Times*, May 27, 2011, https://archive.nepalitimes.com/news.php?id=18246

80 shoots his sister: Bearak, 'Nepal gives "synopsis"'

81 'took place after': Barry Bearak, 'As Nepal mourns royals, mystery and confusion linger', *New York Times*, June 4, 2001, nytimes.com/2001/06/04/world/as-nepal-mourns-royals-mystery-and-confusion-linger.html

81 encounter him: Author's interview with a long-time acquaintance of Sumargi, Hetauda, June 2023

81 family's fortunes darkened: Sumargi family friend and a long-time Sumargi acquaintance

81 'boiler chicken': Sumargi family friend

82 illegal logging: 'Ajay Sumargi's unnatural rise: Is this his background?', *Kantipur Daily*, January 11, 2018, kathmandupati.com/news/ajaya-background/2749

82 ponytailed, a dash of lipstick: Hedelius, *Telia*, p. 139

82 make-up around the eyes: Author's interview with Sumargi business acquaintance

82 factotum: Author's interview with a close associate of King Gyanendra, Kathmandu, June 2023

82 helping to transfer property: 'Ajeya Sumargi's unnatural rise'

82 receives a telecoms licence: Emanuel Sidea, 'Korruptionsskandal för 4 miljarder i Nepal', *Veckans Affärer*, October 11, 2012, sidea.se/teliasonera-nepal; author's interview with Nepali media executive. Kathmandu, June 2023

82 his representative: 'We don't have to answer every rumour', interview with Ajeya Sumargi, *Nepali Times*, August 26, 2005, archive.nepalitimes.com/news.php?id=776

82 Sixteen thousand Nepalis: 'Nepal raises conflict death toll', BBC, September 22, 2009

82 disappeared: United Nations Office of the High Commissioner for Human Rights, 'Nepal Conflict Report', 2012, ohchr.org/sites/default/files/Documents/Countries/NP/OHCHR_Nepal_Conflict_Report2012.pdf, p19

83 'Burn the crown!': Tilak P. Pokharel and Somini Sengupta, 'Protests against Nepal's king grow more violent', *New York Times*, April 9, 2006, nytimes.com/2006/04/09/world/asia/09cnd-nepal.html

83 two-bedroom apartment: Mullins and Magistad, 'Why Nepal's crown prince'

83 their own: 'Nepal: Political appointments a friends and family affair', US embassy cable published by WikiLeaks, November 28, 2008, wikileaks.org/cable/2008/11/08KATHMANDU1245.html

83 robbed banks: John Kifner, 'After Nepal killings, a tough king gets US backing', *New York Times*, August 4, 2003, nytimes.com/2003/08/04/world/after-nepal-killings-a-tough-king-gets-us-backing.html

83 ninety million: Aditya Adhikari and Bhaskar Gautam with Surabhi Pudasaini and Bhadra Sharma, 'Impunity and Political Accountability in Nepal', The Asia Foundation, 2014, nepalconflictreport.ohchr.org/files/docs/2014-02-00_report_taf_eng.pdf, p. 92

84 'The unanimous opinion': 'Business intelligence – Nepal', Control Risks report for TeliaSonera, May 24, 2013

84 surpassed even the monarchy's: 'Low road through the Himalayas', *Economist*, May 31, 2011, economist.com/banyan/2011/05/31/low-road-through-the-himalayas

84 shake Prachanda's hand: Author's interview with Lenin Bista, a former Maoist child soldier and now a leader of anti-corruption protests, Kathmandu, June 2023

84 Cash Maoists: 'At crossroads', My Republica, January 10, 2013

84 exonerates him: Tika R. Pradhan, 'UCPN-M endorses Dahal's document', *Himalayan Times*, February 7, 2013

85 flows like a river: 'If I were to tell you everything I know about Prachanda', *Jana Aastha*, September 14, 2012, archive. nepalitimes.com/news.php?id=19640

85 'sleeping with the enemy': 'Public record research – Nepal', Control Risks report for TeliaSonera, December 21, 2012

86 ceremonial phone call: 'Hello Nepal service launched', Hello Nepal, September 24, 2009, web.archive.org/web/20150214063833/http://www.hellonepalgsm.com/newsroom/detail/service.php

87 accused of enriching: 'The distance between the Maoist strategy and their working policy', Voice of Madhesh, January 10, 2011, web.archive.org/web/20140104015030/https://madheshvani.com/uploaded/The%20voice%20of%20Madhesh-1-37-januaиy-10th-2011.pdf; 'Business intelligence – Nepal', Control Risks

87 licences have been doled out: The committee's report, published in 2011, 'concluded that all information and communication ministers after 2006 had been involved in these irregularities'. Adhikari et al., 'Impunity', p. 95

87 'no frills': 'Now more lower end customers will benefit from our services', TeliaSonera, September 11, 2012, web.archive.

org/web/20151004091959/http://www.teliasonera.com/en/
newsroom/blogs/my-blog/?blogId=9
87 eighty-nine thousand: 'Management Information System',
   Nepal Telecommunications Authority, July 2011, web.archive.
   org/web/20120502013835/http://www.nta.gov.np/
   articleimages/file/NTA_%20MIS_52.pdf, p. 5
87 worth no more than sixty million dollars: Fairness opinion
   report by the Swiss bank UBS for TeliaSonera on the
   acquisition of Nepal Satellite, Hello Nepal's parent company,
   June 2013. The UBS report also posits a far larger valuation
   based on avoiding the hypothetical scenario of some
   competitor buying Nepal Satellite instead. A respected market
   analyst called Dan Davies described this valuation to me as
   'speculative bordering on silly'
87 'It was a pleasure': Email from Mohamed Amersi to Ajeya
   Sumargi and his partner, Arjun Sharma, November 9, 2010
87 'with Mr Sumargi': draft documents headed 'Conclusions',
   laying out the proposed Hello Nepal acquisition, with two
   TeliaSonera employees and Amersi named as the authors.
   Amersi gave me this document, saying he and the two others
   wrote it
88 worth a billion: TeliaSonera board memo on Nepal Satellite
   from 2013
88 'a well-established': Tero Kivisaari, presentation titled 'Hello
   Nepal', December 3, 2010
88 Thirty million dollars: TeliaSonera Asia Holding BV's 2011
   annual report, p. 3
88 opaque British Virgin Islands company: When TeliaSonera in
   2013 reversed its acquisition of the mobile network Hello
   Nepal from Ajeya Sumargi, it said it would 'sell back' its stake
   'to Zhodar Investment'. 'TeliaSonera exits Nepal Satellite,
   focuses on Ncell in Nepal', TeliaSonera, September 11, 2013,
   news.cision.com/telia-company/r/teliasonera-exits-nepal-
   satellite--focuses-on-ncell-in-nepal,c9464055. Multiple
   TeliaSonera internal documents and correspondence with
   Sumargi refer to Zhodar Investments of the British Virgin
   Islands, owner of Hello Nepal, belonging to him

88 writes a cheque: Records of bank transactions in a report by the money-laundering department of the Nepali police's Central Investigation Bureau, Kathmandu

88 Sumargi's wife's sister: Yubaraj Ghimire, 'Prachanda's house may get confiscated', *Indian Express*, February 12, 2012; indianexpress.com/article/news-archive/web/prachanda-s-house-may-get-confiscated; 'Business intelligence – Nepal', Control Risks. An English-language blog recorded the numbers that were reported in the Nepali press. Anand Nepal, 'Prachanda's new residence – purchased for Rs 103 mil?', xNepali, January 24, 2012, xnepali.net/prachands-new-residence-purchased-for-rs-103-mil

88 even more of TeliaSonera's money: TeliaSonera bought 51 per cent of Hello Nepal's owner Nepal Satellite's parent company Airbell Services for $30 million in June 2011, says TeliaSonera Asia Holding BV's 2011 annual report. For a further $44.4 million TeliaSonera increased its stake in Airbell to 100 per cent in April 2012, at which point Airbell owned 75 per cent of Nepal Satellite, TeliaSonera Norway Nepal Holdings AS's accounts for 2012 state

89 two hundred million: UBS fairness opinion. By this point Sumargi has received $75 million. The UBS report gives the final value of the transaction, if all the stages are completed, at $270 million

89 meets the mighty: Nirmal Kumar Thapa and Arunraj Sumargi, 'Ajeya Raj Sumargi', 2016, multiple photographs of Sumargi with Nyberg in meetings with influential Nepalis

89 itinerary: Arjun Sharma email to Mohamed Amersi, March 7, 2011

91 delivered almost everything: Mohamed Amersi email to TeliaSonera executives on the status of the Nepal Satellite deal with Ajeya Sumargi, May 8, 2013; TeliaSonera board memo on Nepal Satellite from 2013

91 'Issues to be solved': TeliaSonera memo, May 2012

92 delegation's itinerary: Mohamed Amersi email to TeliaSonera, March 7, 2011, forwarding an itinerary for the Kathmandu visit

92 asked the telecoms minister … paperwork authorising it: 'Study report of the committee for frequency distribution of Nepal Telecommunication Authority'. Public Accounts Committee of Nepal's parliament, 2011, pp. 41–2

93 jail for corruption: 'Nepal talks after cabinet minister Gupta is jailed', BBC, February 22, 2012, bbc.co.uk/news/world-asia-17125968

93 minions show up: François Pilet, 'La princesse a perdu la clé de son trésor genevois', September 30, 2012, francoispilet.net/la-princesse-a-perdu-la-cle-de-son-tresor-genevois (French). Although Akhmedov, in the witness statement he gave to the Russian authorities, says he was not involved in opening these accounts, it seems the bankers perceived a connection to him, and that was enough to make them raise the alarm

94 establish a link: 'TeliaSonera's "partner" – Karimova's closest confidant', SVT, September 20, 2012, svt.se/nyheter/granskning/ug/teliasoneras-partner-karimova-s-closest-confidant

94 'The allegations directed at TeliaSonera': 'Lars Nyberg – introductory comments Q3 results', October 17, 2012, TeliaSonera, web.archive.org/web/20130203025521/http://www.teliasonera.com/Documents/Presentations/2012/121017%20Lars%20Nyberg's%20introduction%20Final.pdf

96 'discreet source enquiries': 'Business intelligence – Nepal', Control Risks

101 'reversal': I have seen several pages of Norton Rose's reports to TeliaSonera

101 'The decision': Mohamed Amersi's email to TeliaSonera executives, July 15, 2013

102 'constant problems': Amersi email to TeliaSonera executives on Nepal Satellite, May 8, 2013

102 'I do not like': Christian Luiga email to Mohamed Amersi, July 15, 2013

102 opened a criminal corruption investigation: Mannheimer Swartling report, p. 52

102 'Legal opinions': TeliaSonera board memo on Nepal Satellite from 2013

103 a letter: Hedelius, *Telia*, p. 217; TeliaSonera board memo on Nepal Satellite from 2013 refers to a letter from Sumargi of July 10, 2013

103 sixty million dollars: 'TeliaSonera exits Nepal Satellite' says TeliaSonera made a loss of 0.4 billion Swedish krona. The average 2013 exchange rate of 6.5 krona to the dollar gives a dollar equivalent of just over $60 million

103 'regulatory reasons': 'TeliaSonera exits Nepal Satellite'

103 'We wonder': Muddy Waters letter to TeliaSonera, October 15, 2015 muddywatersresearch.com/tou/?redirect=/content/uploads/2015/10/MW_TLSN–OpenLetter_10152015.pdf

103 'Throughout its dealings': Norton Rose report to TeliaSonera

104 'Agreements with': 'Summary of the Board of Directors' review of transactions in Eurasia and measures taken during the past year', April 1, 2014, TeliaSonera, web.archive.org/web/20210513221822/https://www.teliacompany.com/globalassets/telia-company/documents/investors/annual-general-meeting/2014/teliasonera_summary-of-the-board-of-directors-review-of-transactions-in-eurasia_agm_2014-04-01.pdf

105 'no official records': I asked the head of Transparency International in Nepal, Ashish Thapa, whether Maoist leaders maintained illicit business relationships through no-paperwork, handshake-only deals. That was indeed his understanding. 'These are deals of mutual benefit, not done on paper for obvious reasons'

Eight: Making sense

107 'Great. Well': Blavatnik School of Government, 'Book launch: Making Sense of Corruption', YouTube, March 8, 2017, youtube.com/watch?v=6HlsC81_Ix0

107 He's given money: Mohamed Amersi CV, Institute for New Economic Thinking, April 2017, ineteconomics.org/uploads/cv/MOHAMED-AMERSI-April-2017.pdf

108 his Ten Corporate Commandments: 'Ending corruption: Mohamed Amersi outlines Ten Corporate Commandments', One Young World, July 10, 2017, oneyoungworld.com/blog/

ending-corruption-mohamed-amersi-outlines-ten-corporate-commandments

108 no borders: Inclusive Ventures business plan

108 support for schools: Peg Tyre, 'Can a tech start-up successfully educate children in the developing world?', *New York Times*, June 27, 2017, nytimes.com/2017/06/27/magazine/can-a-tech-start-up-successfully-educate-children-in-the-developing-world.html

108 Supplying the Chinese: Karen Freifeld, 'China Post Group sued by investors in joint venture', Reuters, January 13, 2016, reuters.com/article/china-post-lawsuit-idUSL2N14X2FM20160113; archived Post Mart website, http://www.china-postmart.com/products/post-mart-brands

109 Armenian e-waste: Inclusive Ventures website, inclusiveventures.com/investments/re-apaga

109 son's master's degree: Amersi interview with me, July 2023

109 equip Nepal's rural youths: 'IVG fuels Rural Shores expansion into Nepal', Inclusive Ventures, August 10, 2014, inclusive ventures.com/ivg-fuels-rural-shores-expansion-into-nepal

109 reward youths who excel: 'Social Service' section of Ajeya Sumargi's website, accessed October 2023, ajeyarajsumargi.com/biography.html

109 local press: 'Muktishree going social', *New Business Age*, September 15, 2014, newbusinessage.com/magazine_articles/view/913

109 A project is under way: Inclusive Ventures business plan

109 unable to make these dreams reality: Mohamed Amersi's interview with me, July 2023

110 'one of our most': Pogrund and Zeffman, 'Access capitalism'

110 Ben Elliot's Quintessentially clients: Pogrund and Zeffman, 'Access capitalism'

110 'Dear Mohamed': Pogrund and Zeffman, 'Access capitalism'

112 to know his own part: Amersi, in his written responses to me in August 2023, said: 'I was prohibited legally from sharing details of my time at Telia as it was confidential and still under enforcement investigation.' However, he also said 'my CV where my role at Telia is described was in the public domain'

112 budget of the FBI: Ray, 'The continuing façade'

113 commitments: Deferred prosecution agreement in US Department of Justice v Telia Company AB, September 21, 2017, pars 3–6, justice.gov/criminal-fraud/file/998601/download

113 full of ambition: Jonathan Aitken, *Nazarbayev and the Making of Kazakhstan*, Continuum, 2009, pp. 27–9

114 call him Papa: Viktor Khrapunov, *Nazarbayev: Our Friend the Dictator*, Ibidem Verlag, 2015, p. 51

115 middleman has put millions: Tom Burgis, *Kleptopia*, William Collins, 2020, pp. 156–7

115 Sugar: Burgis, *Kleptopia*, pp. 111–16

115 article was headlined: Glenn R. Simpson and Susan Schmidt, 'Kazakhstan corruption: Exile alleges new details', *Wall Street Journal*, July 22, 2008, wsj.com/articles/SB121667622143971475

116 Kazakh economist: Aigul Nuriyeva profile page, Forbes Kazakhstan, forbes.kz/ranking/object/63, accessed June 1, 2023. For a detailed examination of Aigul Nuriyeva's role in Kazakh telecoms, see Thomas Mayne, Leila N. Seiitbek, Fatima Kanji and Erin K. Schornick, 'Bad Connection: Corruption in Kazakh telecoms', Freedom for Eurasia, 2021, freedomeurasia.org/wp-content/uploads/2023/06/Bad-Connection-Corruption-in-Kazakhtelecoms-0.pdf

116 study finance … Swiss bank: Aigul Nuriyeva CV on Kazakhtelecom website, August 6, 2013, web.archive.org/web/20130806181333/http:/www.telecom.kz/page/single/sostav-soveta-direktorov-ao-kazahtelekom?lang=en

116 inculcate: Joshua Kucera, 'Nazarbayev U', Slate, August 3, 2011, slate.com/news-and-politics/2011/08/nazarbayev-u.html

117 unfinished business: Amersi witness statement in Almaty Engineering Company v Sonera Holding, par 36

118 valuation provided: 'Project Artist: Fairness opinion report', UBS, January 30, 2012

118 looks iffy: 'Project Ortus: Business case presentation – DRAFT', TeliaSonera, November 24, 2011; draft briefing for

TeliaSonera by Clifford Chance, May 3, 2012, shown to me by Amersi

118 another valuation: Project Tornio: Valuation Report, ScholzvonGleich, August 2015 (marked draft)

119 'If you want to receive': Viktor Khrapunov, *Nazarbayev: Our Friend the Dictator*, 2015, p. 101

119 shoot up a public square: Burgis, *Kleptopia*, chapter 19

119 shuts down the internet: Dmitry Solovyov and Robin Paxton, 'Kazakh leader orders curfew after oil city riots', Reuters, December 17, 2011, reuters.com/article/kazakhstan-clashes-president-idINDEE7BG05X20111217

119 links to the Kazakh elite: TeliaSonera compliance presentation

119 sources are unanimous: Due diligence report on Aigul Nuriyeva for TeliaSonera

120 'All of the sources': 'White Paper: Tele2's operations in Kazakhstan', Tele2, December 17, 2014, tele2.com/files/globalassets/global/tele2_whitepaper_kazakhstan.pdf

120 'I deny any suggestion': I wrote to Aigul Nuriyeva, putting thirty-two factual points to her and asking whether she disputed or wished to comment on any of them. She did not answer any of them directly, instead giving broad responses, which are quoted here. Email from Aigul Nuriyeva, August 5, 2023

122 told American diplomats: 'Kazakhstan – Government taking further measures against Rakhat Aliyev in wake of WSJ article', US diplomatic cable published by WikiLeaks, wikileaks.org/cable/2008/07/08ASTANA1375.html

123 paperwork: 'Kcell Transmission: M&A opportunities discussion document', Kcell, September 27, 2010

125 letters from Aigul's people: Letters from Amun, one of Aigul Nuriyeva's companies, to TeliaSonera, February 10, 2014, April 28, 2014, and May 6, 2015

125 she controls: Amersi confirmed in his July 2023 interview with me that Nuriyeva owned this company, called Amun; TeliaSonera's internal compliance records say so too, and Nuriyeva did not dispute it in her response to my questions

125 'corruption, money laundering': Request for arbitration in Almaty Engineering Company v Sonera Holding, April 29, 2016

126 Estimating the probability: Ola Espelund, Memo to the board of TeliaSonera on settlement of the claims from AEC and Amun, July 6, 2017

126 TeliaSonera did promise: Mohamed Amersi witness statement in Almaty Engineering Company v Sonera Holding. He refers to Aigul Nuriyeva not by name but by her company, Amun

126 fifteen million: Espelund, Memo to the board

127 nothing improper: Aigul Nuriyeva's email to me

127 Aigul be named: TeliaSonera compliance presentation 'Telia Company has completed its divestment in Kaztranscom', TeliaSonera, November 5, 2018, web.archive.org/web/20221018040559/https://www.teliacompany.com/en/news/news-articles/2018/closing-kaztranscom

127 split eleven million: TeliaSonera 2018 annual report, mb.cision.com/Main/40/2767049/1010210.pdf

127 she says if anyone asks: Email from Aigul Nuriyeva to me

128 someone inside TeliaSonera: I put this account to a spokesperson for Telia Company, as TeliaSonera is now known. She did not reply to my email. In response to my earlier one, listing the facts and allegations about the company in this book, she wrote: 'We do not wish to comment on your book or any of the claims/statements in it'

129 cannot grasp the realities: Carter-Ruck letter for Mohamed Amersi to Norton Rose, March 18, 2022. Copy provided to me by Mohamed Amersi

132 not party to corruption: Email to me from Gulnara Karimova's lawyers, August 7, 2023

132 'shadow elites': Kristian Lasslett and Nadja Capus, 'Shadow state structures and the threat to anti-corruption enforcement: Evidence from Uzbekistan's telecommunications bribery scandal', *Crime, Law and Social Change*, October 19, 2023, link.springer.com/article/10.1007/s10611-023-10122-w

Nine: Two scenes from a park in lockdown

139 temperature climbs: UK Met Office data supplied to me; Time and Date data, timeanddate.com/ sun/@12262020?month=9&year=2020

139 entrepreneur, philanthropist and thought leader: 'Our founder', Amersi Foundation website, amersifoundation.org/ our-founder

139 malicious: The word is used in a written response Amersi sent to questions from me on June 30, 2021. Amersi gives his account of the meeting in his reply to Charlotte Leslie's defence in his data-protection proceedings against her, Mohamed Amersi v CMEC UK & Mena Ltd and Charlotte Leslie in the High Court, January 11, 2022

139 newsreader announces: *Today*, BBC Radio 4, September 25, 2020

140 'Cheating': Tweet by @realDonaldTrump, September 25, 2020, 12.31 a.m., archived by the American Presidency Project, presidency.ucsb.edu/documents/tweets- september-25-2020

140 been shielding: Charlotte Leslie WhatsApp message to Mohamed Amersi, August 31, 2020. Disclosed in the defamation proceedings Amersi brought in the UK High Court against Leslie

140 'Out of safety': Amersi's WhatsApp exchange with Leslie, disclosed in his defamation proceedings against her

140 Party has asked: Amersi's reply to Leslie's defence in his data-protection claim against her

140 Coronation Gardens: TICL website, ticl.me/Southfields/ headlines/13684/view

140 failed MP: Amersi's interview with me, July 1, 2021. Amersi disclosed the transcript in the defamation proceedings he brought in the UK High Court against Leslie

140 Spiteful: Letter from Amersi's lawyers at Carter-Ruck to Charlotte Leslie's lawyers, February 12, 2021. Disclosed in the defamation proceedings Amersi brought in the UK High Court against Leslie

140 making money: Amersi's responses to questions from me during research for a *Financial Times* article, June 30, 2021. Disclosed in the defamation proceedings Amersi brought in the UK High Court against Leslie

140 buys crisps, nuts and sandwiches: Mohamed Amersi, 'Chronology of dates & events relating to CMEC and Comena (March 2019–January 2021)'. Disclosed in the defamation proceedings

141 fifty thousand pounds: Amersi's reply to Leslie's defence in his data-protection claim against her

142 I am having to drive myself: Amersi, 'Chronology of dates'

142 after an honour: Leslie's defence in the data-protection proceedings Amersi brought against her

142 two packets of crisps: Author's fact-checking with Charlotte Leslie

142 wants recognition: Leslie's record of their conversation in the memos she wrote, published as exhibits to Amersi's defamation claim against her

143 buy the chairmanship ... gala dinner: Leslie memos

143 I can have this: Amersi second witness statement in the Leslie defamation claim, par 33

Ten: Cakeism

145 Cucumber, potato: Mikey Smith, 'UK hit by two crises but PM still finds time to lord it up at £25 billion Tory ball', *Daily Mirror*, February 26, 2020, mirror.co.uk/news/politics/inside-25-billion-ball-top-21584553

145 white burgundy: '2017 Jeroboams White Burgundy', Jeroboams, jeroboams.co.uk/product/2017-jeroboams-white-burgundy-12-x-bottle

145 'Can we arrange': Email sent on February 25, 2020 to Mike Chattey, the Conservatives' head of fundraising, and three other Party officials. Their names and that of the sender are redacted. Disclosed in Amersi's defamation proceedings against Leslie

146 arranged by one of tonight's guests: Jonathan Calvert and Sian Griffiths, 'Phone tycoon called in a favour for Johnson's

Mustique freebie', *Sunday Times*, February 16, 2020, thetimes. co.uk/article/phone-tycoon-called-in-a-favour-for-johnsons-mustique-freebie-k0zvl5vzc

146 missed a few meetings: Jonathan Calvert, George Arbuthnott and Jonathan Leake, 'Coronavirus: 38 days when Britain sleepwalked into disaster', *Sunday Times*, April 19, 2020, thetimes.co.uk/article/coronavirus-38-days-when-britain-sleepwalked-into-disaster-hq3b9tlgh

146 'Political donors': 'Book launch: *Making Sense of Corruption*', YouTube

146 'I am sure you will find': Pogrund and Zeffman, 'Access capitalism'

147 5 Hertford Street: Joy Lo Dico, 'How 5 Hertford Street became the most influential members' club in London', *Evening Standard*, December 12, 2019, standard.co.uk/lifestyle/5-hertford-street-members-club-a4308816.html

147 the campaign ... 'Nothing. Has. Changed': Tim Shipman, *Fall Out*, William Collins, 2017, pp. 304–11

148 a non-dom: Mohamed Amersi correspondence with me, August 2023

148 not on the British electoral roll: Mohamed Amersi correspondence with me, August 2023

148 for the cameras: 'Jacques Azagury fashion show in aid of the National Osteoporosis Society', Getty Images, November 16, 2016, gettyimages.co.uk/detail/news-photo/nadia-rodicheva-attends-the-jacques-azagury-fashion-show-in-news-photo/623722826?adppopup=true

149 helped to put on: Amersi written response to me, June 30, 2021

149 House of Garrard: Captioned pictures of the event posted on the National Osteoporosis Society Flickr feed, November 17, 2016, flickr.com/photos/national-osteoporosis-society/30906494542

149 names there: Pictures of the event published by Shuttershock, November 16, 2016, shutterstock.com/editorial/image-editorial/nadejda-roditcheva-mohamed-amersi-7449991r

149 broke her rib: Bridie Wilkins, 'Duchess Camilla recalls traumatic memory from mother's battle with life-changing condition', *Hello!*, October 25, 2021, hellomagazine.com/healthandbeauty/health-and-fitness/20211025124761/duchess-camilla-duchess-of-cornwall-mother-osteoporosis-memory

149 Mohamed himself is the source: English Story filings at Companies House, the UK corporate registry

149 email to arrange: Correspondence with Conservative representatives given to me by Amersi

150 bank receipt: Email from David Poole of Union Bancaire Privée to Mohamed Amersi, May 1, 2017; copy given to me by Amersi

150 an invoice: An invoice for a donation sent by the UK think-tank Rusi to the Amersi Foundation, July 2, 2021

150 seems to control: I wrote to Amersi: 'If there is evidence to demonstrate that this is Nadia's account, please provide it.' He replied: 'None of your business.'

151 The donation has already covered: Peter Walker, 'Tories spent £18.5m on election that cost them majority', *Guardian*, March 19, 2018, theguardian.com/politics/2018/mar/19/electoral-commission-conservatives-spent-lost-majority-2017-election

151 the average Brit: 'Median annual earnings for full-time employees in the United Kingdom from 1999 to 2023', Statista, statista.com/statistics/1002964/average-full-time-annual-earnings-in-the-uk/

151 less than a day's worth of the fees: Amersi told me TeliaSonera paid his Emerging Telecom Ventures $63 million over six years, an average of nearly $29,000, or about £19,000 a day

151 ministers are defeated: 'Election results 2017 summary: Key points at-a-glance', BBC News, June 9, 2017, bbc.co.uk/news/election-2017-40190964

151 backbencher of the year: 'Charlotte Leslie is "Backbencher of the Year"', ITV, November 8, 2013, itv.com/news/westcountry/update/2013-11-08/charlotte-leslie-is-backbencher-of-the-year/

Notes

152 'a well-connected': Amersi second witness statement in his defamation claim against Leslie

152 with the Prince of Wales: Amersi Foundation website, amersifoundation.org/our-founder/

152 police to protect: Ashley Cowburn, 'Theresa May flies back to London amid crucial Brexit negotiations to attend lavish Tory ball with millionaire donors', *Independent*, February 7, 2019, independent.co.uk/news/uk/politics/theresa-may-tory-donor-ball-cabinet-fundraising-event-black-white-ball-brexit-a8767496.html

152 auctioned for the price: Mikey Smith, 'Inside the Tory Black and White Ball where £75k buys you a night out with Theresa May', *Mirror*, February 7, 2019, mirror.co.uk/news/politics/inside-tory-black-white-ball-13968469

152 two lots: Jon Ungoed-Thomas, 'Give me back my £200,000, major donor tells Tories', *Observer*, February 5, 2022, theguardian.com/politics/2022/feb/05/give-me-back-my-200000-major-donor-tells-tories

152 former illusionist's assistant: Sarah Ridley and Michael Hamilton, 'Penny Mordaunt praised for previous role as magician's glamorous assistant', *Sun*, July 16, 2022, thesun.co.uk/news/19224949/penny-mordaunt-praised-for-previous-role-as-magicians-glamorous-assistant/

153 'So I've got': Mohamed Amersi, 'Mohamed Amersi thanked by Theresa May on behalf of Brasenose College', YouTube, April 3, 2022, youtube.com/watch?v=-78i4vPw5ug

153 his dream: Amersi call with me July 5, 2021

153 hallowed stone lists: Clarendon Arch, Oxford

153 skilfully matched: 'The Amersi Foundation Lecture Room', Brazen Notes, issue 28, 2019, bnc.ox.ac.uk/downloads/MU24959_Brazen_Notes_28_-_Online.pdf

153 touchscreen: web.archive.org/web/20220816012454/https://staff.bnc.ox.ac.uk/amersi-technical-guide/

157 a constituency costs: Rajeev Syal, 'Conservatives spent £16m on 2019 election win, figures show', *Guardian*, 7 October 2020, theguardian.com/politics/2020/oct/07/conservatives-spent-16m-on-2019-election-win-figures-show

158 'From my side': Mohamed Amersi email to Conservative officials, February 24, 2020, disclosed in his defamation claim against Leslie

158 deliver forty seats: 'How to do foreign policy in a multi-ethnic society', *Economist*, May 20, 2021, economist.com/britain/2021/05/20/how-to-do-foreign-policy-in-a-multi-ethnic-society

158 Conservative Friends of Israel: Peter Oborne and James Jones, 'The pro-Israel lobby in Britain: full text', openDemocracy, November 13, 2009, opendemocracy.net/en/opendemocracyuk/pro-israel-lobby-in-britain-full-text

158 Conservative Friends of Russia: Luke Harding, 'Tory blushes deepen over activities of Conservative Friends of Russia', *Guardian*, November 30, 2012, theguardian.com/politics/2012/nov/30/activities-of-conservative-friends-of-russia

158 from Mohamed Mansour: Amersi written responses to me, June 2021

159 Lord Polak: Mohamed Amersi's WhatsApps with Lord Polak, disclosed in the Amersi v Leslie defamation case

159 persuading the Iranians: Amersi's second witness statement in the Leslie defamation case, par 10

159 ambassadors: Amersi's second witness statement in the Leslie defamation case, par 28

159 bestowed: Mohammed bin Rashid Al Maktoum Knowledge Award, 2018, mbrf.ae/knowledgeaward/en/#laureates|laureatesTab3

159 auction lots: Smith, 'UK hit by two crises'

160 chatted it over: Amersi WhatsApp to me, July 6, 2021

160 saw Boris again: Amersi, 'Chronology of dates'

160 'Go for it': Amersi WhatsApp to me, July 6, 2021

160 needed in the vanguard: Amersi in his interview with me, July 2021: 'parliamentarians are itching for this organisation [Comena] to be fully up and running, so that, post-Brexit, the UK can start to build its relationships individually with countries of the MENA region. It's fundamental, okay?'

160 'The doubters': James Blitz, 'Boris Johnson's first speech as prime minister – decoded', *Financial Times*, July 24, 2019, ig. ft.com/boris-johnson-prime-minister-speech

161 shakes hands: Amersi, 'Chronology of dates'

161 an email introducing: Email from Myles Stacey, the Conservatives' head of outreach, to Charlotte Leslie and Mohamed Amersi, March 3, 2020, disclosed in the Amersi v Leslie defamation proceedings

Eleven: The boxer

167 Leslie still loves: The account of Leslie's life is drawn from my interviews with people who have knowledge of it, and who asked not to be identified because of the action Mohamed Amersi has taken against her

168 left her to die: Tom Burgis, 'Thomas Mair: The making of a neo-Nazi killer', *Financial Times*, November 23, 2016, ft.com/mair

169 two-faced creep: Leslie WhatsApp to a colleague, disclosed in the defamation proceedings

169 LinkedIn profile: Ilma Bogdan profile page, accessed March 2021

170 Russian influence in the UK: Charlotte Leslie's first witness statement in Amersi's defamation proceedings, June 21, 2022, par. 11

170 'The UK welcomed': 'Russia', Intelligence and Security Committee of Parliament, July 21, 2020, isc.independent.gov. uk/wp-content/uploads/2021/03/CCS207_CCS 0221966010-001_Russia-Report-v02-Web_Accessible.pdf

171 He too, she reads: Leslie's first witness statement in Amersi's data claim against her, July 14, 2021, par. 24

171 'a mysterious figure': 'The incredible shrinking Metromedia', Forbes, October 10, 2006, forbes.com/2006/10/09/ metromedia-kluge-putin-bankruptcy-biz-cz_ hb_1010metromedia.html

172 Russian influence operation ... worries Leslie: Charlotte Leslie's first witness statement in the Amersi defamation proceedings, June 21, 2022, pars 11–12

173 so he can pass it on: Charlotte Leslie email to Julian Lewis, January 5, 2021, disclosed in Amersi's defamation proceedings against her

173 'Charlotte Leslie who is the director': Nicholas Soames email to Ben Elliot, January 4, 2021, disclosed in the Amersi v Leslie defamation proceedings

Twelve: The libel factory

175 Peter seizes the haddock: Peter Carter-Ruck, *Memoirs of a Libel Lawyer*, Weidenfeld & Nicolson, 1990, p. 3

175 enjoys the urgency: Carter-Ruck, *Memoirs*, p. 7

176 say what he wants: James Morton, 'Peter Carter-Ruck obituary', *Guardian*, December 22, 2003, theguardian.com/media/2003/dec/22/pressandpublishing.guardianobituaries

176 Robert Maxwell's … Michael Heseltine: 'Peter Carter-Ruck obituary', *Daily Telegraph*, December 22, 2003 and Emma Brockes, 'A country practice', *Guardian*, August 8, 2000, theguardian.com/g2/story/0,3604,351667,00.html

176 asks for this to be corrected: 'Peter Carter-Ruck obituary', *Daily Telegraph*

176 Four homes: David Hooper, 'The Carter-Ruck chill', *Guardian*, December 23, 2003, theguardian.com/media/2003/dec/23/pressandpublishing.comment

176 Silver Shadow: Morton, 'Peter Carter-Ruck obituary'

176 *Fair Judgment*: Carter-Ruck, Memoirs, pp. 71, 172, 197

176 cigarette box: Brockes, 'A country practice'

177 Carter-Ruck can discern a libel: Morton, 'Peter Carter-Ruck obituary'

177 'It is *untrue* that Peter Sellers': 'Libel news', *Private Eye*, August 17, 1990

177 When the tears are flowing: Hooper, 'The Carter-Ruck chill'

177 twenty thousand pounds: Morton, 'Peter Carter-Ruck obituary'

177 sex smear: 'Peter Carter-Ruck obituary', *Daily Telegraph*

177 twelve times as much: Hooper, 'The Carter-Ruck chill'

177 one of his partners concludes: Hooper, 'The Carter-Ruck chill'

Notes

178 'He's a very': 'Ready, willing and libel', *The Lawyer*, October 20, 2003

178 'had overseen': Mrs Justice Tipples' judgment in Rosneft v HarperCollins and Belton, Annex, Meaning Two, November 24, 2021, judiciary.uk/wp-content/uploads/2022/07/Rosneft-v-HarperCollins-judgment-241121.pdf

179 waves a copy: Catherine Belton, Twitter post, January 19, 2021, twitter.com/catherinebelton/status/1351575121773948936?lang=en

179 'suppressing free speech': April French Furnell, '60 second interview with Nigel Tait, Carter-Ruck', Citywealth, April 9, 2019, web.archive.org/web/20220308045424/www.citywealthmag.com/news/60-second-interview-nigel-tait-carter-ruck

180 'set out improperly': Carter-Ruck letter to me, August 15, 2023

180 what Nigel Tait calls it: Nigel Tait, 'The Trafigura story: Who guards the Guardian?', Inforrm, October 13, 2011, inforrm.org/2011/10/13/the-trafigura-story-who-guards-the-guardian-nigel-tait/

180 defied it: David Leigh, 'Trafigura drops bid to gag Guardian over MP's question', *Guardian*, October 13, 2009, theguardian.com/media/2009/oct/13/trafigura-drops-gag-guardian-oil

181 'right to rewrite': Jamie Grierson and Ben Quinn, 'Google loses landmark "right to be forgotten" case', *Guardian*, April 13, 2018, theguardian.com/technology/2018/apr/13/google-loses-right-to-be-forgotten-case

181 won an apology: Jessica Hodgson, 'Mail pays out immediately to Elliot', *Guardian*, August 8, 2001, theguardian.com/media/2001/aug/08/dailymail.pressandpublishing

181 got with Jade Jagger anyway: Adams, 'An Englishman'

181 'The day free speech': 'Privacy on parade', *Private Eye*, May 27, 2016

182 lawyers' fees: The most comprehensive account of lawfare against the media is Susan Coughtrie, 'London calling', Foreign Policy Centre, April 2022, fpc.org.uk/wp-content/uploads/2022/04/London-Calling-Publication-February-2023.pdf

182 Every time he reads: 'Luvaduck, it's Carter-Fuck!', *Private Eye*, November 10, 2008, 2008

182 cost of a UK libel trial: Coughtrie, 'London calling', p. 16

183 defence solicitor for Belton: Catherine Belton's testimony to the Foreign Affairs Select Committee of the UK Parliament, March 15, 2022, committees.parliament.uk/oralevidence/9907/pdf/

183 defending the book: Belton testimony

185 said countless times: Belton testimony; Jennifer Rankin, 'Russia ordered to pay $50bn in damages to Yukos shareholders', *Guardian*, July 28, 2014, theguardian.com/business/2014/jul/28/russia-order-pay-50bn-yukos-shareholders-khodorkovsky-court

185 'put up': Tipples judgment

186 Or all those other clients: 'Nigel Tait', Spears 500, 2023, spearswms.com/nigel-tait-4; Carter-Ruck correspondence with the author

Thirteen: Reputation hit

187 his hardworking staffers: 'Findings of Second Permanent Secretary's Investigation into Alleged Gatherings on Government Premises During Covid Restrictions', May 25, 2022, assets.publishing.service.gov.uk/government/uploads/system/uploads/attachment_data/file/1078404/2022-05-25_FINAL_FINDINGS_OF_SECOND_PERMANENT_SECRETARY_INTO_ALLEGED_GATHERINGS.pdf

188 record fundraising: Rowena Mason, Luke Harding, Harry Davies and Simon Goodley, 'How Ben Elliot supercharged Tory donations by targeting world's ultra-wealthy', *Guardian*, October 5, 2021, theguardian.com/politics/2021/oct/05/how-ben-elliot-supercharged-tory-donations-by-targeting-worlds-ultra-wealthy

188 membership of the secret: Tom Burgis, Sebastian Payne, Kadhim Shubber and George Parker, 'Elite Tory donors club holds secret meetings with Boris Johnson and Rishi Sunak', *Financial Times*, July 30, 2021, ft.com/content/f8a48bfd-8902-4667-93a6-1b903ca48e7e

Notes

188 'Everything has changed': 'The world after COVID-19: A new luxury era? How the global pandemic has influenced the behaviour of the affluent consumer', Quintessentially, quintessentially.com/assets/pages/homepage/The-World-After-COVID-19-A-New-Luxury-Era.pdf

189 'Mohamed has 3': Ben Elliot email to Conservative officials and Mohamed Amersi, July 2, 2020, disclosed in the Amersi v Leslie defamation proceedings

189 funnel for donations: Email from Mike Chattey, the Conservatives' head of fundraising, to party officials, February 25, 2020, disclosed in the Amersi v Leslie defamation proceedings

189 'Let's get going': Ben Elliot email to Conservative officials and Mohamed Amersi, December 7, 2020, disclosed in the Amersi v Leslie defamation proceedings

190 'As you may know': Mohamed Amersi's letter announcing the formation of Comena, January 4, 2021, disclosed in the Amersi v Leslie data proceedings

191 who sent: Amersi's amended particulars of claim in his defamation claim against Charlotte Leslie, July 29, 2022, par. 86

192 Brownlow emailed Ben: Simon Walters, 'Number 10 makeover scandal: New leaked memo shows Conservative Party chief knew £58,000 donation was earmarked for Boris Johnson's Downing Street flat', *Daily Mail*, April 20, 2021, dailymail.co.uk/news/article-9492829/Leaked-memo-shows-Tory-chief-knew-58-000-donation-Boris-Johnsons-Downing-Street-flat.html

192 should have been declared: 'Report of investigation into the Conservative and Unionist Party – recording and reporting of payments', Electoral Commission, December 9, 2021, dailymail.co.uk/news/article-9492829/Leaked-memo-shows-Tory-chief-knew-58-000-donation-Boris-Johnsons-Downing-Street-flat.html

192 illegal: James Dean, 'Tory chairman Ben Elliot's company admits making illegal payments', *The Times*, May 13, 2021, thetimes.co.uk/article/tory-chairman-ben-elliots-company-admits-making-illegal-payments-vpts7nkqb

192 public money: Dominic Kennedy and George Greenwood, 'Reveal all about £1m contract to pamper super-rich, Boris Johnson is urged', *The Times*, March 16, 2020, thetimes.co.uk/article/reveal-all-about-1m-contract-to-pamper-super-rich-boris-johnson-is-urged-dhl7ll06m

195 Less than an hour ago: Congressional Record for the Senate, February 10, 2021, pp. 628–35, congress.gov/117/crec/2021/02/10/CREC-2021-02-10-pt1-PgS615-4.pdf; other details of the riot come from 'January 6th Committee Final Report', House Select Committee, December 22, 2022, govinfo.gov/content/pkg/GPO-J6-REPORT/pdf/GPO-J6-REPORT.pdf

196 the housing secretary, Robert Jenrick: Oliver Wright, 'Conservative chairman Ben Elliot apologises over his part in Richard Desmond dinner', *The Times*, July 22, 2020, thetimes.co.uk/article/conservative-chairman-ben-elliot-questioned-over-his-part-in-richard-desmond-dinner-5wp2vcqjx; Gabriel Pogrund, Emanuele Midolo and George Greenwood, 'Robert Jenrick overruled civil servants to push through Tory donor's £1bn housing plan', *The Times*, June 27, 2020, thetimes.co.uk/article/were-going-ahead-with-this-jenrick-has-made-his-mind-up-lets-get-this-sorted-2rskbwhnf

197 Huawei ... Mansour: Kadhim Shubber, Tom Burgis, George Parker and Jim Pickard, 'Tory donors use PR firm part-owned by chief fundraiser Ben Elliot', *Financial Times*, August 6, 2021, ft.com/content/363377cc-5769-42cc-9469-fb657231aadd

199 'I can go to': Oliver Wright, 'Exclusive: Tories under fire for links to pro-Russia lobbyists', *Independent*, July 4, 2014, independent.co.uk/news/uk/politics/exclusive-tories-under-fire-for-links-to-prorussia-lobbyists-9583023.html

200 Within a week: Donation filing at the Electoral Commission, published June 1, 2021, search.electoralcommission.org.uk/English/Donations/C0545182

Fourteen: A world of pain

201 life changes irrevocably: Charlotte Leslie's first witness statement in Amersi's defamation case

201 writes to my publisher: Letter from Mishcon de Reya to HarperCollins, January 26, 2015

202 threaten legal proceedings: Letter from Mishcon de Reya to Daphne Caruana Galizia, March 20, 2017

202 car bomb: Ben Taub, 'Murder in Malta', *New Yorker*, December 14, 2020, newyorker.com/magazine/2020/12/21/murder-in-malta

202 Dear Ms Leslie: Mishcon de Reya's letter to Charlotte Leslie on behalf of Mohamed Amersi, January 7, 2021

203 The stuff that's said: Letter sent by the law firm Ince on behalf of Charlotte Leslie and CMEC to Carter-Ruck on behalf of Mohamed Amersi, April 1, 2021

204 Leslie's toxic lies: Letter sent by Carter-Ruck for Mohamed Amersi to Charlotte Leslie, February 2, 2021

204 'And it overran': Leslie's recording of her calls with Carl Hunter; Simon Walters, 'Former MP "felt threatened" by top Tory adviser in phone calls: Charlotte Leslie contacted police claiming senior party activist asked if she could "walk the dog at night and sleep well"', *Daily Mail*, January 19, 2022, dailymail.co.uk/news/article-10415927/Charlotte-Leslie-contacted-police-claiming-senior-party-activist-asked-sleep-well.html

205 purveyor of maritime technology: Carl Stephen Patrick Hunter OBE LinkedIn profile, accessed December 2023, linkedin.com/in/carl-stephen-patrick-hunter-obe-1ab55a4a

212 The headline: *Financial Times*, July 7, 2021, ft.com/content/5dab0a3e-687a-446f-8e55-58c999d4321f

212 instigates mediation: Charlotte Leslie's second witness statement in the defamation proceedings, par 19

213 If it succeeds: Tom Burgis, 'Tory chair accused of mixing business and political interests', *Financial Times*, August 3, 2021, ft.com/content/acf45616-76e4-4e31-8252-a661c1ee4608

213 join the legal action: Lord Hunt will neither confirm nor deny that this happened; Amersi says he said no such thing; Fridman's spokesperson said: 'Mr Fridman has had no relationship with Mr Amersi for 15 years. He was not aware

of these allegations, finds them deeply offensive and categorically denies any involvement in any threats of legal action against Ms Leslie.' Tom Burgis, Sebastian Payne and Max Seddon, 'New claims raise questions over Tory donor's Russian business links', *Financial Times*, ft.com/content/4b922f07-9919-4648-915e-065011221906

Fifteen: Statements of truth

215 falling apart: Christian Edwards, 'Why is Britain's health service, a much-loved national treasure, falling apart?', CNN, January 23, 2023, edition.cnn.com/2023/01/23/uk/uk-nhs-crisis-falling-apart-gbr-intl/index.html

215 conspiracy to steal: Jack Nicas, Flávia Milhorance and Ana Ionova, 'How Bolsonaro built the myth of stolen elections in Brazil', *New York Times*, October 25, 2022, nytimes.com/interactive/2022/10/25/world/americas/brazil-bolsonaro-misinformation.html

215 advanced: Megan Specia, Ivan Nechepurenko and Thomas Gibbons-Neff, 'Russian mercenary group says it has taken contested Ukrainian town', *New York Times*, January 10 2023, nytimes.com/2023/01/10/world/europe/ukraine-soledar-bakhmut-wagner.html

215 meat-grinder: Peter Beaumont, 'In the "Bakhmut meat grinder", deadlocked enemy forces slog it out', *Observer*, 10 December 2022, theguardian.com/world/2022/dec/10/russia-ukraine-war-bakhmut-meat-grinder-deadlock

215 Prigozhin had business: Jim Fitzpatrick, 'Revealed: UK government helped sanctioned Putin ally sue British journalist', openDemocracy, January 23, 2023, opendemocracy.net/en/prigozhin-government-russia-ukraine-hack-libel-slapp/

216 'Yes,' says the judge: All quotes from court are from the official transcripts

217 'resounding success': Rami Ranger email to Carter-Ruck, July 15, 2022, disclosed in the Amersi v Leslie defamation proceedings

217 bestowed his charity: Particulars of claim in Amersi's defamation proceedings against Leslie, April 6, 2022

Notes

221 where he's held: Léonie Chao-Fong, Jamie Grierson, Emily Dugan and Helen Sullivan, 'Family of Briton missing in Ukraine "very worried"; German foreign minister pledges more weapons – as it happened', *Guardian*, January 10, 2023, theguardian.com/world/live/2023/jan/10/russia-ukraine-blog-live-almost-no-walls-left-in-soledar-says-zelenskiy-as-fierce-fighting-continues

221 data-protection law: Particulars of claim in Amersi's data-protection proceedings against Leslie

225 confirmed to a *Private Eye* reporter: Mohamed Amersi's email to Richard Brooks of *Private Eye*, July 24, 2021, a copy of which Amersi gave me

225 'I cannot now recall': Amersi's written responses to my questions, November 2023

225 'conduct ourselves': I wrote to Nigel Tait and Carter-Ruck to ask them about this seemingly false evidence, and to put to them the other main points about them in this book. They did not answer any of my questions directly but made broad points, which I've quoted. Letter from Carter-Ruck, August 15, 2023

226 'They are both': Leslie second witness statement in the defamation case, par. 16

226 down tools: Internal Conservative email, January 10, 2021, disclosed in Amersi v Leslie defamation proceedings

226 'Can you do': Internal Conservative email, April 25, 2021, disclosed in Amersi v Leslie defamation proceedings

227 'peddled access to Charles': Gabriel Pogrund and Henry Zeffman, 'Tory chairman "peddled access to Charles"', *Sunday Times*, August 1, 2021, thetimes.co.uk/article/tory-chairman-ben-elliot-peddled-access-to-prince-charles-hsw5t5bzr

228 private spies of K2: Amersi says, in his written responses to me of August 2023, that neither he nor Carter-Ruck retained K2. I emailed K2 to ask about this, including whether they undertook their work on Leslie in the hope of securing such a retainer. There was no reply

228 Lady: K2's response to Charlotte Leslie's Subject Access Request, June 23, 2022

228 messages from Phil Hall associates: For example, 'Press release: Mohamed Amersi', sent to journalists by Phil Hall Associates, October 4, 2021

229 What clients he's had: Phil Hall LinkedIn profile, accessed December 2023, linkedin.com/in/philhallpha/

229 Nigel Tait's son: 'A right Carter-Fuck-up', *Private Eye*, December 10, 2021. Confirmed in an email to me by Phil Hall Associates, October 16, 2023

229 He's been warned: Amersi's second witness statements in his defamation proceedings against Leslie, par. 75

Sixteen: The very fabric of this country

231 Dear Mr Speaker: Mohamed Amersi's letter to the Speaker of the House of Commons, July 21, 2023

231 'abusing Parliament's privilege': On August 8, 2023, a parliamentary clerk replied to Amersi on the Speaker's behalf and said: 'Members are responsible for what they say in parliamentary proceedings and must use their own judgement in deciding how to exercise the privileges of the House of Commons'

232 'an industry that hides evil': 'Lawfare and UK court system', Hansard, January 20, 2022, hansard.parliament.uk/ commons/2022-01-20/debates/4F7649B7-2085-4B51-9E8C-32992CFF7726/LawfareAndUKCourtSystem

232 'It is iniquitous': Letter sent by Carter-Ruck's for Mohamed Amersi to David Davis, February 16, 2022

232 refund two hundred thousand: Jon Ungoed-Thomas, 'Give me back my £200,000, major donor tells Tories', *Observer*, Feb 5, 2022, theguardian.com/politics/2022/feb/05/give-me-back-my-200000-major-donor-tells-tories. A Conservative spokesman confirmed that the money was refunded

233 lunchtime auction: Electoral Commission filing published on June 16, 2022, search.electoralcommission.org.uk/English/ Donations/C0557888. Anna Mikhailova, 'The £500k donor the Tories just can't shake off ...', *Mail on Sunday*, May 15, 2022, dailymail.co.uk/debate/article-10817199/ANNA-MIKHAILOVA-500k-donor-Tories-just-shake-off.html

233 'Ben Elliott's resignation': Mohamed Amersi's post on Twitter, September 5, 2022, twitter.com/moamersi/status/1566826347279818754

233 'Losing Our Moral Compass': Letter from Carter-Ruck to King's College London, May 25, 2022

234 report is withdrawn: Hodge later used parliamentary privilege to republish it; Amersi complained to the parliamentary authorities that this was an abuse of privilege, because the report still contained 'inaccuracies'

234 recent study: John Heathershaw, Alexander Cooley, Tom Mayne, Casey Michel, Tena Prelec, Jason Sharman and Ricardo Soares de Oliveira, 'The UK's kleptocracy problem: How servicing post-Soviet elites weakens the rule of law,' Chatham House, December 2021, chathamhouse.org/sites/default/files/2023-01/2021-12-08-uk-kleptocracy-problem-heathershaw-mayne-et-al.pdf

234 'the intermediary for payment': Carter-Ruck's correspondence with Chatham House

234 offered to donate: Amersi's written responses to me, August 2023. He says the offer of a donation had no bearing on his requests for amendments to the report

235 letter goes to Michaela Ahlberg: Correspondence between Carter-Ruck for Mohamed Amersi and Taylor Wessing for Michaela Ahlberg

235 One victim: Strategic Lawsuits Against Public Participation (SLAPPs): Government response to call for evidence, July 2022, gov.uk/government/consultations/strategic-lawsuits-against-public-participation-slapps/outcome/strategic-lawsuits-against-public-participation-slapps-government-response-to-call-for-evidence

235 target of a 'reverse-Slapp': Mohamed Amersi post on Twitter, June 29, 2022, twitter.com/moamersi/status/1542084332273156096

Seventeen: Reality

237 the 'well-known' fact: Shaun Walker, Isobel Koshiv, Pjotr Sauer, Morten Risberg, Liz Cookman and Luke Harding, 'Mariupol: The ruin of a city', *Guardian*, February 23, 2023, theguardian.com/world/ng-interactive/2023/feb/23/mariupol-the-ruin-of-a-city

238 epistemological bankruptcy: I came across this term used in this way listening to Sam Harris on his Making Sense podcast, 'What do we know about our minds?', April 20, 2023, samharris.org/podcasts/making-sense-episodes/317-what-do-we-know-about-our-minds

239 to dissent, to dispute: This is unimprovably expressed in the fourth chapter of Christopher Hitchens' *Letters to a Young Contrarian*, Basic Books, 2001

239 happy to donate: Kate Devlin and Adam Forrest, 'Scandal-hit Tory donor opens wallet to Starmer', *Independent*, independent.co.uk/news/uk/politics/tory-donations-rishi-sunak-labour-b2399420.html

239 'Mohamed Amersi is also': 'FPRI welcomes Mohamed Amersi to its board of trustees', Foreign Policy Resreach Institute, June 29, 2023, mailchi.mp/fpri/bt-news-23-06-24?e=07f6866fd0

239 'What a few days': Mohamed Amersi's post on Twitter, September 17, 2022, twitter.com/moamersi/status/1703247157996786019

240 'I have a right': Mohamed Amersi post on X, November 23, 2023, twitter.com/moamersi/status/1727669702472691839

240 'Mr Amersi': @twittetwist post on X, November 24, 2023, twitter.com/TWITTETWIST/status/1727996658351251640; I asked Amersi whether he controlled this account and he said he did not

241 'The Claimant has': Particulars of claim in Amersi v BBC, January 31, 2023

ACKNOWLEDGEMENTS

Those who deserve the highest praise are, as ever, the ones who cannot be named. They risk a lot to reveal the truth in the knowledge their courage will never be recognised. Several experts and fellow journalists have generously helped me. Although I'm not thanking them by name either, to spare them entanglement in the threatened legal retribution that awaits this book, I'm hugely grateful all the same.

Once again, I'm in awe of my publisher, Arabella Pike. If there is anyone who fights so fiercely to defend free speech while remaining so irrepressibly cheerful, I'm yet to meet them. The rest of the HarperCollins team, including Iain Hunt, Matt Clacher, Katherine Patrick, Sam Harding and Julian Humphries, is likewise indispensable. Tom Jarvis and David Hirst bring such insight to the legal review that at times it becomes – almost – a pleasure. I owe a lot to their wisdom, and to Simon Dowson-Collins' and Nicola Boulter's. Steve Leard designed a sizzler of a cover.

Sophie Lambert, my agent, walks the whole road with my books: she's there at the beginning, the middle and the end, and great company too. Thanks also to her colleagues at C&W, especially Alice Hoskyns and the rights team.

I'm obliged to Charles Kaiser for a bad review and some good advice. Fran Jakobi, Joe Burgis, Magid El-Amin, Lorna Dodds, Quentin Peel and Yinka Ibukun were kind enough to give me both encouragement and honest criticism of drafts. In Nepal, I was fortunate to work with the brilliant Bhadra Sharma. For open-source fact-checking, I drew on dazzling young talents: Liam Travers and Sasha Mahuli and, younger still, Annabelle Campbell (standing on the shoulders of Vix Campbell). The responsibility for any errors that remain is entirely mine.

The finest parents, family, in-laws, friends and neighbours a frazzled writer could hope for are a blessing. There's only one Camilla Carson. Wonderfully, she's married to me, even though I keep saying terrible things like, 'I'm thinking of doing another book'. And finally, thanks with all my heart to my daughter Delilah and my son Fred. What they mean to me, what it is to have them as companions – that's where I run out of words.

INDEX

Index

Index

Index

Index